THE HUMAN FACE OF THE ALASKA GOLD RUSH

IT WAS A RIOTOUS TIME WITH SAINTS AND SCOUNDRELS LIVING SIDE-BY-SIDE

STEVE LEVI

MASTER OF THE IMPOSSIBLE CRIME

PUBLICATION
CONSULTANTS
We Believe In The Power Of Authors

PO Box 221974 Anchorage, Alaska 99522-1974
books@publicationconsultants.com—www.publicationconsultants.com

ISBN Number: 978-1-63747-007-7
eBook ISBN Number: 978-1-63747-008-4

Library of Congress Catalog Card Number: 2021930239

Manufactured in the United States of America

Acknowledgements

The Human Face of the Alaska Gold Rush would not have been possible without the ongoing, high-quality assistance of many people who worked at the now-defunct National Archives in Anchorage—specifically Judy Petersen, Tammy Carlisle, Diana Kodiak, Bruce Parham, and Tom Wiltsey; and the State of Alaska Archives—specifically Abigail Focht and Chris Hieb; and the University of Alaska Anchorage Archives—specifically Arlene Schmuland, Gwen Higgins and Veronica Denison. A special thanks to the Institute of Historical Study in San Francisco, whose grants allowed me to travel to archives in Washington (state and D.C.) San Francisco, and Los Angeles for on-the-ground document searches.

And here's to my wife, who never lost faith I'd FINISH the book!

The Human Face of the Alaska Gold Rush

ALASKA!

E ven today, the word sets the imagination of the world ablaze. It is the Land of the Midnight Sun, where Eskimos eat blubber and polar bear prowl wind-swept sheets of the polar ice pack. Here glaciers calve into ice-floe choked sounds where walrus bellow and *orca* cruise the depths in search of king salmon while overhead the *Aurora Borealis* dances from horizon to horizon across the winter sky.

But it is more than that. It is the land of the Alaska Gold Rush, where nuggets were said to be the size of goose eggs, where men froze to death in search of the elusive yellow metal and dancehall girls lured sourdough who turned overnight into millionaires into marriage. Honky-tonk pianos punctuated the howl of the north wind in towns that were half-tent and half-ramshackle collections of driftwood, whalebone and packing cases. It was a time of whiskey and gold and long, lonely trails behind a dogsled. It was, in a word, ALASKA.

In truth, the Alaska Gold Rush was all of that. It was a riotous time with saints and scoundrels living side-by-side. In the cities, rugged men and women walked on planks set across streets so deep with spring mud horses could be swallowed. On the tundra, life was a living hell with mosquitoes, gnats, white socks and biting flies that descended on warm-blooded creatures in clouds. On the flipside of the seasons the temperature could drop to 50 or 60 degrees below zero, cold enough to freeze a can of oil so solid it could be cut in half with a saw. With the wind blasting at 100 miles an hour, the chill factor could go down to 100 degrees below zero, cold enough to freeze a person to death in a matter of minutes if he could not find proper shelter. In whiteout conditions, visibility could be cut to a foot in a matter of minutes.

Then there was the gold, unending rivers of it from dust to nuggets so heavy they would rip out the seams of your pockets. It could be panned out of the beach sand, dug out of the ground, plucked from quartz veins deep in mining tunnels or found just lying around in a streambed. There was enough to build an empire. Juneau alone took *five times* more gold out of the Treadwell and Alaska-Juneau mines than the United States paid for all of Alaska—and that was twenty years *before the* booms in Nome and Fairbanks or the hundreds of other strikes that stretched from the Arctic Ocean to the Inside Passage.

Besides the gold there was the **adventure** of it all for this was Alaska, a land where anything was possible. And so they came by the thousands. They were called *Argonauts*, like the famous men of Jason's men who went in search of the Golden Fleece in the annals of Greek Mythology. In 1898, the Argonauts lived again, but in this era, seeking gold in the form of dust and nuggets and bullion. Not a lot of Argonauts became wealthy, but every person who came north was touched by the spell of Alaska and was changed forever. Each argonaut took a bit of the north home with them to Des Moines and Paris and Tokyo and a thousand other cities and towns. Around the world, Alaska became the byword for adventure, where dreams could come true and wealth was within the reach of the common man.

To this day, travelers from the four corners of the earth still flood to Alaska believing that as they walk the streets of Juneau, Nome and Fairbanks, they can still hear the ghostly honky-tonk of the saloon pianos echoing across a century, drawing them back to the wild and woolly days when the very word "Alaska" set the imagination of the world ablaze!

While there is a solid date for the end of the Alaska Gold Rush – April 8, 1944 when the Alaska-Juneau Mine in Juneau closed permanently – there is no real starting date. Gold had been found in the Nome area by Americans as early as 1866 but those men were more interested in staying alive than digging in the permafrost for the yellow metal. The first sizeable strike in Alaska came in 1880 when Chief Cowee of the Auk Indians, who lived outside of what is now Juneau, went to George Pilz, a prospector in Sitka. Pilz, a German metallurgist, was paying Indians 100 blankets if they could lead him to a gold strike.

Cowee was interested in the blankets.

But Cowee had come at a bad time. Pilz's best men were out looking at prospects and the only people he could send were the dregs of his organization, a drunk by the name Richard T. Harris and an illiterate named Joe Juneau. These unlikely partners took a small boat to the present site of Juneau, quickly traded their food and supplies for rotgut booze from a nearby Indian fishing camp and spent the next three weeks on a drunken binge. They returned to Sitka and told Pilz, that there was no gold.

But Cowee, who had returned to Sitka on his own, emphatically told Pilz that his two men hadn't so much as gotten off the beach much less sampled the creek where Cowee knew there was gold. Pilz was outraged! He ordered Juneau and Harris back under notice that if they didn't look precisely where Chief Cowee instructed them to look, they would not be paid. When they went back the second time, the two sots discovered what turned out to be the richest gold find in Alaskan history.

But the rise of Juneau is not the saga of a solitary prospector searching for nuggets in an ice-cold mountain stream. Rather, it is the story of large mining companies who dominated the history of that community. The gold in Juneau was in the hard rock of the mountains and the only way to retrieve it was to bore tunnels into the very heart of the rock walls. Hundreds of miners spent their lives underground, following the elusive veins wherever they led. Over six decades the Juneau mines produced $4.5 billion in 2010 dollars – and today Juneau lives comfortably on that legacy. It is a sedate, cultured community with a population of about 30,000. The gold industry has long since abandoned the area and another has taken its place. Now, instead of plucking nuggets from the veins in Mt. Juneau, the residents of Alaska's capitol city extract money from the wallets of tourists. At the most, Juneau only saw about $36 million a year during the height of the Alaska Gold Rush. Today the city sees more than three times that each year mining the tourists. The tourists come north to see the land of the Gold Rush and the tourism industry mines the tourists so you can see that the Alaska Gold Rush is not yet dead in Juneau.

Historically, by the time of the Klondike Rush in 1898, Juneau was a well-established city. It had an operating court system and was a regular stop on the steamship line. For many tourists at the turn of the last century, Juneau was Alaska and that did not change until gold was discovered in the Klondike.

The first, real indication there was gold in the north – and specifically from the shores of the Klondike River in the Yukon Territory of Canada – came on July 17, 1897, when the steamer **Portland** landed in Seattle with what the newspapers reported was a ton of gold on board. The wharf was mobbed with people who watched awe-struck as bearded sourdoughs sauntered down the gangplank laden with the golden ore.

"Show us your gold!" the crowd cried and many of the miners did.

Within a matter of hours, Klondike fever swept Seattle. By the end of the week it had swept the West Coast and by the end of the month everyone was talking of nothing but the Yukon Territory and gold, gold, gold.

This was the start of the Klondike Gold Rush, the strike that was to draw the likes of Jack London and Robert Service – though Robert Service didn't actually get to Dawson until it was a ghost town. The heart of the strike was the city of Dawson, at the confluence of the Klondike and Yukon Rivers. For 18 months, this was the center of attention for the world with 100,000 men and quite a few women rushing north as fast as they could go by whatever means was at hand.

But getting to Dawson was an arduous task for most Argonauts. For Americans it meant getting to a West Coast city to take a steamship north. This meant getting to Seattle or Portland – but San Francisco or Los Angeles would do. Then there was the matter of gathering the necessities of surviving in the Yukon. Correctly fearing the prospect of having tens of thousands of starving men gunning down each other for a mouthful of food during the winter, the Canadian government required 1,000 pounds of food for every man who crossed the border from the District of Alaska into Canada. (Alaska would not become a Territory until 1912.) This half-ton of food *was in addition* to the gold mining equipment so it didn't take long for the poundage to add up. For a syndicate of four men, 6,000 pounds of equipment was not unusual. While it was not difficult moving these three tons of supplies by rail to the West Coast or by steamship to Skagway or Dyea, once the men got off the steamer, they had to travel by foot and every ounce became a concern.

But there was reason to be concerned long before any Argonaut ever arrived in Skagway or Dyea. With so many stampeders trying to get north, there was a staggering demand for transportation. This, in turn, led to a large number of unscrupulous men putting together steamship companies whose sole asset was one or two steamers which had been pulled out of a salvage yard or off a beach where it had been washed ashore decades earlier. With a fresh coat of paint, a few timbers and a lot of crossed fingers these ships were offered to the Argonauts as seaworthy ships. But just as quickly as they went to sea, they came apart. Many sank. Those that survived made the voyage so hazardous – not to mention unpleasant – that horror stories of the sea voyage north were both common and frightening. Many of the ships reeked of the smell of their previous career and it was impossible to spend much time below decks. Other passengers wrote of ships so decrepit that caulking could actually be pulled out from between the hull timbers.

But this was not even half the problem. These ships were overloaded to the point that many of them "turned turtle," or flipped over. Every cubic inch below decks was filled with cargo, often with no thought of how the ship would be balanced. Horses, pigs, and dogs were jammed in what space remained. Sometimes there was so much cargo that it was just piled on deck and tied down with ropes. Cargo doors were jammed open with luggage that made every storm potentially fatal. Then, after the cargo and animals had been stowed, the passengers were overbooked. Ships that normally were allowed 30 passengers booked 150. Bunkrooms were built wherever there was room and men slept in rotation. They ate in rotation as well, sometimes waiting for hours to get a meal. The galleys had to run around the clock to feed the passengers and even then the food was more gruel than a meal.

The epitome of overloading was the **Al-Ki** which left Seattle on July 19, 1898. The ship carried 110 passengers, 900 sheep, 65 cattle, 30 horses, and still managed to load 350 tons of supplies. Another dilapidated wreck, the **Colorado**, left Seattle with 350 horses, 150 cattle and 100 dogs. Once aboard, these animals had to be fed and watered daily, a chore that fell to their owners. The combined smell of animals, flatulence, manure and feed in these ocean-going stables added to the onboard stench. Dead animals were not uncommon and extracting their cadavers was a chore worthy of Hercules.

Then there were the crews. Or what passed for "crews." When hundreds of seasoned sailors abandoned decks for the gold fields, men whose maritime experience was limited to rowboats on calm country lakes often filled their places. Unscrupulous men claimed years of sea experience to get a free ride north. Farmers, bartenders, cardsharps and derelicts signed on as seaman, many of them so unfamiliar with the ocean they were unsure what their job entailed. When manpower became tight, men were shanghaied. Fighting was not uncommon and drunkenness a hazard to the safety of the ship.

That any ship managed to arrive in Skagway and Dyea at all was amazing. That many did not is not surprising. More than 50 ships went down in 1898, the first year of the stampede. One of the strangest was the **Clara Nevada**, Alaska's ghost ship. On her maiden voyage, the **Clara Nevada** went down on the night of February 5, 1898, near Eldred Rock, midway between Juneau and Skagway. The ship was on her return trip from Skagway, headed south, with as many as 165 passengers and at least 100,000 ounces of gold – $18 million in today's dollars. The ship sank under mysterious circumstances. But what makes the **Clara Nevada** so noteworthy is that ten years later, she re-surfaced, the bones of her dead littering the shore of Eldred Rock. While it is certainly true that many ships have gone to the bottom of the sea, very few have resurfaced, whatever the reason. Of note to treasure hunters, the 100,000 ounces of gold onboard the **Clara Nevada** has never been found.

Arriving in Skagway or Dyea, the Argonauts were still not out of danger. While they had faced the raw fury of Mother Nature, now they had to contend with the wickedness of man. Skagway was run by the notorious Jefferson Randolph Smith, also known as "Soapy Smith," a conman and gang leader who sought to rob as many stampeders as he and his gang possibly could. They tried mightily but they could not rob them all. But they scammed quite a few. In addition to crooked card games, loaded dice, fake fundraising efforts, and hoodwinks of every variety; they ran rampant over law and order. Murder was a common affair and between February and July of 1898, the Royal Canadian Mounted Police estimated there was a murder a day. One stampeder noted with gallows humor that "doctor's would not thrive well," in Skagway, "for there are but 4 [burials] in the cemetery and I have not heard of anyone being sick." In Skagway people didn't get sick; they got shot.

The reign of Soapy Smith did not last long. In July of 1898, his gang robbed one too many prospectors and a sleeping vigilante movement sprang to life. Meeting at the end of a Skagway pier, the forces of law and order were debating what to do when Soapy made the mistake of approaching the group with a loaded Winchester. An altercation ensued in which Soapy was killed instantly. With their leader gone, the gang was quickly rounded up and sent to Sitka for trial. Of interest to trivia enthusiasts, when the United States Army sent a contingent of soldiers to bring law and order to Skagway, they sent buffalo soldiers.

While the focus of the Seattle newspapers was on Skagway, most of the attention of the Argonauts was on Dyea, the head of the Chilkoot Trail. This was the preferred route into Canada. Though it was steeper, the Chilkoot Pass was a shorter route into Canada than the White Pass out of Skagway. In fact, the Chilkoot Pass is probably the best known and most identifiable aspect of the Klondike Gold Rush, with men walking up the ice staircase in a long line at a place named "The Scales," so-named because of a generation of tramways located here which charged by the pound. The trail rose 1,000 feet in two miles. At the top was Canada.

Though this trail was tougher, the walk was shorter and this was the key to speed when it came to getting to the Klondike. For most of the men, the journey from Dyea to Lake Lindeman would be on foot, continuous trips of 50 to 75 pounds per man. Moving forward was strictly a job for the fit. A man would load up a pack of 75 pounds, walk a few miles and deposit – or cache – his load. Then he would return for another 75 pounds. This process would continue *ad nauseam* until the entire 1,500 pounds, his portion of the syndicate's supplies, had been moved forward a few miles. Then the process would start again.

Statistically, every man had to pack a total of 59 miles to move all his food and supplies forward a single mile. If it was during the summer, the packers had to contend with deep mud on the trail and the clouds of mosquitoes and biting flies that swarmed them. During winter, blizzards would bury their cache in a matter of an hour. Time was lost on bad weather, avalanches, blockage on the trail, weighing food at the Canadian border, seas of mud and traveling only as fast as the slowest member of the syndicate.

The shortest route to the top of the Chilkoot Pass was straight up the slope. While there was a tram, many of the Argonauts could not afford the rate – or preferred not to pay it – and carried their own cargo, 75 pounds at a time, up the 1,200 ice stairs. The men stood in line, shoulder-to-shoulder, for hours waiting for their chance to ascend the narrow staircase. With everything from needle-and-thread to pieces of a boat, the men ascended the 30-degree ice walkway, step-by-step-by-step, going the speed of the slowest man ahead of them.

There are quite a few myths which cling to the staircase. One of them is that there were so many men moving up the stairs that if one stepped out of line he might have to wait for hours to rejoin the rush. This is not true. Businessmen who saw the value in charging each man who used their facility had constructed the staircase. Since every syndicate was moving at the rate of about 75 pounds per man per trip, each person would have to make multiple trips. That, in turn, meant multiple fees to use the staircase. The men who built and maintained the staircase had every incentive to make sure the men didn't get what were called "cold feet" and go home. The men who stepped off the staircase were known as "cold footers" and from this comes the expression, "to get cold feet" meaning to become frightened and quit a project that was underway. To keep the Argonauts from getting cold feet, the staircase was made as functional – and therefore profitable – as possible. A rope handrail ran to the top of the Chilkoot Pass and every 20 or 30 steps there was a level area where the Argonauts could step out of line for a rest. Those wily entrepreneurs were so successful that there is even a report of a peg-leg man making it over the Chilkoot.

Note the men resting alongside the staircase

Don't forget that all the men you see walking up the ice staircase of the Chilkoot Pass had to come back down to get more supplies and gear. While going up was difficult, coming down for the next load was a breeze. It was simply a matter of sliding down what became known as the "Grease Trail," a shoulder-deep channel that had been worn smooth by men sliding to the bottom, as one stampeder recalled, "on a gee pole, a spade, or a bit of canvas." Since the Grease Trail was so narrow, each Argonaut had to time the men ahead of them. If someone got hung up in the trail it might mean a dangerous pile-up in the snow channel.

But the wild and wooly days of the Chilkoot Pass were fleeting. As men were lock-stepping their way up the ice staircase, a railroad was being built over the White Pass out of Skagway. The completion of that railway, the White Pass and Yukon Railroad, came on July 29, 1900, and the face of the northland changed forever. Before the railroad, the only way into the gold country was on foot and it took a special breed of person to be willing to submit himself to the rigors of the trail, the mosquitoes and mud in the summer and ice fog in the winter, moving forward at the rate of two or three miles a week, and then facing the terrors of white water travel in frail, overloaded, undependable, handmade boats. It had been a culling process with the weak quitting and selling their goods along the trail or simply abandoning the cargo where it sat. The railroad changed all that. After July 29,

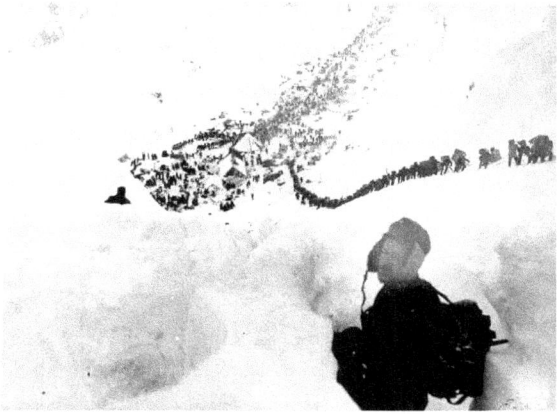

View of the "Grease Trail" from above

1900, it was possible for a stampeder to place his 1,500-pound load on the train and ride all the way to Whitehorse in a single day. Dyea died that day and Skagway saw a new birth.

But it wasn't to last long. Within a year the news of a new strike in Nome on the coast of the Bering Sea was drawing men out of the Dawson and Whitehorse by the boatload. By the end of 1900, the White Pass & Yukon Railroad would be nothing more than a metal ribbon connecting two towns shrinking in population as fast as they had grown the previous year. But before the Klondike Strike was concluded, it created one of the greatest disasters of that century: the Valdez Stampede.

To have called the Valdez Stampede a disaster would be like saying the Vietnam War was an incident. Three thousand stampeders rushed into Valdez on their way to Dawson. The geographic logic of this is hard to understand today because Dawson is more than a thousand miles from Valdez. But then again, if you were selling passage on a steamship, every ticket bought for Valdez was money in your pocket. That being said, history does not record anyone reaching Dawson from Valdez by foot before Dawson went ghost. Also unknown is how many died but the destitute numbered well over a thousand men who had tried to cross the treacherous Valdez Glacier lured by the promise of gold the size of goose eggs. Instead they found starvation, destitution and death.

The disaster began when unscrupulous steamboat companies convinced stampeders that there was another way to get to Dawson, a way that would avoid the congestion at the Chilkoot Pass. This was the so-called All American Route because almost the entire trail was through American territory. It started in Valdez on Prince William Sound and went along the spine of the Valdez Glacier and then up the Copper River watershed. Then it went over a few mountain ranges and dropped into Dawson. And, of course, if someone were to find gold in the Copper River watershed, well, then there would be no reason to continue on to the Klondike. Thus, in the Fall of 1898, 3,000 Argonauts – not one of whom had a map as to the country they were entering – left Valdez and slowly began making their way across the glacier. Since they were on ice, it made sense to move their cargo by sled. Each was loaded with around 200 pounds of cargo and moved several miles at a time. Back and forth the men went, 200 pounds per load, until all the food and gear for the syndicate had been moved forward. Then the process would start again. It was not easy work, as stampeder George Hazelet learned when he began moving his supplies over the glacier. After pulling two, 200 pounds sleds a day every day for weeks, he wrote that he had referred to himself as a beast of burden with long, floppy ears like a donkey.

The route was tortuous. The sun beat down on the stampeders and cooked their flesh. Rain created floods that washed away their camps. Snow froze them, the wind whipped their equipment across the glare ice and accidents dwindled their ranks. Then, cruelest of all, when they arrived in the Copper River watershed, they found no gold at all. The rush over the glacier had been a fraud, a scam to make money for the shipping companies. Exhausted, many of them starving, Argonauts by the hundreds stumbled back over the glacier to Valdez. No one knows how many died on the way but the number could have approached a thousand. Those that were lucky enough to make it back found the city teeming with the destitute, packed like sardines in abandoned cabins, frostbitten and living in a stench that was indescribable. They would have died in that condition had not the United States Army under the command of Captain William Randolph Abercrombie come to their rescue.

Abercrombie convinced the steamships to take the destitute back to Seattle at half the price of a ticket and then hired those who were able to work as manual laborers to create what is now the Richardson Highway. The destitute were paid a dollar a day plus board and were kept on payroll for 32 days, just long enough to enable them to pay for a ticket to Seattle and to leave them with $5.00 when they arrived.

Further north, a similar disaster was being played out the same year. Again, sparked by unscrupulous steamship companies who were only interested in selling tickets north, these companies started a rumored there was gold enough for every man on the Kobuk River. Once again, without a map or any idea where to look for the yellow metal, several thousand men rushed north through the Bering Sea for Kotzebue Sound. But the Kotzebue Rush was different because the Bering Sea and the Kobuk River are only ice-free for a few months each.

A very few months.

There were only about 120 days of ice-free travel across the Bering Sea and up the Kobuk River. If you could not get into your claim and back out before the ice covered the river and ocean, you were stuck until the next spring. Many of the Argonauts did not understand this and found themselves ill prepared for the long and ferocious winter of 1898. Hundreds of them ran out of food before spring and tried to walk out through a winter wasteland where temperatures fell to 50 below zero with regularity. Some tried to walk to the new settlement of Nome, 183 miles to the west, and never arrived. Others tried to make it over the mountains into the Koyukuk River basin where there were rumored to be settlements. Hundreds more died on the slopes of the mountain range. The next spring, the Revenue Cutter Service – the forerunner of the United States Coast Guard – had to rescue more than 70 destitute miners on the beach of Kotzebue. How many froze to death or died of starvation on the merciless landscape of the Arctic will never be known but some sources estimate the dead were as high as 1,200, almost half the people who went in – and a significant number of these were women.

* * *

When it comes to the Alaska Gold Rush, perhaps the best known strike was at Nome on shores of the Bering Sea. Ironically, the discovery of gold in Nome came by accident. Perhaps the man most responsible for the Nome Strike was an Englishman who never made it to the northland and died six years before the Alaska Gold Rush set the world ablaze. Further, it was the *failure* of this Englishman that brought about the Nome Strike, not his success.

The Englishman in question was Cyrus Field. As a young man, Field dreamed of building a Transatlantic Cable for telegraphic communication that would link Europe with America. Further, he envisioned a worldwide cable system where telegraph messages would speed along wires strung across land and laid on the bottom of the seas. A successful merchant, he retired at 33 and formed the New York, Newfoundland, and London Telegraph Company. After three failed expeditions, he was able to lay a working cable between England and Ireland in 1858. Then, in 1866, after the American Civil War, he successfully laid the first transatlantic cable.

But even as Field was laying his submarine cable, his competitors saw an opportunity for themselves. While the undersea cable across the Atlantic was certainly an admirable idea, it was still a very expensive proposition. A more economic idea was a landline linking the cities of world. Whether Field succeeded or failed, there was still going to be a need for a spider web of telegraphic wires on land to link the world's cities. Realizing that a less expensive means of running a telegraph cable from North America to Europe would be across Siberia and under the narrow waters of the Bering Strait, Western Union raised money to link North America with Asia. One member of the expedition to lay the cable was a 22-year old Civil War veteran by the name of Daniel B. Libby. On September 16, 1866, Libby and a Western Union construction crew of 40 men landed at Port Clarence, 100 miles north of Nome, and spent the next ten months stretching wire along 23 miles of the Seward Peninsula.

Then came a brutal winter – not that there are any other kind in the Arctic. The expedition had not packed properly and by April, months before the mantle of ice broke on the Bering Sea, the small party ran out of food. Facing imminent starvation, Libby stopped work on the telegraph and sent his men out, individually and in different directions, to forage for food. "It was with great difficulty that they got enough to eat," Libby said of his men and it was no small blessing when the supply ship arrived on June 28, 1867. But there was bad news aboard. Cyrus Field had succeeded in laying the cable under the Atlantic and Western Union was abandoning its Trans-Siberian project. On July 2, 1867, the Libby party, less two men who had been interred "beneath the frozen sod," departed.

But the winter on the Seward Peninsula had not been without some promise. Libby had seen "unmistakable evidence" of gold. For the next 30 years, he talked of going back and searching for the elusive yellow metal. Then, in 1897, when the story of the Klondike Strike captured the imagination of the world, Libby set about organizing an expedition north. He had no trouble finding partners and on August 18, 1897, Libby and three partners left San Francisco for Port Clarence – this time with enough supplies "to last the four-man party for several years." Libby clearly was not going to face starvation again. By July of 1898, the men had struck it rich.

With the success of the Libby party there was an undistinguished rush that led to the formation of a miner's district and community of Council City a handful of miles from where Nome is today. It was on his way to this remote outpost of civilization that one of the so-called Three Lucky Swedes made the discovery that established Nome. Eric Lindblom, a Swedish tailor, abandoned ship at a small Native village on his way to Kotzebue and hid out with a family of Eskimos until his ship gave up searching for him. Hitching a ride with his hosts to Council City, Lindblom made the first discovery on the future site of Nome when the Eskimos stopped at the mouth of the Snake River to fish. Lindblom returned to the spot in August of 1898 with two partners, Jafet Lindeberg and John Brynteson, and made the strike that made history.

Thereafter the history of Nome was one of boom. It wasn't a city that grew or a community that bloomed from the tundra overnight. Nome erupted to into maturity. One moment it was a deserted stretch of Alaskan coastline on the Norton Sound. The next it was so white with tents set peg-to-peg that the landscape appeared to be snow-covered. And it was one of the most desolate places on earth. Located 2,300 miles north of Seattle, the strike was on treeless, flat country that saw fewer than 120 days a year of ice-free ocean for steamship travel; June 1 to October 1. In addition to its desolation and climatic conditions, it had no harbor and the water off the coast was so shallow ships could not approach closer than a mile from shore. Everything had to come ashore on shallow draft barges and small boats. During the winter there were months of unbroken, frigid weather accented by ferocious snowstorms, whiteouts and very short daylight hours around the winter solstice. During the summer it was a strip of beach sand immediately adjacent to an unending, low, flat, swamp that teemed with every kind of biting, sucking, stinging, swarming insect. Travel across the tundra was circuitous where possible and unless there was a wind blowing, a man could be driven mad by the sheer number of insects descending upon him.

It was also the least likely place to find gold. There were no nearby mountains from which gold veins could drop nuggets into a river system. The land was ancient in geologic terms and the rivers that did exist were so sluggish they could not be used for sluicing. Nome had a tide of two feet and during the winter the ocean was covered with an ice plate that stretched all the way to Siberia. Eight months a year the ground froze solid to the permafrost making mining virtually impossible.

Even the naming of the area was unusual. It began half a century before the Alaska Gold Rush when a British mariner from a rescue mission identified the cape on which Nome is now located with the handwritten notation "? Name." Back in London, a cartographer misread the scribbling as "C. Nome" or Cape Nome. Other sources contend that Nome was a corruption of the Yupik expression "ka-no-me" which translates as "I don't know" or "I don't understand."

The initial beneficiaries of the gold in the area were known as "The Three Lucky Swedes" and it did not take long for greed to set in among the other Argonauts. Recognizing that it would be easier to jump good claims then look for gold on their own, a mass meeting was called to declare all claims in the area null and thus open them up for re-staking. So sure were the perpetrators this scheme would work, wood for bonfires was piled in strategic locations so that once the ruling was made that all claims were voided, bonfires could be kindled so men in the field could rush in and stake the best claims for themselves and their partners in town.

It was a bold scheme that might have worked except for a handful of soldiers who broke up the meeting. But the handful of soldiers could not hold off popular sentiment long and it was the accidental discovery of gold on the beaches that turned Nome from a seething cauldron of discontent to a town where everyone who could find a pot, pan or cradle was on the beach panning for gold. And since no one can own tidelands, they were open to all.

With the discovery of gold on Nome's beach – which was in the public domain – the strike changed from one of large mining operations squeezing out smaller ones to a poor man's paradise. Some of the claims on the beach were as small as 16 square feet; but they were yielding a thousand dollars a square foot or, as stampeder Robert Easton estimated, "$256,000 from a piece of ground no larger than your living room floor." That's about $5 million dollars today.

When it came to beach property, "you owned the land you were standing on," wrote one stampeder, "but you lost your right to it the minute you left." All manner of equipment and inventions were used. While most of the miners worked with traditional pans, sluices and rockers, there were some bizarre contraptions as well. Several companies experimented with a "caisson," or shallow water rig. At least one of them was 16 feet long and four feet wide and high. At low tide, the caisson was rolled out 120 feet into the surf where it sucked up sand from the bottom of Norton Sound and ran it through a sluice system. That operation was fairly successful and netted about $6 for every shovelful of sand that came through the sluice.

It was estimated in today's dollars that Nome's first year produced $64 million in gold, half of it from off the beaches. "Numerous" miners were making between $160,000 and $320,000, "scores" made between $50,000 and $128,000 while "hundreds" were making between $24,000 to $32,000. When gold was discovered on the beaches, men were making between $320 to $16,000 per day – and spending $600 a day of it in the saloons and gambling houses.

It was the discovery of the gold on the beaches that turned Nome from a city of destitute Argonauts to a boomtown. There was gold on the beaches and it was just a matter of picking it up. The simplicity with which the gold could be taken immediately generated a double rush, one down the Yukon River from Dawson and the other by steamship from the Pacific Northwest. Every ship in Dawson that could be loaded with passengers was rushing to Nome.

By the Fall of 1899, Nome wasn't a town; it was a landing zone. Argonauts were coming into the city so fast there was no place to house them. Carl Lomen, later to become one of the most respected men in the area, recalled that the "confusion was appalling. Machinery, hay and grain, hardware, provisions, liquor, tents, pianos, mirrors, bar fixtures, household furniture were all stored in the open. Stovepipes were every-where, all breathing out a slow black smoke that settled in a dark fog over everything, biting at a man's throat and making his nose run." Cargo from incoming ships was lost overboard and washed up on shore where it was snatched by whoever happened to be nearby. In town, "claims to town lots were jumped. The cabins that had been erected were hauled away at night by horses brought by gangs of men, some of the owners still in the cabins, and before they could get back to their location an-other structure would be occupying the ground." When one stampeder arrived in Nome he recalled that the horizon was white with tents with "the dark silhouettes of buildings [which could be seen] among the tents which spread back for miles on the tundra in great white blobs."

In the history of gold rushes, Nome was unique. Access to the gold bearing sands was simply a matter of buying a steamship ticket. It did not require any particular stamina to reach the gold fields. While the Argonauts on their way to the Klondike over the Chilkoot Trail were moving ahead at the rate of 50 pounds at a time, in Nome it was simply a matter of being barged ashore with your supplies. This led to an entirely different breed of Argonaut. Anyone from a lounge lizard to a bank president could be a miner. All it took was finding a vacant space on the beach after the tide came in. No one owned any property so there was no expense to get into the mining business. All it took was a willingness to put up with hardships. By September of 1899, the Revenue Cutter Service estimated there were between 2,000 and 3,000 residents of Nome with another 1,000 expected to arrive from Dawson. About 2,000 were expected to leave Nome before the ice came in, but Nome would still have to accommodate about 2,500 people all winter long "with very limited building accommodations and a great lack of fuel." Food supplies were estimated at 1,700 tons for the next six months. The Revenue Cutter Service did its part to alleviate part of the problem. They illegally seized a number of known malcontents, most of them with criminal records in the lower states, and gave them what came to be called a "blue ticket." In Alaskanese, a "blue ticket" is a one-way ticket out of town on the first available means of transportation in any direction. Blue tickets were being regularly used as late as 1905. (They were called "blue tickets" because the Alaska Steamship Company tickets were blue. The term stuck.)

With so many Argonauts and so few supplies and services, prices were "jumping stiff legged," as one Argonaut wrote disconnectedly. Prices in Nome were astronomical compared to Seattle. In today's dollars, meals in Nome ranged from $40 to $80 depending on the quality. A bed in a tent was $24 a night. Drinks were $8 for beer. Some items, such as the copper plate used in the gold rockers, were going for its weight in gold. If copper couldn't be bought, other metals were substituted. One miner even used 64 silver dollars to plate his rocker.

With so much gold and so little law and order, it is was only a matter of time before corruption would set in. But no one expected corruption to be on the scale in which it came. "In chaos there is profit," as Alaskan humorist Warren Sitka noted, and no one understood this better than one of the most powerful political bosses in the United States in 1899, Alexander McKenzie.

As the Republican National Committeeman from North Dakota, McKenzie had controlled politics in his state for more than two decades and exercised tremendous influence in Washington D. C. The possibility of reaping great personal rewards in Nome came to McKenzie's attention when he was approached by Oliver P. Hubbard of the Nome law firm of Hubbard, Beeman and Hume, the firm who was representing the Argonauts intent on jumping all claims filed by the Three Lucky Swedes. McKenzie immediately saw the possibility of a scam beyond even his wildest imagination and arranged to have a corrupt judge, Alfred Noyes, appointed to the Nome bench. McKenzie and Noyes came to Nome in July of 1900 and proceeded to legally seize every rich claim they could lay their hands on. Stating that they were only holding the gold until a judicial decision could be reached, they legally seized $16 million in today's dollars and waited to catch the last boat out of Nome. They were only stopped at the last minute by a ruling from a San Francisco judge that arrived on the very ship which McKenzie and Noyes expected to depart with their booty. It was a close call and it was only the concerted action by the lawyers of Nome that stalled what amounted to blatant theft by duly appointed legal officers.

The citizens of Fairbanks should have been so lucky. Fairbanks, like Juneau and Nome, was founded by accident. In August of 1901, Elbridge Truman Barnette convinced a gullible steamboat captain that his steamship could easily ascend the Tanana River without striking bottom. However, when it became apparent that Barnette did not know what he was talking about, the steamboat captain angrily evicted the protesting Barnette along with 135 tons of his supplies onto the nearest shore – which happened to be on the Chena Slough. As Barnette's supplies were being off loaded, a sourdough by the name of Felix Pedro suddenly appeared on the bank. He had just made a major find in the area and was wondering if Barnette would have any food to sell since he, Pedro, did not want to walk the 360 miles round trip to Circle for supplies. Then and there was established Chenoa City, later to become known as Fairbanks.

Barnette, ever the entrepreneur, was not about to let his location – quite literally in "the middle of nowhere" – stop him from making his fortune. The first winter he traded for furs from local Indians and prospectors and took the pelts to the lower states where he and wife, Isabelle, spent the winter. The next spring he and his wife returned with a new steamship, the **Isabelle**, with a very shallow draft that he had sent in pieces to St. Michael at the mouth of the Yukon River. It was there he met and conversed with United States Judge James Wickersham of the Third District and changed the map of Alaska.

At that time Wickersham's court was in Eagle, a community diminishing in population. Wickersham had a judicial district that was about 300,000 square miles in size, larger than the state of Texas, and he wanted to move his court to a different community. But he had a problem. Other communities wanted an exorbitant price for land and money was in short supply with the federal government. Barnette offered Wickersham a free lot on which to establish his court, which was no particular problem for Barnette as it would cost him nothing to make the offer. But then again, his wasn't much of town either.

Wickersham suggested that Barnette rename his city Fairbanks, in honor of Senator Charles Warren Fairbanks from Indiana, the man who had made Wickersham's appointment to judge possible. Barnette, not one to pass up a chit when it cost him nothing, agreed. Both men probably left the meeting assuming that they had not agreed to anything. Wickersham couldn't move his court to a flyspeck of civilization even if the land was free and Barnette's renaming of few cabins in honor of a United States Senator who would never come to Alaska was an empty gesture at best.

History had a little surprise for both of them.

In April of 1902, while Barnette was in the lower states, his brother-in-law, Frank Cleary, was operating Barnette's general store. Cleary has been given specific instructions not to give *any* goods or supplies to *anyone* wanting credit – and particularly prospectors like Felix Pedro who was broke. But when Pedro came to the cache he was able to talk Cleary into giving him a season of supplies against $100 cash. Cleary took the money and put the rest on account. While Cleary was undoubtedly wondering what he was going to tell Barnette when he returned, Pedro made a dazzling discovery less than 12 miles from the general store. At first he tried to keep it a secret but it leaked and there was a general rush into the area.

By the time Barnette returned to his cache on September 8, the first news he heard was of Pedro's strike. The crew of the **Isabelle** immediately quit their jobs and began staking the nearby creeks. Barnette was not slow in taking advantage of this flash of fortune and staked for himself, his wife, and a half-dozen relatives in Ohio whose power of attorney he had acquired earlier. Two days later a miner's meeting was held in Felix Pedro's tent. A new mining district was voted into existence with Barnette as its recorder. When Barnette suggested the name of the community to be formed be called Fairbanks, no one objected. Thus was Fairbanks officially named.

But it was still not a city. It had no people. Basically Fairbanks was nothing more than a few cabins and a seat of a mining district, the last being simply a political designation. But Barnette was not above a little more chicanery. A gold rush into the area would give the population base a budge so he sent his cook, Jujira Wada, to Dawson to spin the tale of the gold of Felix Pedro's discovery to draw people to Fairbanks. Spin a tale he did for Wada was no fool. He did such an admirable job that he was able to get front-page coverage for this new strike, possibly as big as the Klondike. The story made the front page of the *Yukon Sun* on January 17, 1903, and as many as 1,000 men hit the trail for Fairbanks. Considering it was the middle of winter with the Mercury at 74 below in some places, this rush was a dangerous undertaking at best.

Some of the entrepreneurs in Dawson were concerned enough about the alleged strike in the Tanana Valley to do some investigating on their own. A strike that close to Dawson could put them out of business. If there really was a strike, it might be in their best interest to set up subsidiary businesses in Fairbanks. But before they made the move, they needed to know if there really was a strike in the vicinity of Barnette's cache. Pooling their resources, they sent a respected mining operator, James "Coatless" Monroe – also known as Curley – to investigate the claims made by Fairbanks. "Coatless" had earned his nickname by never wearing a parka or gloves no matter how cold it got. Coatless made it to Fairbanks and on his return in March, 1903, he reported that the only money in circulation was that from the rushers' pockets. While there might be a strike in the Tanana Valley someday, that day was not in 1903.

But Coatless wasn't saying anything the locals around Barnette's cache didn't know. Rather than making living conditions better, the discovery of gold had made them worse. They couldn't mine during the winter and there wasn't a job to be had. A local by the name of Ford was quoted in the *Alaska Forum* as stating that in terms of gold "$20 will cover the entire output" in Fairbanks that winter and that was "the poorest excuse for a foundation to base a stampede on I ever saw."

It didn't take long for the rushers to realize they had been bamboozled. When they got to Fairbanks area they found no gold, primarily because it was winter and mining was difficult to perform. The lack of a boom, understandably, led to ill will particularly as Barnette's was the only store in the area and his prices were sky. Particularly galling was his requirement that every man buying a bag of flour for $500 in 2020 dollars also had to buy three cases of canned goods, which some men claimed were spoiled.

Tensions were running high. The rush had happened in the dead of winter, meaning that men had put their lives on the line to make it to Fairbanks. All they found was snow, unemployment, high prices, and too many men competing for what jobs were there. At first the anger of the newcomers focused on the man who had lured them west, Jujira Wada.

It did not take long before the miners held a mass meeting to decide what to do. No one appeared interested in eating horse or dog, as one miner recalled, and Barnette's prices were too high for many of the men to eat bread. Since talking about their problems did not resolve the matter, a mob was formed and Wada was grabbed and dragged before the council. Wada, terrified he would be lynched, didn't give the mob enough satisfaction so they went looking for Barnette with a "nicely noosed rope." They found him exactly where they expected him, at his store. But he was flanked by a dozen men each carrying a high-powered rifle. There was a brief verbal confrontation and a compromise was reached. For Barnette's part, he cut the price of flour in half and did not require the acquisition of a case of canned goods with the flour. Shortly thereafter, Barnette headed out for the winter. This eased tensions considerably.

But there was indeed gold in the area and Fairbanks did grow. It became a wild city, a rollicking town, the kind that no Hollywood producer need invent for the screen. No less a character than Dawson's Swiftwater Bill Gates, who certainly knew saloons, said of Fairbanks that it was "only one sidewalk. If you fall off one side, you fall into the mud. If you fall off the other, you fall into a saloon." The railroad came and soon Fairbanks was a transportation and cargo hub for the Alaskan Interior.

Barnette's stature grew as well and it was not long before he established one of the first banks in the city, the Washington-Alaska Bank. It proved to be a very profitable venture until January of 1911 when Barnette fled town with the bank's treasury, an estimated $16 million in today's dollars. He was eventually arrested in Los Angeles and brought back to trial in Valdez. But with the best legal assistance money could buy, he was found guilty of only one charge, a misdemeanor. The judge fined him $1,000. Barnette paid the fine and left Alaska. The *Fairbanks Daily News-Miner* called the trial the "rottenest judicial farce the North has ever witnessed." and for years used the term "barnette" as the verb "to rob."

There has long been debate as to how much money Barnette might have stolen. It was clear to his 1,400 depositors that Barnette had absconded with their money – 5,600 ounces of it which was subsequently seized in Cordova as it was being shipped out of Alaska. That amount that left Alaska was substantially high enough for Barnette to live comfortably for many years to come.

He did. As late as 1920 Barnette still owned a palatial estate in Mexico. Thereafter he disappears from the historical record. All that is known for certain is that Barnette died in the abyss of obscurity. When he died accidentally of a fall in his home in Los Angeles on May 22, 1933, his passing was not even recorded by the Alaskan papers.

* * *

No history of the Alaska Gold Rush would be complete without revealing the human face of the era. No collection of people is truly a community until it has the amenities of civilization, chief of them being an operating newspaper. Single sheet, tabloid or daily, the press is the heartbeat of the town. Nothing is news until it's in the press; then its history.

The Alaska Gold Rush spawned hundreds of newspapers, many of which lasted only a few issues. Many did not make it that long. They appeared like lonely crusaders on milk white stallions armed to do battle with the forces of evil – usually represented by corrupt businesses, sniveling government officials, petty bureaucrats and, when no other target was available, other newspapers. Today, fewer than a handful remain.

It is important to note that newspapers were far more influential in the Alaska Gold Rush than in any other part of the country. Unlike the rest of the nation, Alaskans did not have the option of being able to speak frequently with neighbors from the next town. In Alaska, there were no "next towns." As a result, news items from each community were often reprinted in other papers so anyone reading a paper would get a snippet of news from Nome, Juneau, Valdez, Kodiak or Fairbanks. Just as important, news organizations produced leaders. Four of Alaska's appointed governors were newspapermen – Alfred P. Swineford, John F. A. Strong, Scott Bone, and John Troy – and several others had newspaper experience outside of Alaska.

But running a newspaper in Alaska was like to trying to drink tea on the subway. Many of Alaska's early papers were the product of small printing presses that could be carried in a rucksack and set up in a tent. Using a cabin, even temporarily, was an improvement. Sometimes the sheets were typewritten or run through hand-fed printers much like a medieval printing press. Perhaps the most expensive newspaper in the history of Alaska was hand-typed by James Wickersham. To finance his Mt. McKinley expedition, Wickersham typed the May 9, 1903, edition of the *Fairbanks Miner* and sold the copies – all seven of them – for $250 in 2020 dollars. It was eight pages in length using every sheet of legal paper that was in Fairbanks that day.

No chapter on newspapers in Alaska would be complete without a section on the most-sued member of the Alaska press corp, George Hinton Henry. Henry published six papers in four cities between 1907 and 1915, all of them going broke, and he probably holds the record for the number of times an editor has been sued for slander, though the true number is unknown as most of the records for that period have been lost.

His most celebrated journalistic target was Commissioner Henry Bathurst of Hot Springs. In those days, the commissioner was the only local representative of law and order. Bathurst had filed five indictments against George Hinton Henry but none of them had stopped the editor from sniping. Finally Henry went one editorial too far and Bathurst sentenced him to 90 days in jail.

Not to be out done, Henry got a "tramp printer" to continue to publish his paper which continued to criticize Bathurst while he, Henry, was in jail. Bathurst then issued a warrant for the arrest of the actual press and had it installed in the cell next to Henry. When Henry was released, the press was not. Henry left town and eventually the press was tossed onto a garbage heap. Years later, in 1923, Judge James Wickersham rescued it and sent it the University of Alaska, Fairbanks.

It should also be pointed out that the bulk of the Argonauts were men, this does not mean that there were no

women present. Even excluding the dance hall girls, there were more than a handful of women who came north, many of them alone. A stampede might not have been the most proper place for a woman in those days but this did not deter all of them.

Fanny Quigley made a living cooking for the stampeders. Whenever there was a new strike, Fanny would hitch up her cooking wares and hike to the next boom, thus her nickname "Fanny the Hike."

Today Fanny is memorialized as the driving force behind the formation of Denali National

Fanny Quigley

Park, the most visited tourist attraction in Alaska. Sinrock Mary, an Eskimo, was the richest woman in Alaska. Her wealth was in reindeer, many of which she sold to the stampeders in Nome.

Sinrock Mary and her husband courtesy of the
Wilson & Erskine Collection at the Kodiak Historical Society.

Women also held jobs as cooks, postmasters, secretaries and many worked alongside men in the goldfields.

The Alaska Gold Rush was not a white man's strike either. Felix Pedro, who discovered the gold that made Fairbanks, was Italian. The "Three Lucky Swedes" in Nome – only two of whom were Swedish – were naturalized citizens and the man responsible for the Juneau boom was an Auk Indian, Chief Cowee. Non-Native women and minorities made up about one quarter of the total population of Argonauts.

One of the sad facts of the Alaska Gold Rush was that while the big winners were the stampeders who struck it rich, the big losers were the Natives. Little thought was given to the rights, status or privileges of Alaska's indigenous people and they were trampled whenever and wherever the Argonauts stampeded. This is not to say that no one cared for the rights of the Natives. This would be inaccurate. Many people fought to protect the rights of the Natives. But they were in the minority and until the Argonauts left, the Natives were often left to starve, their natural sources of food depleted by rushing hordes of miners.

Not a lot of the Argonauts of '98 ever became wealthy. Of the 100,000 Argonauts, only a few hundred ever came home with enough gold to call themselves wealthy. But all came home changed by the grandeur of Alaska. From San Francisco to Paris to Moscow, the returning stampeders talked of the walrus and grizzly, the Eskimo and bellying up to the bar with Wyatt Earp. Madison Square Garden had its roots in the Alaska Gold Rush as do Boca Raton, Florida, and the Guggenheim Art Gallery. An entire century after the madness swept the world, the works of Jack London and Robert Service can still be found in bookstores though they only wrote of the Klondike Strike. Rex Beach, who wrote of the Nome Strike became a script writer in Hollywood and his classic *The Spoilers* had been turned into the movie NORTH TO ALASKA several times, twice starring John Wayne. Hollywood continues to reach into the Alaska Gold Rush for the stories continue to astound us. And north the tourists still come, by the millions, to the land made famous by gold.

In terms of perspective, the total gold output for all of Alaska from 1880 to 1906, 26 years, was $5.6 billion in 2020 dollars. A century later Alaska experiences an economic impact of $3.4 billion *per year* from the tourism business alone, many of them coming north to see the land made by the Alaska Gold Rush. And every community in Alaska is mining the dollars in the pockets of the tourists. Tourism has become the new Alaska Gold Rush, Is the Alaska Gold Rush over? Well, it's all a matter of perspective.

THE SMALLER STRIKES

I t would be impossible to develop a composite list of all of Alaska's Gold Rush communities. There are just too many and their size varied from a handful of prospectors in tents to boomtown communities which evaporated as quickly as they appeared. There were other strikes which were mentioned briefly in the newspapers of Alaska and then ceased to be leaving the historian to wonder if the strike had ever been more than the wild talk from the pickled brain of a barfly.

For many of the larger communities, there is nothing left save diaries scattered in archives across the United States, a few photographs of a vibrant city and maybe a reference or two in a newspaper. In some, the dilapidated buildings still stand, solitary sentinels against the ravages of time. For others, all that remains is a reference on a map. But together the names to titillate the imagination: Iditarod, Independence, Hope, Candle, Ophir, Wiseman, Livengood, Railroad City, Ruby, Circle, Tolovana.

CIRCLE

Circle was originally established and named in 1896 because it was believed the community was on the Arctic Circle. In fact, it was not. It was about 50 miles south of that demarcation. Though it started as a speck of civilization, within a year a resident, Nora Crane, counted 300 log houses in Circle. Further, she noted, "there is a layer of about a foot of tin cans over the whole place."[1]

At one time it was considered the "Paris of North." It boasted the largest log cabin in the world along with streets 60 feet wide so that four dog teams could careen down the main avenue side-by-side. In addition to the 28 saloons, 8 dance halls and opera house, it also had a library with the complete works of Darwin, Carlyle, Irving and Macaulay as well as a copy of the Encyclopedia Britannica.[2]

But the boomtown didn't last long. By October of 1897, Circle was a ghost town. With the strikes in the Yukon Territory, the Argonauts left as rapidly as they had come. Lots that had sold for between $2,000 to $3,000 – with $800 extra for corner lots—were abandoned. "You can now have a lot in the city for the taking and have the business house or cabin thrown in," reported the *Seattle Times*. "About the only thing Circle has left is the post office and postmaster."[3]

But Circle wasn't dead. There was enough of a population to keep at least one saloon open, Herrington's. But even this saloon hit hard times. In August of 1898, A. H. Brown reported that "the saloon stock had been watered over and over again until there was very little taste to it."[4] It had a rebound and in 1899 at least one traveler found it a proverbial hole in the wall. Harry de Windt described it a "motley collection of sodden dwellings and dripping roofs."

With specific regard to the gayety one might have expected of a city of entertainment, de Windt noted sadly that "every tenth house was either a gambling or drinking saloon, or a den of an even worse description." There were some theaters and a "so-called" Music Hall. Alas, noted de Windt, "although legitimate drama of the blood-curdling type found many admirers, the dancing saloons were infinitely more popular." The dance halls were just as austere in their decor as the community. There was bar at one end of the room "where a wrangle took place, on an average, every five minutes." Music, if that is what it could be called as he noted, was "execrably played" by a violin and guitar which were often drowned by the din at the bar. The "mud-stained men and painted women" danced to the strains of "Donau-Wellen." For each dance, the miners were charged one dollar. Each woman was allowed to get $.25. The guests, de Windt noted wryly, "numbered about sixty, and quite a third of that number of dogs had strayed in through the open doorway from the street."[5]

In January of 1899, Dunham noted Circle had a population of 599 white people – including 32 women and 7 children. On September 15, 1899, the population had dropped to 55. Of these 20 were soldiers and 13 were women. The rest of the population had left for the Nome rush. But left in the wake were three stores stocked with liquor that did not go to Nome. This amounted to 3,000 gallons of whiskey and 437 barrels of beer.[6]

EAGLE

Of all the boomtowns in Alaska, Eagle had the most colorful founding. Its seminal roots began in Dawson in 1899 with an unsavory character by the name of Old Man Martin. An elderly man, Martin was doing "three months on the woodpile" for some minor infraction, when he told the Hudson brothers, similarly sentenced,

> Yuh know, I'd like to live in a country where they could take every jasper that can't say 'H' without hobbling it, and – say, I got an idea! You know what this country needs more 'n anything else? It needs a good, hell-roaring' git-up and git thar American town, and by Hokey, I'm going to start one, if you two jaspers will back me up.[7]

As the Hudson brothers had nothing of importance to do at the time, they agreed and the three went in search of converts – after they had finished their stint on the woodpile. Their derelict crew of founding fathers and mothers included the

> Professor Howard, an owlish gentleman with a white beard who had "a number of honorary letters" from eastern colleges.

> Barney Gibbony, a gambler and saloon man who had just made a killing at the Dewey House in Dawson. Gibbony was looking

for a site to build his own saloon and a new town sounded a lot better than trying to fight the high land prices in Dawson.

George Graves and his partner, One Thumb Jack, who were professional gamblers. Their inclusion in the partnership may have been because they came with their tools of the trade: a faro table and roulette wheel.

Jenny Moore, who had a somewhat successful small lunch counter business.

"Black" Becky White, a Black woman whose specialty was 'Plain and Fancy Washing.' White, however, stipulated that her being part of the founding of Eagle were contingent upon her washtubs and wringers be included as cargo. Precious they were for they were the only such tubs in the Klondike.

A medical practitioner of questionable education, "Doc" Pernault.

A drifter known as "The Kid," "The Pest" and "Hey You."[8]

Professor Howard had the ideal spot in mind for a city, which was fine with the rest, particularly since it was only 110 miles south of Dawson. This made it just over the international boundary into the United States and, as Old Man Martin stated with an entrepreneurial gleam in his eyes, "Just within good stampeding distance."[9]

As this menagerie of characters set sail down the Yukon there were more than a few old timers on the shore who suspected that this might be the start of a rush. Perhaps these individuals knew something they didn't. After all, Dawson's pay dirt wasn't what it used to be. Little did these sourdoughs know just how accurate their hunch was.

The soon-to-be founders of Eagle maneuvered down the river until they had crossed into the United States and settled on an island where the breezes kept the clouds of mosquitoes at bay. A somewhat permanent settlement was established whereupon a fight immediately broke out over the name of the community. Votes were evenly split between American City and Eagle City so a coin was flipped. Barney Gibbony, "being the only one with *cheechako* money in his pocket," flipped a $20 gold piece. The coin landed with the eagle up and thus was the city named Eagle.[10]

For the next six weeks, the crew plotted out streets and cut down trees to make way for the expected hordes coming downstream to this new city. An American flag was made from three California blankets and raised on a tall, stripped spruce.

Now came the delicate work. The rascals then pooled all of their gold dust. With 400 ounces, three miscreants slipped into Dawson. Their ploy was simple. One of them would go into a saloon, buy drinks for the house and then let it slip that the gold came from the "American side of the border." After quenching his thirst, the sourdough would leave and give the gold bags to another Eagle-ite who would pull the same stunt in another saloon. His appearance would be followed by a third. Ten days later, the three sourdoughs headed south back to Eagle, *apparently* unaware of the mob of men from Dawson who were following them. The moment the three allegedly unsuspecting sourdoughs landed in Eagle, a great land rush followed.[11]

Eagle, like Dawson, was a boomtown for a shade more than a year. Then Nome drew its population away, down the Yukon River to the golden sands on the shore of the Bering Sea. Eagle was large enough in 1900 to warrant the establishment of a Federal Judicial District overseen by none other than James Wickersham. But the ebb and flow of history passed the city by. The Argonauts swarmed through Eagle from Dawson and Whitehorse on their way to Nome. Fort Egbert, established near Eagle, was closed in 1911 except for a small Army Signal Corps depot which lasted until 1925.

In terms of population, Eagle exploded from a handful of residents in 1897 to more than 1,700 by the fall of the next year. Jack London, not yet the famous writer he was to become, passed through Eagle in June of 1898 in the middle of the community's building boom. He arrived at 4:00 a.m. and reported that even the early hour "did not prevent [some residents] from stopping their faro game long enough to try to sell us a corner lot."[12]

But Eagle's population boom did not last long. Within months it was back to 300. Then the seat of the Third Judicial District was moved to Fairbanks and that, in essence, finished Eagle.

SITKA

The first discovery of gold in Sitka was made in 1871 by Edward Doyle, a soldier, who found "float gold" in the Indian River just outside of town.[13] Pilz came north to this strike, as did others whose names would be synonymous with Juneau. Joe Juneau and Frank Harris were both in this rush.

There was also a momentary flash of interest in 1898 when glacial moraine was discovered to have "$100 to $900 a ton." The gold-bearing gravel lay between a glacier and a lake which were a mile apart. The gold, the discoverer of the site noted, could be found in great supply as he believed the lake could be "easily and cheaply drained." [14] That never happened.

In April of 1995 Anne Shepard of the Sitka Convention and Visitors Bureau was contacted regarding the authenticity of this strike. Shephard checked with local historians who expressed surprise that there had been a strike in 1898 and, for that matter, that there was a glacier near a lake as had been described in the *Seattle Times*. The fact that the story was probably released on April 1, which may be a clue as to the authenticity of the facts involved.

YAKUTAT

The best ground, staked by the "Kayak boys" who discovered the strike was on White River. But there was only 6 miles of river. They made 100 ounces a week in November of 1902 – $78,000 a week in 2020 dollars. The gold in Yakutat, was also on the beach, and the diggings could only be worked at low tide.

The gold strike area overlay some oil leases in the area. This was not surprising as the oil leases stretched for about 100 miles down the beach. Some of the oil finds were so promising that there was oil actually leaking at the surface level. There was also coal in the area.[15]

Yakutat is probably best known for the disastrous adventure of Arthur A. Dietz. Eighteen men started in a rush which started on the broad breast of the Malaspina Glacier. Alaska's largest glacier, the Malaspina is 850 square miles in size and feeds into ice fields which have an accumulated 2,000 square miles, making the entire ice complex about the size of Delaware. Only Deitz and four others survived, two them blinded. Dietz told a highly stylized tale of his trek in MAD RUSH FOR GOLD IN FROZEN NORTH in 1914.

BRISTOL BAY

There were reports of a strike in the Bristol Bay area but after a small rush in September of 1900, it was declared a "big fake." After going directly to the spot where the alleged strike was made, a number of miners declared there wasn't enough gold "to buy a postage stamp." The man who claimed to have made the original strike had gone home to Virginia.[16]

LAKE ILIAMNA

In September of 1909, it was determined that the alleged strike in Lake Iliamna was, after all, a fake. A man by the name of Swanson had boosted the area so well that he got a Seattle lawyer, George Murphy, to grubstake him. But part of the deal was that the brother of the lawyer, Ed Murphy, would go north. Swanson agreed and the two men headed north on the steamship **Senator**, trying to boost the area along the way. Initially they had no successes.

Leaving the steamer at St. Michaels, they took a boat south to Nushagak from where they intended to journey up the Nushagak River and portage over the mountains to Lake Iliamna. Swanson sent Murphy to look for a boat to carry them up the river and while the man was gone, Swanson ran for the hills – with the grubstake money.

While Murphy was looking for his fleet-footed partner, a rush of 19 men from Nome arrived. While Swanson and Murphy had been unable to generate any enthusiasm for the strike on the steamship **Senator,** news of the strike in Nome had created a minor rush. When it was discovered that the strike was a fake, the 19 Argonauts, broke, were forced to hitch rides back to the United States on cannery vessels. Murphy headed south as well. Swanson made a 200 mile hike to Iliamna from where he took a steamer to Kodiak. Afraid he would run into some of the Argonauts or his former partner, he "took a small boat and struck out for some place along the coast" and from there disappeared from the pages of history.[17]

COOK INLET

In November of 1898, the *Seattle Times* reported a string of rich strikes in the Cook Inlet area. Some creeks were completely staked and men were getting ".90 to a $1 a pan" on Willow Creek, about 70 miles north of the present site of Anchorage. The outlook was good, according to the locals, and a bustling town was expected any year. Other parts of Cook Inlet were equally as rich. Further south, on Knik Arm, "only thirty miles from tidewater," two Mexicans had taken out "$2,000 in six weeks" – $72,000 in 2010 dollars. The rest of the creek where the Mexicans made the strike was staked.

The diggings were so good in the Cook Inlet area and the Susitna into the Interior that government officials hinted at the possibility of a road linking the Inlet with the Tanana River. A road could be put through "without much difficulty" un-named officials were quoted as saying. "Little or no heavy work" would have to be done since "the country is rolling, after passing the summit [with] as easy grade down the other side." These same officials claimed that the Tanana side was "dry" with "very few mosquitoes or flies."[18] However, few Alaskans who have camped along the Alaska Highway during the summer could claim that there were "very few mosquitoes or flies."

A decade and a half before Anchorage was founded, there was a strike on the shores of Turnagain Arm, 40 miles south of what was to be Alaska's largest city a century later. At one time the gold bearing rock of Cook Inlet – around the present community of Hope – was thought to be so large that it would rival the Klondike. Unlike other strikes, when this statement was made by the *Seattle Times,* the newspaper was deluged with outraged Alaskans demanding the truth be printed. A group of Alaskans including sourdough Jack Rener, in Seattle at the time and had been reputed by the *Times* to have earned a "princely fortune" in the gold mines of Cook Inlet, was verbally abusing the paper when a reporter walked by. To the crowd Rener said, "Say boys, here's a reporter; what'll we do with him? We ought to hang him for such a pack of lies as that. [The publication of the lies in the *Seattle Times]* will crowd a lot of poor men into the country by their stories, and there is absolutely no need of it."

Rener and a group of Alaskans formed a delegation to set the record straight and voted that H. A. Schmesar speak for the group. "There seems to be a scheme to boom the Cook Inlet Country," Schmesar told the *Times.* Further, the only people who could possibly benefit from such a untruth were "a few men who own claims which have become white elephants of which they cannot dispose of unless it is through some stock company, and [we, the assembled miners] don't propose to see the scheme go through." At the most, Schmesar estimated the amount of gold pulled out of the Cook Inlet Country was $150,000 which was a far cry from the $1,000,000 initially reported by other miners.[19]

Rener spoke the *Seattle Times* two days later in which he offered the best route to the Copper River was to pole up the "Buchitna" for 200 miles before making cresting a pass into the upper reaches of the Copper River. This author could not find the "Buchitna" on any map of Cook Inlet and the State of Alaska, Division of Natural Resources could find no such river either. There was only a small lake named "Bulchitna" which feeds the Yentna River which, in turn, flows into Cook Inlet.

But by following the Yentna, a prospector would be moving away from the Copper River watershed, not winding his way toward it. Thus it is possible that Renner was "absurding" the *Seattle Times,* telling a non-Alaskan a tale that was just-about-true. This is a tantalizing possibility as the word "Buchitna" is very close to "Bulchitna," the Alaskan version of "bull shit," the documented source of its name.[20]

KETCHIKAN

At the southern tip of Southeastern Alaska is Ketchikan, hardly a likely place for a strike. Yet, in April of 1899, there was a "well-defined rush of miners." One miner, Captain Charles P. Dyer, claimed to have taken 337 ounces of gold worth $6,347 out of six tons of ore at his Gold Standard Mine.[21] Further, according to the *Seattle Times,* there was a good reason for the rush. "When a man can take $30,000 out of a little hole in the rock – when his first blast, impossible to be confined, sprinkled the woods for a block in every direction with rich, yellow gold – there certainly is a reason for a rush." The gold had been found in a vein that ran right to the water's edge and had been discovered by men who had "scruples against doing any work." Further, "it was against their religion to try to trace the ledge into the interior."[22] (This quote has never been understood, historically or religiously.)

SUSITNA

There was a reported strike in Susitna in 1907 which turned out to be a bust. But no one knew it at that time and it proceeded much the same as any other major strike. First the word was passed that there was the possibility of a major strike at hand. "Dogs went up in price," the *Nome Pioneer Press* reported, "when some forty Fairbankers suddenly decided that they had business in the Susitna and each proceeded to quietly gather up an outfit in the hopes of leaving town before anyone else could get away." Once on the trail, the Argonauts gave "evasive answers as to where they were heading" when they met incoming miners.

But Fairbanks was small and it didn't take the newspapers long to report who was heading out of town, a list that was picked up and printed by a Nome newspaper a month later. The strike was a bust, probably much to the disgust of some of the men who had left jobs to rush into the watershed at the end of November.[23]

KOYUKUK

Though many Americans assume that Nome is in the Arctic, in fact it is slightly below the Arctic Circle. The best known strike above the Arctic Circle was actually on the Koyukuk River. It was a brief strike when about 1,000 men rushed to the southern face of the Brooks Range and the originating watershed of the Koyukuk River. During the summer of 1898, the river was clogged with steamboats. Landing was easy enough that mining companies established their own cities, like Beaver City, Union City, Arctic City, Bergman, Peavy, Soo City and Jimtown.

None of these communities lasted very long and none of them was particularly expansive. But some of them were notable. Arctic City had electric lights and Bergman sponsored the first professional boxing match north of the Arctic Circle. For the record, the contenders were Jack Kelly of Denver and J. C. Cox of Los Angeles.

But the area was abandoned as rapidly as it was built primarily because there wasn't that much gold to find. After a miserable winter, almost all of the Argonauts left. One prospector from Beaver City had few regrets. "After I left the old shack I never turned back to take a last look," he wrote, "for there was nothing to see or remember."

A GLIMPSE OF THE ALASKA GOLD RUSH

The symbol of law and order in Candle City, 1903, courtesy of the Perry D. Palmer Collection at the University of Alaska Fairbanks, UAF-2004-120-22.

The photograph was taken at 10 pm on June 28, which gives an indication of how much sunlight there is in Nome around the Summer Solstice. Because the water was so shallow passengers and cargo had to be lightered ashore. You can see the larger ships in the deep water in the distance. This photograph is courtesy of the B. B. Dobbs Collection at the Alaska State Library, ASL-PCA-12-059.

Pressroom of the *Iditarod Pioneer* courtesy of the Alaska State Library, ASL-P277-004-110.

Ruby in 1911. Even though the city had been established almost a decade earlier there were still prospectors living in tents. This photograph courtesy of the Candace Waugaman Collection at the University of Alaska Fairbanks, UAF-2003-183-22.

Discovery City courtesy of the Alaska State Library, ASL-PCA-277-045. While there were business on both sides of the street, cross the mud was treacherous. Note the plank mud crossing in for the foreground.

Fairbanks fire of 1906 courtesy of the Albert Johnson Collection at the
University of Alaska Fairbanks, UAF-1989-183.

Saloon in Dishkaket courtesy of the George & Lilly Clark Photograph Collection at the University of Alaska Fairbanks, UAF-1986-109-15.

Contrary to the Nome presented in John Wayne's NORTH TO ALASKA, the real Nome is a flat, windswept plain. There are no trees and little driftwood. So coal had to imported, in this case in 108,000 sacks. This photograph is courtesy of the Alaska State Library, ASL-P137-013.

Nome utilities in 1900 courtesy of the Anchorage Museum of History and Art B87-7-60.

Sheep sled courtesy of the Anchorage Museum of History and Art B-70-35-6.

"SAY, WHAT WAS YOUR NAME
IN THE STATES?"

"Say, what was your name in the States?
Was it Thompson or Johnson or Bates?
Did your murder your wife and fly for your life?
Say what was your name in the States?"

. . . old American folksong[24]

Argo Bill – came to St. Michael on the **Argo**.[25]

Baldwin, E. J. "Lucky" – of San Francisco, known as a "lecherous, cigar-smoking, card playing and blasphemous" highroller." He made a substantial fortune in the Comstock Lode in Nevada and enhanced it further in Nome. By the time he died in 1909 – at the ripe age of 81 – he had accumulated a fortune of $25 million ($725 million in 2020 dollars) and a half-dozen former wives and paramours to argue over the estate. Baldwin's saloon, modestly named the Baldwin, had heavy mahogany doors which had come from his hotel in San Francisco – also named the Baldwin. It had burned down in 1898, just before the Alaska Rush.[26]

Barstow, "Tubby" – In Nome, 1900, he was "gaunt and cadaverous, skinny as a match" and once went for 29 straight days without eating anything.[27]

Bear Kid – a husky individual who gained the name by wrestling a tame black bear.[28]

Biddy the Heart Smasher – In Nome, 1900, had "bushy, ginger-colored hair which he kept slicked down with a sweet-smelling lotion" who fancied himself a lady killer.[29]

Bill the Turk – see Eric the Strong

Bill the Owl – "had eyes that very much resembled an owl's, perfectly round, and he never seemed to move them when talking."[30]

Billy the Dog – in Nome, 1900, so-named because he was always "chasing from place to place, picking up odd jobs."[31]

Billy the Horse – so-named because he was the first man to bring horses over the trail into the Klondike. Other sources indicate that he got the name because he had stolen a horse in Spokane, Washington, by leading it across a trestle with coal sack pillows to hide its hoof prints. Years later in Nome, Billy met the man from whom he had stolen the horse. Billy asked the man if he had ever found his horse or who had stolen it. The man replied in the negative and Billy allegedly stated,

> "Well, I'm the gent that 'borrowed' the horse, and as he wasn't working, and I needed help, I just coaxed him along on my journey to some other place. Nice animal, that, chief, and he done nobly, so I thank you for his use. Have a drink?"[32]

Billy the Horse was well-known for his encounter with Bishop Rowe. They were coming from opposite directions on the same trail and, as the Bishop was completely bundled up, Billy didn't know he was talking to a man of God. When asked about the trail he had just traveled, Billy replied "that trail is the god-damndest trail that any dirty son-of-a-b%^&* ever went over." Then Billy asked how the Bishop had found the trail he had just come over, "Just about the same as you, brother."[33] (Billy was booming until as late as 1913 and died in April of 1916.[34])

Billy the Horse was also alleged to have been in a poker game of notoriety in Dawson where Swiftwater Bill Gates slipped a man named Jack Blackburn a sixth card. It was well into the game when Jack asked for some beer and sandwiches. No one objected and they continued the game after a quick bite. When it came time to show cards, Jack laid down four aces. Swiftwater Bill immediately objected and said that Jack had six cards and was thus disqualified.

"Six cards," said Jack. "You're crazy."

Search as they could, the three other men could not find the extra card they knew Swiftwater Bill had slipped to Jack. So Jack walked away with the pot.

About six months later, Billy the Horse ran into Jack on the trail and asked him about that game. Jack smiled and said, "I saw that card as soon as it got in my hand. That's when I got powerful hungry and thirsty. Reason you didn't see no sixth card in my hand was because I just slipped it into that there sandwich and ate it." Thereafter he was known as Eat-'em-up Jack.[35]

Once, when Billy was down on his luck and was refused a drink, he got a can of peas and doctored it to look like a dynamite stick. He attached a fuse to the can and went back to the saloon that had refused him the drink. He entered the saloon, lit the fuse and watched while everyone cleared out. Alone, he had several drinks, took a few full bottles of booze before he casually left the saloon.[36]

Black Hand Charlie – never washed his hands.[37]

Black Sullivan – see Hootch Albert

Blond Kid[38]

Blueberry Johnnie – grew tired of his Native wife and child and took them blueberry picking. He returned alone. Later he went down river with Fiddler John and John's dance hall girl lover. Fiddler John had $15,000 in his pocket and his girlfriend $5,000; but only Blueberry Johnnie was ever seen again.[39]

Blueberry Kid – in 1916, the Blueberry Kid was in a poker game with two slickers from San Francisco, the Coon-Can Kid and Curley Harris. The men had been gambling for several days and the table was ringed with people watching the betting. At the last hand, the "weight of the gold nuggets made the table sag." The Coon-Can Kid dropped out and Curley called. The Blueberry Kid had four aces. Curley said he had "five aces and a six-shooter." The Blueberry Kid got up and left the table.[40]

There was another Blueberry Kid who shot Flatfoot Kelly and Hobo Smith along with their wives, Pale Mary and Silvertoed Helen. He hid the money and fled Alaska. Later, during a murderous attack while in the trenches of World War One, the Blueberry Kid revealed himself to a fellow Alaskan who subsequently reported Kid's whereabouts to the authorities. The Kid was captured in Seattle, tried, convicted and sentenced to San Quentin. Before he was sent to prison, he revealed where he had hidden the $30,000 he had stolen. The alleged name of the Blueberry Kid was James Ryan.[41]

Bobo the Bosco – in Nome, 1900, a cantankerous man who was eventually killed by Doc Spencer, "The Killer." (See Doc. Spencer)

Bonnifield, Sam "Silent Sam" or "Square Sam" – a card dealer in Circle City that so impressed a young Tex Rickard, the man who would build Madison Square Gardens, that Rickard always gambled "as if Sam Bonnifield was looking over his shoulder." It was said no miner was ever cheated by Sam's Bank. Bonnifield was later declared insane by a Fairbanks court but this did not stop him from starting at least one more bank, this one in Beloit, Kansas. Then he suffered from a strange mental derangement which took his memory. Arrested for drunkenness in 1909, Bonnifield mind "was a blank," a condition that continued until his death in Seattle in 1943. He died broke.[42]

In Klondike Gold Rush annals, Bonnifield is remembered as the man who won $50,000 in two sitting against the legendary "Yukon Tiger" and the "King Gambler of the Klondike," Louis Golden.[43]

Bourbon Kid – in Nome, 1900, the nickname of Tom Nestor, the "liquor warehouse tycoon." [44]

Braying Kid – in Nome, 1900, a singer which a deep bass voice who could only sing one song: "Asleep in the Deep."[45]

Broken Nose Jake – see Whiskey Jim

Brown, "Conscientious" – refused to do things because his conscience bothered him. [46]

Brown, Jr., J. J. "Power of Attorney" – a well-known claim jumper in Nome in 1901 famous for his jumping of Mickey Hayden's property. When Brown went to take control of Hayden's claim, Hayden "perforated" the seat of Brown's pants with his rifle. Brown, the *Nome News* reported, "left Hayden in undisputed possession of discovery claim." Reached for comment, Hayden remarked that he was "getting pretty wise" about how to handle claim jumping.[47]

Bull Frog Johnson – in Nome, 1900, was known for blowing his nose in the napkins of the Paris Cafe.[48]

Bunch-Grass Bill – an individual in Nome who, along with Mrs. Strong – later to be the First Lady of Alaska when her husband became Governor – ministered Reverend S. Hall Young back to health with a "diet of milk and whiskey."[49]

Burns, "Agreeable Billie" – a "dyed-in-the-wool Democrat" who was first elected to the Territorial House in 1913 as a "No Party," served in the Territorial House from 1913 to 1917. He was regarded as the "most universally liked men in the Territory."[50]

Buteau, Frank – "King of the Fortymile"[51]

Captain Jack – Also known as Sablok, he was a "notoriously bad character," who was arrested on St. Lawrence Island for breaking into the home of the government school teacher and threatening him. Captain Jack was turned over to authorities in St. Michaels in July, 1899. He was eventually sentenced to six months.[52]

Carew, "Boozey" – was always drunk.[53]

Carrol, "Malamute Joe"—awaiting trial for carrying a concealed weapon in August of 1910, the law enforcement establishment of Fairbanks "agreed not to press charges on condition the he would migrate." He did so in a small boat at which time he stated he expected to see "salt water before the freeze up."[54]

Cheechako John[55]

China Joe – registered in the 1880 census as Hi Ching and known colloquially as Joe the Baker, he ran a small bakery in Juneau. Joe endeared himself to the children of Juneau by always passing out cookies or goodies in his store. As a consequence, it was said that his was one of the few stores to be spared Halloween pranks.[56]

During the Great Yellow Scare some non-Alaskans tried to run China Joe out of Juneau. When the anti-Yellow mob reached the home of China Joe they were met by a contingent of Alaskans armed to the teeth and told them to leave China Joe alone and be on the next ship out of town. They were.

Chinese Joe[57]

Club-foot Al[58]

Cockney – arrested for disturbing the peace for using foul language in Tanana and was fined $30.[59]

Cold Hand Charley – in Nome, 1900, who was always talking about the cold weather he had encountered and survived. He liked to talk about the "old days" when temperature was judged by a bottle of Perry Davis' Painkiller. "It froze at 70 degrees below zero," he would say. "Whenever the Painkiller froze, we knew enough to stay indoors."[60]

Costa, "Happy Jack" – an Italian who struck it rich and was known to say, over and over, "Oh, by Godda, I gotta de gold!"[61]

Cowdon, C. G. "The Kennel Kid" – in Nome, 1900, a cheechako who bet Big Mike Sullivan $50 that Sullivan didn't own a dog team. Sullivan made a dog team by surreptitiously gathering stray dogs where he could find them. After he had won the bet, Big Mike released the dogs. "The sensible thing to do would be to keep your dogs in a kennel," said Cowdon. "Why let them run loose?" After that, he was known as The Kennel Kid.[62]

Crawford, Bob "Megaphone Kid" – a seven-year old in Fairbanks in 1906 who was earning $2 an hour for his "spieling" ability.[63]

Croaker Kid – in Nome, 1900, the sobriquet of Eddie Grigsby, Nome's surgeon.[64]

Cutty Sark Yank – in Nome, 1900, because he was from Vermont and came to Nome on the **Cutty Sark**.[65]

Dancing Kid[66]

Davenport, Diamond Lil – dance hall queen in Skagway, 1898.[67]

Deacon Eakin – In Nome, 1900, was so named because he would mutter "But is there a God?" when he got drunk. [68]

Deaf Dan[69]

Deep-water Gus – a halibut fisherman who disliked shallow water. [70]

Deetering, William "Caribou Bill" – acquitted of murder for shooting Jack Ridenour in the back after being ordered off Dome Creek properties in August of 1908.[71]

Diamond Dick – was famous for converting his gold to diamonds and then giving the diamonds to dance hall girls.[72]

Diamond Tooth Lil – so-named for a diamond which she had set "between two buck teeth."[73] (Other women with similar names included "Diamond Tooth Lou," "Diamond Hattie," and "Diamond Tooth Gertie.")

Dick the Dude – a Native from a village near Sitka, Dick the Dude had learned carpentry aboard the man-of-war **Jamestown**. In

1891, he constructed a two-story home in his village at a cost of $2,500 and then threw a potlatch – which cost him another $1,000. Dick the Dude was a credit to his race, the *Sitka Alaskan* wrote. "Dick's present comfortable position illustrates what a thrifty Native can accomplish when he adopts the white man's ways." He gained the sobriquet "the Dude" because he dressed in the latest American fashion in spite of the fact that he lived in a Native village.[74]

Dickey, "One-Armed"[75]

Double-Cross Dinzy – in Nome, 1900, an untrustworthy individual. For the genealogical record, his real name was Dan Plasteid from Haverhill, Massachusetts.[76]

Double-0 Kid[77]

Duncan, Thompson – also known as the "Bughouse Barber." He operated the O.K. Barber Shop at the foot of Paradise Alley in Skagway until March 9, 1899 when he gunned down his former roommate and intimate friend in the O. W. Johnson Saloon. Then the former roommate turned the gun on himself.

Dutch Helen[78]

Dutchy[79]

Dynamite Joe – of Ketchikan[80]

Eat-em-up Frank – owned a cabin on the Tanana River between Fort Gibbon and Fairbanks. When he got drunk, "which [was] often," he would shout at the crowd that he would eat up any man. Eat-em-up Frank only weighed 100 pounds.[81]

Eric the Strong – lived with Bill the Turk on Mooseheart Mountain.[82]

Erusard, "French Pete"[83]

Ethel the Moose – Dance hall girl in Skagway, 1898.[84]

Evaporated Kid – so named because he looked like a "human string bean with the bean left out."[85]

Fewclothes, Molly – dancehall girl in Skagway.[86]

Fintzen, John "Gold Stick Johnnie" – around Ketchikan, Gold Stick Johnnie was known for his divining rods which were supposed to detect gold. He never could boast of a large strike.[87]

Flying Dutchman[88]

Fortier, Albert "Hootch Albert" – Tanana mail carrier[89]

Foster, W. F. "Slim Jim" –one of "Soapy" Smith's lieutenants.[90]

Frisco Sue – in Nome, 1900, a prostitute.[91]

Garden Island Cesspool – named given to J. H. Caskey's newspaper, the *Alaska Citizen*, by readers of "Wrong Font" Thompson's *Fairbanks Daily News Miner* – until Thompson bought Caskey out in 1921. The name derived from the area where the *Alaska Citizen* was published, Garden Island, and from where the *Fairbanks Daily News Miner* is published today.[92]

Gayhart, Gus "The Dago Kid"[93]

Gimmie Kid[94]

Goldilocks Gus – in Circle about 1900, Gus was found with a piece of buttered bread. It was suspected that the butter in question had been stolen from Perry the Dog's five pound box. Gus could not explain where he had gotten the butter so a miner's council was convened and Gus was ordered out of Alaska and his claim auctioned off.[95]

Good Enough Larry – always said "Good enough" when asked about the gold he was taking from his claim.[96]

Grant, Six-Shooter – known for his twin six-shooters which he wore everywhere he went, in spite of the fact that no one else in Ketchikan felt afraid to walk the streets without a six shooter. Apparently he only shot his guns once, when the sailing craft he was in tipped over. Grant drew his guns and shot the "sheet-ropes and halyards" forcing the sails to fall so the boat could right itself.[97]

Gravity Grant – was always asking "Why is there gravity?"[98]

Greasy Jim the Pearl Diver[99]

Half-Kid – see Wilson Mizner.

Ham Grease Jimmie[100]

Handsome Kid – in Nome, 1900, the partner of Scotty Allan who shared
In the mail run between Nulato and Nome.[101]

Hair Lip Mary – a "noted and notorious" madam who was known for her "uninhibited flow of witty and scurrilous invective." Dragged into court, she was being harangued by a District Attorney when she launched into a "resume of his pedigree" and finished by stating "[I] remember that you haven't paid yet for the window that you broke the last time you were drunk and squabbling with the girls down at my place."[102]

Hard Luck Sam[103]

Hardluck, Evan[104]

W. J. "Six-Shooter Sam" Harris.
Photograph courtesy of the
Alaska State Library.

Harris, W. J. "Six Shooter Sam" – a character on the Juneau waterfront who was alleged to be a "marshal" though no such documentation exists. (Court records list him as a "special police officer"[105] but the newspaper lists him as a City Marshal.) Harris was an ego maniac bully-with-a-badge in 1909 who was ravaged by the *Alaska Daily Record* to a large part because he had been appointed by Mayor Emery Valentine who was not liked by the *Alaska Daily_Record*. The paper referred to Harris as "a pair of long legs above of which was to be seen a broad white sombrero, of the Alkali Ike class and underneath it and between the ends of the legs there was a Seymour coat." Harris's clothing was so out of character for Juneau that more than one person mistook him for a "bum."

Harris carried at least one pistol – unusual in that Juneau didn't see that much violence – had several belts of ammunition wrapped around his waist, carried a blackjack and Bowie knife and smoked a large cigar on duty. Residents referred to the badge which he flourished upon occasion as an "oyster can tied to his vest." (Can openers in those days made triangular holes. To remove the top of the can, the holes had to be made around the circumference of the lid. Once removed, the lid looked like a star, thus the reference to the "oyster can.")[106]

The blackjack was later taken away from him by an irate citizen of Juneau when "Six Shooter Sam" tried to use it without provocation. Harris was able to recover his black jack and, on the night of September 20, 1909, beat a staggering drunk senseless. The drunk, Jerry O'Neil, was on his way home walking down Front Street in Juneau when Harris suddenly demanded to know where he was going.

"Home," replied O'Neil.

"Well, you had better go," replied Harris.

O'Neil then asked who Harris was whereupon Harris "shouted his favorite slogan [that] he would show him 'hew is hew'" and struck O'Neil mightily on the head. O'Neil senseless body was then dragged to the police station.[107]

The story of Six-Shooter Harris and the confrontation with the newspaper editors is also historically accurate. In 1909, Juneau had a bumper crop of editorial conflict. On April 9, 1909, A. R. O'Brien of the *Alaska Daily Record* published rude statements about one Charles A. Hopp, the editor of the *Douglas Island News*. Hopp, the newspaper printed tongue in cheek "hopped around the recent political fight over in Douglas" until he saw which side was going to be "successful and then came out strongly for the winners." Hopp was compared to a "star harlot" in the "tenderloin [of] the newspaperdom in Alaska" who believed that by attacking the "Western Federation of Miners" that he would "get [a] job printing at Treadwell."[108]

Hopp responded on April 14, 1909, when he published of "Gloomy Gus O'Brien" of the *Alaska Daily Record,* took time from "tearing down everything that is good, decent and holy in the city of Juneau to hurl a handful of his filth at the editor of this paper." Insinuating that O'Brien had "either escaped from a penitentiary or a lunatic asylum," Hopp further suggested that in the few months since O'Brien had come to town, "he has done nothing but vomit forth the most villainous rot ever read in this part of the North." A man without friends, O'Brien's "very name has [gotten to be] a curse" on the streets of Juneau. But the script strayed over the line and Hopp was indicted for libel.

Hopp and O'Brien were not the only editors in trouble. The same grand jury also indicted L. S. Keller, editor of *The Daily Alaskan* in Skagway. Three months earlier, Keller had published an attack on Judge Lyons in Juneau that ended with an indictment for libel. The *Daily Alaskan* editorialized that the confirmation of Lyons as a judge was the "severest blow that could have been struck at public confidence in the administration of justice in Alaska" because Lyon was in the pocket of "Big Business" and would serve as their "servant on the bench."[109] Hopefully, the editor mused, the Judge would "rise superior to the influences that have elevated him to his present position."

All three editors were indicted by the grand jury of August 18th. Three days later, the remaining two editors in the area, Edward C. Russell of the *Daily Alaska Dispatch* and W. C. Ullrich of the *Juneau Daily Transcript* took the Grand Jury to task. On August 21, Russell had published an editorial attacking the credibility of the Court Clerk and Jury Commissioner:

> "There would be a nice condition of affairs with Judge Lyons on the bench, Big Clem [Summers] jury commissioner and all around fixer Clerk Shattuck paying political debts with court printing and furnishing wet nurses for the gang and Brother Louie Shackleford floor leader. What a nice deal this would be."[110]

Not to be left out, the next day Ullrich summed up the feelings of the Judge Lyon his crew succinctly under the heading "THE 'RULE OR RUIN' GANG:"

Robert A. Kinzie, Gov. Wilford B. Hoggatt, Clem M. Summers, Louis P. Shackleford, Thomas Lyons, Henry A. Shattuck, charter members. John Boyce, honorary member. Gloomy Gus O'Brien, valet and editor o[f] rule or ruin organ. Principal place of business, Juneau, Alaska. Principal object, GRAFT.[111]

Two days later, Ullrich ran yet another libelous editorial for which he was indicted.[112]

Thus all five editors were indicted by the Grand Jury. That was a known fact. What happened next is a matter of conjecture. On August 21, C. M. Summers, smarting from the attacks on him in the papers, was in the company of A. R. Russell when the two men happened to run into Edward C. Russell in the Friedman Brothers Cigar Store in Juneau. The confrontation resulted in Summers and Russell "knowingly, willfully and unlawfully" assaulting Russell, wounding him in the eye. Then O'Brien proceeded to wipe the cigar store floor with Russell's body – the actual indictment language being that O'Brien did "knowingly, willfully and unlawfully grapple with, hang on and drag said Edward C. Russell on and along the floor of [the] room."[113]

Two other men, C. F. Cheek and Henry Shattuck, who had also been attacked editorially by Russell were also present. So was special policeman W. J. Harris, also known as "Six-Shooter Sam." Harris attempted to take custody of O'Brien but Cheek and Shattuck, stopped him by standing between the policeman and the man under arrest. When Harris reached for his billy club, Shattuck took it from him. Harris then arrested all three men.[114]

Since the men were so well known in Juneau – Summers was the President of the First National Bank of Juneau and the "jury commissioner" while Shattuck was the Court Clerk – the case was moved to Ketchikan. The case against Summers was dropped but O'Brien was fined $230. Ullrich's paper went under the same month and libel charges against Hopp and O'Brien were dropped.[115]

Haslan, "Step-and-a-half" – had one leg shorter than the other. [116]

Hastings, Rat-faced[117]

Hemple, "Oklahoma Bill" – in Valdez, 1898, Hemple, paralyzed on one side, attempted to cross the glacier. After cresting several benches – almost being killed by a number of his party who became drunk and were sitting on him by accident – he came off the glacier and opened the General Merchandise and Outfitting Store in Valdez as well as that community's first bank. He never sold liquor in his store.[118]

Herrold, Robert "Hot Air" – so named because he worked for the Hot Air Mine or because he was responsible for putting up the telephone lines for the Hot Air Mine.[119]

Higrade Kid – a thief.[120]

Hobo Kid[121]

Hold-Up Fanny – in Nome, 1900, a prostitute.[122]

Hold-Up Kid[123]

Hoo-Hoo Henderson – in Nome, 1900, a prostitute who would fake an orgasm and cry out "HOO-HOO!"[124]

Hootch Albert – in Circle, circa 1900, bought up a shipment of spoiled potatoes and made a fortune selling potato whiskey.[125] Along with Black Sullivan, he was famous for distilling liquor, both of which were strictly illegal in Alaska. But it was close to impossible to get arrested much less prosecuted for the transgression.[126]

Hood, "Snow Goggle" – always wore sun glasses.[127]

Hook Ole – replaced his lost hand with a hook which was "deadly in barroom brawls."[128]

Hootlanana Kid[129]

Horsemeat Kid – in Nome, 1900, bought up all of Nome's dead animals, butchered the cadavers and sold them as dog food.[130]

Hosfold, John, "Missouri Jack" – Was known throughout Alaska as "Missouri Jack."[131]

Hot Springs Joe[132]

Hungry Kid – man of whom it was said was "able to eat at any and all times and never to refuse a meal."[133]

In-And-Out Kid – in Nome, 1900, so-named because he had the habit of rushing into a saloon, gulping down a drink and then rushing out.[134]

Indian Jim[135]

"Jack the Swede" – In 1906 "Jack the Swede" had a contract to cut ice for the drinks of several saloons in Council City.[136]

Jackson, Arthur "Cook'em Two Days Beans" – In 1898, Arthur Jackson and his father made it over the Valdez Glacier and into the Cooper River watershed. Supplies were pretty easy to come by because so many boats flipped in the Klutina River and the banks of the river were littered with supplies. Jackson and his father found a bag of beans and, after two days of cooking, found the beans still hard. A sourdough came by and asked what they were cooking. Jackson said they had been cooking the beans for two days and the vegetable was still hard. The sourdough took one look at the beans and laughed. "Well no wonder they're still hard. They're coffee beans!" Thereafter Jackson was known as "Cook'em Two Days Beans."[137]

Jackson, "Hand Logger"[138]

Jekyll-and-Hyde Smith – a man whose moods would swing wildly.[139]

Jimmy the Pirate[140]

Jimmy the Tough[141]

Joe Whiskers[142]

Johnson, "Cut Throat" – in Circle about 1898, Johnson tried to cut his throat while he was drunk. But he was so inebriated that all he did was slash his jawbone on both sides deeply. He was saved from bleeding to death and after he sobered up he was told by those who had patched him up that if he wanted to kill himself he was at liberty to do so but they wanted to watch. Johnson declined and allowed a heavy beard to cover his scars.[143]

Johnson, Ed "Frozen Foot" – a gambler in Nome who moved to Funter Bay in Southeast Alaska in 1917. Frozen Foot ran booze out of Funter Bay until 1922 when two federal agents shut him down. Johnson bribed his way out of being arrested and the two Federal agents, J. W. Kirkland and W. Mayburn, proceeded to tell different stories to the grand jury. Kirkland reported that the Johnson's cabin was deserted while Mayburn told three different stories, one to the United States Commissioner and two to two grand juries. When other agents went back to Johnson's cabin and burned it, the Grand Jury indicted Johnson and then censored the federal agents for destroying a man's property. With what should have been *three* open-and-shut cases of bribery, bootlegging, perjury – and the legal assistance of former Judge and Delegate James Wickersham – the United States government could not get a conviction.[144]

Johnson, Skookum[145]

Jones, "Bosun Bill" – a seaman who hired on as a teamster in Katella. Ordered to harness a team of horses, he did not know how to attach the reins. When the barn boss asked what was taking so long, "Bosun Bill" replied, "Well, Boss, I can drive them all right, but damned if I know how to put the rigging on them."[146]

Kelly, "Kangaroo" – an Australian with a long neck.[147]

Kelsey, "Deep Hole" – dug down 212 feet on his claim in Tanana, a record which lasted until W. O. Johnson dropped a hole 319 feet in Chatenika.[148]

The Kid – also known as "The Pest" and "Hey You," he was one of the founders of Eagle.[149]

Laboyteaux, "Alabam"[150]

Lamont, Albert – see Gunny Sack Jack Whitsler

Lamore, "Nellie the Pig" – see Wilson Mizner.

Lathrop, Austin E. "Cap" – Alaska's first millionaire was known as "Turnagain Arm Jim."[151]

Lazy John – a Native who felt complimented when he was told he was lazy and used that with his name for years.[152]

Lee, "Highpockets" – so-named because he was so short that his coveralls from Sears came to his armpits.[153]

Long Shorty[154]

Louis, "Flapjacks" – allegedly ate flapjacks three times a day.[155]

Lousetown Babe – a prostitute who operated primarily out of Klondike

City, across the river from Dawson. Klondike City was also known as Lousetown. The Lousetown Babe used to travel the Alaskan interior plying her trade with a small sign which she would put on her bedroom door, "FRENCHING INSIDE."[156]

Low Grade Tim – "a no-good bum."[157]

Lucky Bob – so-named because he had all his teeth.[158]

Lucky Jim – Chief Conductor of the Alaska Mercantile Comp;any.[159]

MacNit, "Assessment Work" – so named because that was all he ever claimed to be doing on his claim.[160]

Maiden, Andrew Jackson – known as "Sourdough Maiden."[161]

Malamute Kid – known for his fine malamute dogs.[162]

McIntosh, "Wooden Shoe" – so named because his flat feet made him walk as though he was wearing wooden shoes.[163]

Metcalf, Captain C. F. – was nicknamed "Jibboom."[164]

Miller, Henry – "Dutch Kid" was arrested in Fairbanks as a pickpocket. He had "annexed $140 from Jim Peterson" and his "get rich quick" scheme landed him the "arms of the law."[165]

Minchumina John – In 1913 Minchumina John, an Athabaskan, his wife and a child hailed Reverend Hudson Stuck at the 3,600 foot level of Mt. McKinley. Stuck was climbing the mountain with Harry Karstens, the "Seventy Mile Kid." The trio had been following the climbers because they wanted Stuck to baptize their child. Stuck obliged and after he had completed the baptism, Minchumina John said "Now will you marry us?"[166]

Miner, H. H. – Known in the Hot Springs area as "The Man Who Can't Keep Warm," Miner was interviewed in Chicago on his way to Cuba in 1910. Dressed in a fur overcoat, ear muffs, his collar turned up over his ears and wearing a heavy hat and boots for the Arctic, Miner was quoted as saying

> I should have worn my winter underwear. I've on two suits of underwear, but they are not heavy enough. My, but I'm cold! Been cold ever since I put in a winter on the Yukon.[167]

Missouri Jim[168]

Mittenburg, "Muddycreek" – believed that gold was most likely to be found in fast, muddy creeks and spent his times prospecting those areas.[169]

Mit – see Wilson Mizner.

Mizner, Wilson – One of the lovable scoundrels of the Alaska Gold Rush was Wilson Mizner, later of Hollywood fame. He was involved with gambling and prize fighting in Nome and a work stoppage in the Klondike. In Nome he had the reputation of being able to "borrow money from a lamppost and is said to be the only man who ever hired the Nome brass band on credit."[170] In addition to these northern distinctions, in the course of his life he was also a mining engineer, actor, playwright, a Fifth Avenue art dealer, husband of the "second richest woman in the world," proprietor of the legendary Brown Derby in Los Angeles and, with his brother Addison, a founder and promoter of Boca Raton. Mizner died in 1933.

In Nome in 1902 he was involved in a badger game in which he was to play the "damaged husband." He drank too heavily the night before and when he awoke, late for his appointment, he discovered his pistol had been stolen. Looking for a prop, he found a can of tomatoes and stripped of its label.

Thus armed he crashed into the lover's nest and threatened to blow the two lovebirds sky high with the explosive which was, in fact, nothing more than the can of tomatoes. The man paid for his life with his money belt which yielded $10,000 in gold. After the man had fled in fear, his partner asked for her share of the scam. Mizner handed her the tomato can. When she asked what good the can was going to do her, Mizner calmly stated, "It just got me $10,000."[171]

By his own admission, as Deputy Sheriff in Nome, Mizner hid Scurvy Bill and Two Tooth Mike from a posse even though he knew for a fact that Scurvy Bill had stolen at least $40,000 from the Gold Commissioner's office in Dawson.[172] (It is Mizner's claim that he was a "Deputy Sheriff." He probably meant "Deputy United States Marshal.") Just after he had hidden Scurvy Bill in his own attic, Mizner was called to join the posse in looking for the criminals he had just hidden. The posse had followed blood to a cabin where they assumed the criminals were hiding. Mizner then astonished the posse by "rolling a cigarette in one hand and holding a revolver in the other, [and then kicking] in the door of the cabin." (One source lists the three desperadoes as Mit, the Half-Kid, and Two-Tooth Mike.[173])

Mizner was known as the "Yellow Kid." Legend has it he would put syrup in his hair and, during the day when he worked with gold dust as a cashier, he would brush his hands on his hair from time to time. Each night he would shampoo and extract the minute gold particles his hair follicles had been collecting during the day.[174]

According to Mizner he, once robbed a restaurant in Nome for chocolate for his girlfriend "Nellie the Pig" with the words

"Your chocolates or life" and grubstaked the future owner of Grauman's Chinese Theater in Los Angeles, Sid Grauman.

Molly Fewclothes – dance hall girl in Skagway, 1898,[175]

Monroe, James "Coatless" – so-called because he never wore a parka or gloves no matter how cold it got. Apparently he did it for show and once out of sight of Dawson he would don parka and gloves. In town, he usually wore three suits of underwear to maintain his reputation. A highly respected mining engineer in Dawson, he was hired by a conglomerate of Dawson miners to go to Tanana in March of 1903 to see if there really was a great strike there. Back in Dawson, Monroe, the "shirtwaist sage," reported that Tanana might be big in a year or two, but not in 1903. (He was also known as Curley.)[176]

Montana Fillie – a dancehall girl in Skagway.[177]

The Moose – dancehall girl in Skagway.[178]

Moose Hide Charles – always carried a moose hide poke.[179]

Moose John – not to be confused with Moose Meat John of Anchorage fame circa 1935.[180]

Moose Mary[181]

"Most Assuredly" Pebble – a man whose favorite expression was "most assuredly."[182]

Mousetrap Kid – His real name was Pete McGrath and he ran an outfitting shop in Nome, 1900. He earned his name by arguing with a prospector over the price of a mousetrap for 15 minutes while a mining company executive waited for change.[183]

Murphy, Spud – of Mouse Point.[184]

Mystery Knut – kept an air of mystery about everything he did.[185]

Nellie the Pig – "one of the best looking trollops" in Nome in 1900 who "was given this nickname for a good reason."[186] She originally got the name by biting off the ear of a bartender.[187] See Wilson Mizner.

Nels the Ox – "powerful and hardy"[188]

Nigger Jim – In Nome, 1900, he was an "Irishman with a frosty beard" who hired a bummer to boost Teller. The bummer did and started a mild rush. When it was discovered that the strike was a fake, the bummer was found dead alongside the trail in ten feet of snow. The coroner reported that the man had died of exposure but the man who found the body, Wild Jim, reported that the neck had been broken.[189] (See Wild Jim O'Hare.)

Norby, "Yakima Pete" – so named because there were four men on board the **George E. Starr** by the name of Pete so they were given the nicknames of Big Pete, Little Pete, Blubber Pete because "he was fat like a walrus" and "Yakima Pete" because he came from Yakima.[190]

O'Conner, James "Hamgrease" – was arrested for living in a "State of Fornication" with a woman who was not his wife. The case was dropped.[191]

O'Hare, "Wild Jim" – at Cape Lisburne in 1900 Jim was living with an Eskimo woman named Chechero. When Captain Healy of the Revenue Cutter **Bear** asked him "Have you slept with this girl?" Jim replied "Yis sor." "Then," replied Healy, " I pronounce you man and wife!" When Jim realized he was married, he went on a drunken binge for a week during which he was named "Wild Jim."[192]

O'Hern, Jack – in Fairbanks, circa 1905, he was also known as "Happy Jack" or "Whiskey Jack." Consistently being arrested for drunkenness, O'Hern fled at least one sentence of 40 days and upon recapture was sentenced to another stint of 90. Jail was nothing new to him as he had spent "a good two-thirds" of the previous year in jail. Though he came from a good family, he was a "slave of drink," reported the *Fairbanks Evening News,* and his sober moments were "far and few between." His drunkenness had become such a nuisance that local saloons "cut him off" and the district attorney promised to prosecute anyone selling liquor to "habitual drunkards" like Whiskey Jack.[193]

Old Maiden – a man in Circle about 1900 who always packed 40 to 50 pounds of newspaper with him regardless of how rough the country was. When asked why he carried the papers, Old Maiden replied, "they're handy to refer to when you get into an argument."[194]

One-Eyed Jack[195]

One Thumb Jack – one of the founders of Eagle.[196]

Onespot, Lena – In January of 1910, Lena Onespot, a Native woman who lived four miles outside Tanana, had an unusual funeral. When the woman died, her friends took her corpse to St. James Chapel and then hurried away to attend a potlatch – expecting to be gone ten days. Reverend Peabody "had to take the initiative in having a grave dug, for the mild weather rendered it inadvisable that the interment be long delayed." Lena Onespot was so-called because he was one-eyed.[197]

Oregon Mare – a dancehall girl in Nome who would whinny while in bed with a John.[198]

Paper Nose Tommy – In Wrangell in the late 1880s, an Indian by the name of Tomyot bit off a woman's ear. Her husband cornered Tomyot at the end of a barge and cut off the point of his nose. Sourdough Buck Choquette sterilized the wound and covered it with oil paper for protection. Thereafter Tomyot was known as Paper Nose Tommy.[199]

Perry the Dog – in Circle about 1900, Perry the Dog was known as the cleverest man in town. An ardent gambler, he once kept a game going for 56 hours. He loved butter and had a five pound box sent to him. When the box was stolen, Goldilocks Gus was suspected. Gus was unable to explain how he had come by the butter he had on his bread, butter being a rare commodity in Circle, and was ordered out of Alaska.

One night Perry the Dog and Belching Bob came into a Circle saloon and Perry set up a drink on the house. Twenty men and 8 women lunged for bar stacking themselves two deep as Perry yelled, "Give 'em what they want!" Then he ordered a second round. The bartender was suspicious at this point as to who was going to pay for these drinks but Perry the Dog allayed his fears.

"Me and Bob got a little bet on," Perry told the bartender. "The one that loses pays for all the drinks. That'll be alright with you, won't it?" The bartender agreed.

Perry the Dog and Belching Bob then began looking out the window at Mount Juneau and began talking between themselves and laughing. Hooked, the bartender asked them what they laughing about and what was the nature of their bet.

"Bob and me have a little bet about Mount Juneau there," replied Perry the Dog. "Bob bets that when the mountain falls over, she'll go that way and I bet she'll tumble this way. We're just waiting to see which one of us is gonna lose the bet and stand the drinks."[200]

Pete the Pig[201]

Piano Kid[202]

Pike Pole Slim[203]

Polo Kid[204]

Red-Light Kid[205]

Erwin "Nimrod"
Robertson

Renoir, "Crazy Louis" – was almost hung in Nome in 1900 when he tried to kill a man while drunk. He was given a blue ticket on the next available ship.[206]

Robertson's Plane

Robertson, Erwin "Nimrod" – A resident of Eagle in the early days, Nimrod dreamed of building an airplane. He only needed $1,000 to construct his "bird machine" but failed because, as it was said locally, he could "make anything except a living." Nimrod was a wizard at making things, like gold puzzle rings and jewelry and once made a set of dentures for himself from the jaw of a bear he had shot. Then he ate the bear with its own teeth.[207] Nimrod had a great fear of being eaten by wolves. In November of 1940, when he became stranded on the trail and would clearly die, he chose to lie on the ice of a river where a trickle of water would pass over his body and freeze him solid to the ice floe. After his corpse was found, it took rescue workers almost a week to extract his body from the river ice.[208] Interestingly, Robertson's plane flapped its wings like a bird. The flapping mechanism is housed in the University of Alaska Fairbanks Museum today.

Robinson, "Stikine Bill" – When the construction crews of the White Pass and Yukon Railroad arrived at the international border,

Canadian officials refused to let them cross. Michael J. Heney solved this stoppage by sending "Stikine Bill" Robinson to the top of the summit to soothe Canadian officials. Armed with a bottle of Scotch in each pocket of his jacket and a box of cigars under each arm, Stikine Bill met with the solitary guard patrolling the international border. Two days later, after the guard awoke with a crashing hangover, he discovered that Heney's men were already a mile into Canadian territory and moving fast. While this tale sounds very much like a myth, this particular incident was told by a man who was present at the event, F. B. Whiting, M. D. who, interestingly, was also the doctor who performed the autopsies on both Soapy Smith and Frank Reid and was Michael J. Heney's personal physician.[209]

Rosebud Johnnie – was known to live off such edibles as rosebuds, grass and lichens. Once while guiding a party of starving miners, he noted that there was food atop a certain hill. When the desperate miners made it to the top of the rise, they found Rosebud Johnnie chowing down on, wild rosebuds he had dug up out of the snow.[210]

Rungger, Roadmaster[211]

Salt Water Jack[212]

San Juan Jack – represented the San Juan fish packing company in Ketchikan.[213]

Schmidt, "Two Step" Louie – from Dawson got his name because he was a frequent dancer at, among other places, a dancehall named Alamander Left. Louie once sold a claim for $5,000 and insisted that $1,500 be in chips for dances at the Alamander Left. Louie was rich enough to come into the dancehall and pin a $100 bill on the curtain by the orchestra and telling the musicians to "give the crowd a century's worth of *Turkey in the Straw*." The musicians usually played a few dances of *Turkey in the Straw*, took down the $100 and proceeded to other dance numbers.[214] Legend has it that one night he spent $25,000 on a binge. Victor Durand, a fiddle player who had performed in both Dawson and Nome, reported that one night he played *Turkey in the Straw* 175 times for Louie. Louie died alone in his cabin in Nome in 1946 with a substantial amount of gold. Unfortunately no one other than Louie knew where it had been hidden. The only one to benefit from Louie's death was a wolverine that he had been unable to trap. The wolverine had broken into Louie's cabin and feasted on his corpse before it was discovered by Louie's friends.[215]

"Scrap Iron Jake" – a vagrant in Tanana in 1909 who, when arrested, "improvised a pry [with which] he soon managed to loosen the bars that were holding him and then took himself off to parts unknown."[216]

Scum-doo[217]

Seventy Mile Kid – In the early years of the 1900s, Harry P. Karstens was sleeping in his tent in the Seventy Mile River area in the Yukon Territory when he was awakened by a bright light. The light, as it turned out, was his tent was on fire. He barely made it out alive and there he was, standing in his underwear 30 miles from the nearest cabin in 40 degrees below zero. As quick as he could, Karstens stripped the canvas tarps off his dogsled and fashioned them in pants and a parka. Then he mushed the 30 miles for help, running most of the way to keep from freezing. "One thing in my favor;" he later commented, "I had a good pair of underwear." Two decades later, in April of 1921, Karstens was named the first Superintendent of McKinley National Park, now Denali National Park.[218]

Scurvy Bill – see Wilson Mizner.

Shady Sadie – in Nome, 1900, a prostitute.[219]

Sheep Creek John[220]

Short and Dirty[221]

Simmons, E. R. "Slippery Slim" or "Slim the Barber" ran up gambling debts in Council City and attempted to pay them off by selling his barber chair and tools to Erle Snyder for $30. Alas, "Slippery Slim" had already sold the same chair and tools to W. B. Hart. When the deception was discovered, Deputy Marshal Bienswanger, "armed to the teeth with everything from a tooth pick to a Gatling gun," spent $1,500 tracing the barber to Nome where the miscreant was found "concealed under a bed."[222]

Simp – in Nome, 1900, a cheechako who decided he would mush his own dog team to Candle. He advertised for a dog team and the fun-loving sourdoughs rounded up and sold him a team of stray dogs and then fooled him into buying a rope harness and securing the dogs with a "double reef hitch and a half over." Simp paid for the dogs and was off to Candle. But each time he passed someone who owned one of the dogs, the dog was cut out of the team. By the time he reached Candle, Simp only had two dogs left – and lawsuits for dognapping that took him years to resolve.[223]

Simpson, "Rotary Bill"[224]

Single-0 Kid – in Nome, 1900, so-named because he only bet on the single 0 in roulette.[225]

Sitka Jack – "a murderous looking siwash"[226]

Sitting Maude – in Skagway, 1898, a "dance hall queen."[227]

Six-Fingered Jake – so-called because he had six fingers on each hand.[228]

Skid the Bartender – In Nome, 1900, Skid was the bartender at the Ophir Saloon. He had a stump for a left hand. When the owner of the bar pulled at his right ear indicating that there was trouble brewing, Skid would strap an iron hook onto his stump.[229]

Skinny Dick[230]

"Skoogy Pete"[231]

Skookum Bill[232]

Skookum Jim[233]

Slap 'er Down Louie – known to come into his favorite bar once a year after his clean up and yell "I slap 'er down, boys, an' the drinks are on me!"[234]

Slick-in-Sight Bill – believed that the appearance of a stone that was worn slick by the action of the glacier against the rock was a sign that gold was near. When someone would ask Bill about his claim he would often pull a piece of glaciated granite from his pocket and say "See, I have the slick in sight."[235]

Slow Sam[236]

Smith, "Tarantula Jack" – in July or August, 1900, he and Clarence Warner discovered the copper deposit that made Kennecott.[237]

Sourdough Bill[238]

Spencer, Doc. "The Killer" – in Nome in 1900. Doc was actually a veterinarian who was "pretty good treating a dog or horse but not so good with people." He got his name from his treatment of Bobo the Bosco. Bobo tried to pick a fight with the wrong man in the Ophir Saloon, a man by the name of Eddie Halford. When Bobo turned around he was cold-cocked with a pick handle to the head. He lay on the floor until Doc Spencer arrived and had a few drinks. Then the Doc force-fed Bobo a cup of morphine. Bobo was then taken upstairs where he regained consciousness long enough for a short conversation.

"Do you know who it was that killed you?" he was asked.

"No, and I don't care," snapped Bobo. "But who in hell was it that gave me that morphine?"

Bobo died and thereafter Doc Spencer was known as "The Killer." As an ironic footnote to the affair, Eddie Halford was found innocent of the death of Bobo and Doc Spencer was never brought to trial for murder because, interestingly, he had been one of the jurors at Eddie Halford's trial.[239]

Smiling Albert[240]

Smith, "Brainy" – one of the smartest men on the Koyukuk and the man who took out the largest stake ever made by a single man, over $500,000 – $14 million in 2010 dollars.[241]

Smith, "Forty-Mile"[242]

Smith, "Hungry" – one of the cheapest men on the Yukon River.[243]

Smith, Jefferson Randolph "Soapy" – known for the scam he pulled in Denver with bars of soap. "Soapy" would appear to stick a $100 bill inside the wrapping of a bar of soap and then drop the soap into a basket with identically wrapped bars. After mixing the basket vigorously, he would sell the bars of soap for $5, each person hoping their bar of soap would be the one which had the $100. Soapy was killed by Frank Reid on the night of July 8, 1898.

Snake Legs – North West Mounted Police in Dawson. Of them, Old Man Martin, founder of Eagle noted, "Hell, there ain't a horse in the whole damn shebang, and I'll bet an ounce against a hole in a doughnut there ain't a damn one of 'em could ride if they did have one."[244]

Speedy Stiff – so named after chasing a thief with unexpected speed in spite of the fact that he had chronic stiffness of the joints.[245]

Spitting Maud – dancehall girl in Skagway.[246]

Squaw Tamer[247]

Steam Shovel Pete – was known to be able to run a "muck-stick" better than "any three men on the creek."[248]

Step and a half Johnson – had one leg shorter than the other and was quite fond of footraces – but he preferred a race course that was along the side of a hill which gave his short leg an advantage. [249]

Stufin, "True Story" – rated as one of the worst liars on the Yukon River.[250]

Sundborg, George Walter "Hoodoo" – so named in Rampart in 1897 when he shot and killed a hawk eating a gold finch that was perched on the mast of the steamship **National City.** Some of the passengers said that he had "hoodooed" the steamer. The next day the steamer's mast collapsed and Sundborg was labeled "Hoodoo."[251]

Sweet Marie – dancehall girl in Skagway.[252]

Syphon Kid – so named because he was asked to siphon out a bit of whiskey from a keg in Council City. But he didn't "dare let the free end of the siphon out of his mouth for feat of wasting the precious liquid."[253]

Tague, Charles "Hard Rock Charley" – one of six men charged with stealing gold from Fort Gibbon.[254]

Taku Billy[255]

"Teddy Bear Kid" – in Nome, 1900, the name given to Father Jacquet, the "mad" Russian priest. He would walk the streets of Nome with two trained bear cubs and raise money for St. Mary's Hospital in Nome or to send a stranded miner home. He was known for entering every saloon in search of contributions and with him went the two cubs. He was described as having black, piercing eyes that peered over his "cadaverous cheeks." He had a curly black beard and walked the streets of Nome in a flowing robe with prayer beads for a belt.[256]

Thompson, "Wrong Font" – editor of a number of papers in Fairbanks including the *Fairbanks News, Tanana Tribune, Tanana Miner, Chena Miner, Ridgetop Miner, Daily Alaskan Citizen, Weekly Alaskan Citizen* and the *Fairbanks Daily News Miner* which is still in operation today. When he finally bought out his last rival in 1921, Thompson was quoted as saying that his was a "newspaper graveyard" in which he lived "cluttered up with the remains of the papers" which had once been published in Fairbanks.[257]

Three-fingered Bob[258]

Timber Line Gus – was well over seven feet tall.[259]

Timber Line Kate[260]

Tobin, "Deep Hole" – known for digging deep prospecting holes.[261]

Tommy the Horse – once bet another miner $50 he could pack 200 pounds of flour from Eldorado to Hunker (8 miles) in one hour. While hiking, his pack strap broke and he had to stop to make repairs. This cost his enough valuable time to lose the bet by five minutes.[262]

Truesdale, "Hatless Bob" – in Circle, circa 1900, was accused of selling liquor to the Indians. The only evidence against Hatless was a bottle of whiskey taken from an Indian. The jury heard the case and was then sequestered with the bottle of whiskey. After each member of the jury sampled the evidence to determine the veracity of the claim of the prosecution it was determined that the evidence was missing. Thus was Hatless acquitted.[263]

"Two Tooth Mike" – see Wilson Mizner.

Webber, "Old Man" – ran one of the sloppiest roadhouse in Alaska and was known for his rabbit stew, which was cooked in an old kerosene can on top of a sheet-iron stove. Webber never cleaned the can and just kept adding whatever wild game he had. Charging $2 per serving, legend has it that the meal was wretched but on the Upper Yukon that was all there was. When Judge Wickersham came to Old Man Webber's roadhouse, he said he wanted a special meal rather than the rabbit stew and didn't Webber know who he was? To that Webber replied, "I don't give a damn, if you're Teddy Roosevelt, you won't get any better than the rest of the boys in this roadhouse!" Then Webber explained how Alaska had changed since the "shyster lawyers" had come to the northland had how Alaska was "going to Hell as fast as it can go."[264]

"Two-faced Jack" – also known as "The Double-Bitted Axe" because of his two-faced personality.[265]

The Virgin – dancehall girl in Skagway.[266]

Virgin Annie – a prostitute in Unalaska.[267]

Wallace, "Babe" – dancehall girl in Skagway.[268]

Weiner, "Five Dollar" – so named because he never spent more than five dollars on anything.[269]

Whiskey Pete – a drunk.[270]

Whiskey Jim – was accused of selling liquor to an Indian, Broken Nose Jake.[271]

White, Elmer John "Stroller" – as a newspaper reporter in Dawson, White had a column entitled "Strolling Through the Yukon" and the name stuck. White joined the Klondike Strike and worked for the *Skagway News, Bennett News, Klondike Nugget* (Dawson), *Dawson Daily News* and the *Dawson Free Press* before becoming the editor and publisher of the Yukon Territory's *Whitehorse Star.* He eventually moved to Juneau where he was the editor and publisher of the *Douglas Island News* which later moved to Juneau to become *Stroller's Weekly.* White served in the Territorial Legislature and was Speaker of the Territorial House from 1919 to 1921. After his death in September of 1930, a 5,000 foot mountain to the northwest of the Mendenhall Glacier was named in his honor, Mt. Stroller White. Of humorous note, White's journalistic saga of the "chirping of ice worms" predates Robert Service poem of the ice worm cocktail.[272]

Whitsler, "Gunny Sack" Jack – of Valdez, so-named because he and his partner, Albert LaMont, always carried their supplies in gunny sacks. Their claim was on a creek, naturally enough, dubbed

Gunny Sack Creek. LaMont was the younger of the two and was known as the "Gunny Sack Kid."[273]

Wickersham, James "Sunny Jim"[274] – Wickersham was also known as "James the Terrible," "Flickering Wick," "The Judge Militant" and "Our Jim" after he became a delegate.[275]

"Windy Bill" Morgan – a great talker and it was said that isolated camps loved his presence – along with his portable phonograph and "store of classical records." Morgan was once asked why he had left his home and family and he replied, "Sir, my family is the sort which has frequently been asked to leave a country for the good of that country."[276]

Woodpile Annie – in 1900 in Nome, a prostitute.[277]

Yellow Kid[278]

Yellow Leg John – so-named because he often wore yellow Mackinaw pants which his long legs made conspicuous.[279]

Yes Bay Gus[280]

Young, "French Joe" – a "poke snatcher" in Nome in August of 1900. The event which brought him to the attention of the law occurred in the Madden Bar when a miner dropped a heavy poke on a table and yelled that he was the "real thing from Dawson." French Joe thereupon snatched the poke from the table "like a turkey gobbler on a luscious June bug." With the miner and several more in pursuit, French Joe left the saloon by a back door. The chase continued down the street until Joe tossed the poke aside and made his escape. The crowd in pursuit let Joe fly and fell upon the poke, tearing it open only to discover that it was full of sand. Joe could not be found immediately but was lured from his hiding by a fake fire alarm. Recognized, he was immediately arrested.[281]

Things did not go well for the prosecution at the trial. The victim could not identify Joe as the assailant. French Joe then plead for mercy because he had stolen something of little value. The Judge "rebuked" him and then bound him over for $10,000.[282]

Names without explanation as provided by R. Lynn Smith in Herbert Heller's SOURDOUGH SAGAS (Author's note: This list mixes Alaskan with Klondike names.)

MEN		
Waterfront Brown	Deep Hole Johnson	Montana Pete
Swiftwater Bill	Too Much Johnson	Blueberry Tommy
Billy the Turk	Husky Kid	Dago Joe
Step and a half	Slivers Perry	Two for a Quart
Two Step Louie	Slivers Feiges	Mush-on
Buckskin Harry	Powerful Joe	Snuff Box Olsen
Eat-em-up Frank	Blackie	Snowy
Hard Luck Charlie	Louise Dick	Jimmy the Goat
Muck-Luck Kid	Hot Air Smith	Wise Mike
Scurvy Kid	Brainey Smith	Komoko John
Skylight Kid	Windy Smith	Long Shorty
In and Out Kid	Jumping Smith	Stone-age Bill
Malamoot Kid	Happy Jack	Tanglefoot
The Dutch Kid	French Joe	Three-Fingered Bob
The Daylight Kid	Cock-eyed Shorty	Dog Sam
Dago Kid	John the Greek	The Black Prince
Blueberry Kid	Moose John	The Gambler's Ghost
Forty-mile Kid	Butch Stock	The Coat
Sixty-mile Kid	Ham Grease Jimmy	The Vest
The Crummy Kid	Hungry Mike	Tripod Pete
Honest Ike	Poker Charlie	Diamond Dick

WOMEN		
The Nosey Sisters	Dirty Gertie	Nellie the Pig
The Limping Grouse	Queenie	Sweet Marie
Passionate Annie	Three-way Annie	The Sweet Pea Girl
Bunch Grass	Web Foot	Maggie the Rag
The Virgin	Diamond Tooth	Moosehide Annie
The Oregon Mare	Gertie	Laughing Annie
The Utah Filly	Diamond Hattie	Irish May
The Black Bear	Skagway Kay	Texas Rose
The Cub	May the Cow	Butter Ball
Spanish Marie	Allah, Allah, Allah	The School Marm
Spanish Julia	Kitty the Bitch	Fighting Nell
Finn Annie	The World's Wonder	Fuzzy Knot
Snow Ball	The Merry Widow	Box Car Aggie
Spot	Cheechako Lil	The Doughnut Queen
Moose Mary	The Chinless Wonder	Sixty-Nine
Short and Dirty	French Camille	

Another list of names without explanations also appeared in the *Nome Nugget,* October 11, 1901. Some of the readable names include

Jimmy the Goat	Twelve to Two	Baked Bean Leo
Sawdust King	Chili Dick	Punctual Carp
Gypsy Joe	Pete the Pig	Swiveled Eye Kid
Coon Skin Bill	Three Fingered Bob	Buzzard Kid
Handsome Harry	One Armed Jake	Slaughterhouse Mike
Popcorn Jimmie	Hokey Pokey White	Rotten Egg Mike
Tommy the Skunk	Jimmie Craps	Kangaroo Jack
Possible Straight Kid	Fatty Bill	Shanghai Huber
Ring Tail Squealer	Fifteen to Two	Roulette Joe
Pig-Faced Patsy	Tommy the Rat	Economic Willie
Dead Eye Dick	Peg Legged Jack	Leo the Nonpareil

Another list of names with no explanation can be found in "Fairbanks Nicknames' Curate Finds Malamute Kid had Company Aplenty," *Anchorage Daily Times,* June 23, 1943. That list came from a sourdough by the name of Joseph Ulmer who left some papers at the University of

Alaska Fairbanks. In Box 4, "Notes on Alaska People," is an extensive list of names but with no explanations. A selection of names follows

WOMEN		
Baroness	Forty Mile Rose	Sailor Bess
Bedrock Susie	Gumboot Billie	Short and Dirty
Beef Trust	Hottentot	Sore eyed Sanaa
Black Bear	Irish Queen	Spitting Maud
Brown Gravy	Irish Rose	Sweet Marie
Calamity Jane	Jew Rose	Sweet Pea
Cheechako Lou	Kitty the Bitch	Ten-Cent Sally
Chicken Ridge Fanny	Koyukuk Queen	Texas Hazel
Cockeyed Elsie	Limping Grouse	Texas Rose
Connie the Wiggler	Lousetown Lizzy	Three-way Anne
Cow Miller	Merry Widow	Tin can Anne
Cub Bear	Molly Fewclothes	Tin fiddler
Dago Marie	Nelly the Pig	Utah Filly
Diamond Tooth Lil	Oregon Mare	Weeping Pearl
Doghouse Lizzy	Passionate Anne	White Rat
Dutch Kate	Piledriver Maud	Woodpile Anne
Fighting Pearl	Pissing Jenny	World's Wonder

MEN

40 Horsepower Swede	Bismark	Cannonball Kid
Alabam	Black Jack McDonald	Caribou Bill
Arizona Charlie	Blinky	Cassiar Jim
Austrian Joe	Blue Parka Kid	Cast Iron Kid
Automatic Swede	Blue Ribbon Kid	Charles the Twelfth
Bald Face Kid	Blueberry Tommy	Cheechako John
Bear Kid	Boston Smith	Cheeseham Sam
Bear Paw	Boxcar Reilly	Clawhammer Bill
Big Mitt Stevens	Buckskin Bill	Codfish Tom
Billy the Dog	Budweiser Kid	Coldwater Johnny
Billy the Finn	Bullcon Kelly	Colorado Kid
Billy the Horse	Burn 'em Up Kid	Concrete Johnson
Billy the Kid	Burning Daylights	Cook Inlet Kid

Coolgardie Smith
Cow Miller
Crazy Baker
Crooked Kid
Crooked Neck Jorgen-
son
Crummy Kid
Curly Kid
Curly Monroe
Cyclone Thompson
Dago Frank
Dago Joe
Dago Kid
Dago Smith
Dawson Charlie
Daylight Kid
Deacon Jones
Deephole Johnson
Diamond Dick
Diamond Kid
Dirty Pete
Doctor La Booze
Dogface Johnny
Dogfish Pete
Dogmusher Johnson
Dutch Henry
Dutch Kid
Dynamite Joe
Eat'm Up Frank
Eat'm Up Johnson
Engineer Burns
Evaporated Kid
Fiddler John
Fifteen Two
Fisty McDonald
Flapjack Jake
Foghorn Nelson
French Joe
Gasoline Nick

Geepole Johnson
George the Arab
Gloomy Gus
Going Kid
Goosy Smith
Grabhound Johnny
Greasy Bill
Grizzly Bill
Groundhog Jackson
Ground sluice Bill
Hamgrease Jimmy
Hand logger Jackson
Handsome Harry
Happy Jack
Hardluck Charley
Hatless Joe
Helm Bay Johnson
Herring Pete
High-grade Sweeny
Hobo Bill
Hobo Reilly
Holy Joe
Home Brew Pete
Honest Ike
Honest John
Hootch Albert
Hot Air Reilly
Hotcake Johnny
Hungry Kid
Hungry Mike
Hurry Up Jones
In and Out Kid
Indian Joe
Itchy-Scratchy
Jerusalem Joe
Jew Ben
Jew Bob
Jimmy the Bear
Jimmy the Cheese

Jimmy the Goat
Jimmy the Mule
John the Baptist
John the Finn
Jump-off Pete
Keyhole Jimmy
Kid Brown
Kid Fisher
Kid Marion
King Oscar
Kobuk Red
Kobuk Scotty
Koldyke Kid
Kultus Johnson
Laughing Ole
Lighthouse Johnson
Little Giant
Lonesome Pete
Long Shorty
Mackinaw Kid
Malamute Kid
Midnight Johnson
Mike the Turk
Million Dollar Kid
Missouri Bill
Monkey Wrench John-
son
Montana Pete
Moose Bill
Moose Johnson
Moose Ptarmigan Ben
Moosehide Kid
Mountain Climber
Mukluk Kid
Mulligan Dan
Mush On
Muskrat Johnny
Mysterious Kid
Napoleon

Nigger Jim
Nightgown Kid
Nimrod
Nome Kid
North Pole Johnson
Oklahoma Bill
Oregon Kid
Overland Jim
Packer John
Paddy the Pig
Pale Face Kid
Panginegee Kid
Pelly River Kid
Penny Ante Brown
Pete the Pig
Phonograph Nelson
Photograph Sam
Pistol-grip Jim
Poker Charley
Poker Green
Popcorn Jimmy
Porcupine Paul
Poriugee Pete
Portwine Charley
Powerful Joe
Ptarmigan
Rabbit Nose Rob
Ragtime Kelly
Rambling Sam
Ramp's Peterson
Red Dog Sam
Rescue Pete
Rocky Mountain Ryan
Rosebud Johnny
Roughouse Bill
Roughlock Johnson
Russian Kid
Saint Peter of Tanana
Saltwater Pete

Sandspit Kid
Sawdust John
Scarface Kid
Scotty the Bear
Scow Davis
Scurvy Kid
See Me Felix
Seventy Mile Kid
Sixshooter Grant
Skagway Bill
Skagway Jim
Skookum Jim
Skookum Johnson
Slim Gray
Slim Jim Slivers
Slim Williams
Slippery Jack
Slow John
Smiling Albert
Smokehouse Bill
Snoosebox Olsen
Soapy Smith
Socialist Kid
Sourdough Bill
Sourdough John
Spaghetty Kid
Spanish Joe
Sparerib Jimmy
Sparkplug Kid
Spikehorn Jesus
Spud Murphy
Squaw Brown
Squeaky Pete
Stag-hound Bill
Stampede John
Step and a Half Taylor
Stoneage Bill
Stub Erwin
Swiftwater Bill

Tagish Charlie
Tennessee Kid
Terrible Swede
Three Finger Bob
Tin Ace Pontass
Tommy the Mate
Too-Much Johnson
Tonsina Jake
Too Much Johnson
Turnip Mike
Twostep Louie
Waterfront Brown
Whiskey Jack
White Dog Smith
Whitehorse Smith
Wildcat Anderson
Windy Bill
Wise Mike
Woodchopper Joe
Yellow Kid
Yukon Charley

FACES OF THE ALASKA GOLD RUSH

E. T. Barnette courtesy of the University of Alaska Fairbanks, UAF-1989-12-102.

Wilson Mizner

The Oregon Mare courtesy of the Alaska State Library, ASL-P277-001-192.

China Joe courtesy of the Alaska State Library, ASL-P297-118.

The Gypsy Queen, dancehall girl and wife of Curly "Coatless" Monroe, courtesy of the Alaska State Library, ASL-P277-001-193.

Bishop Rowe courtesy of the Mollie Ward Greist Collection at the Alaska State Library, ASL-P90-014.

Drawings by Amanda Saxton

BREAKOUT!

I t was 6:30 on the morning of July 4, 1905. Roberts, a new guard at the federal prison on McNeil Island, southwest of Tacoma, Washington, was making his morning round when he made a disturbing discovery. While he had been on duty that night, keeping an eye on the desperados under his care, eight of them had disappeared.

Examining their cells he discovered something even more embarrassing. The eight escapees had gained their freedom by tunneling through six brick walls and two ceilings. One of the ceilings was composed of sheet steel. How the eight convicts had been able to complete the work without being heard was a matter Warden O.P. Halligan, United States Marshal Hopkins and a host of news reporters were going to be asking for days.

Immediately after the alarm was sounded, Warden Halligan did a quick nose count. He was missing eight men, confirmed by their empty cells. Seven of the escapees were run-of-the-mill convicts,

> Clyde C. Castle, from Tacoma, who had been sentenced to two years for altering money orders, with his term to expire on October 27, 1905.

> James Leslie, from Alaska, who had been sentenced for larceny with his term to expire on August 18, 1905.

Joseph H. Malone of Fort Gibbon, Alaska, who had been sentenced to six years for rape with his term to end on December 4, 1908.

W. D. McCarthy of Tanana, Alaska, who had been sentenced to ten years for robbery with his term to expire on April 14, 1910.

Matt Moor, one of two Japanese escapees, was from Alaska and had been sentenced to five years for stabbing. His imprisonment was to end on May 16, 1908.

Edward Stickney, from Tacoma, had been sentenced to three years for counterfeiting with his term to end on July 5, 1907.

K. Takenouchi, from Alaska, the second of the Japanese escapees, had been sentenced to 20 years for manslaughter. His term was to expire on May 16, 1918.

The eighth man, however, could hardly have been called run-of-the-mill. He was the one prisoner the warden could have guessed would be in the escape party even before looking over the log book. That convict was George Wade. A master escape artist, Wade had already been in – and escaped out of – McNeil Island at least twice and had slipped from custody twice more at another penal institution. A seasoned escape artist and long-time drug smuggler who knew the United States/Canada border area like the back of his hand, he was going to be a hard convict to catch.

The only real surprise for the warden was the escape of Castle and Leslie. Both men had short sentences and were due to be released fairly soon, Leslie within a matter of weeks. Their escape did not make any sense. But then again, this was McNeil Island and a lot of things that happened on this island didn't make sense.

Originally McNeil Island, located in the chilly waters of Carr Inlet, had been established as a prison site primarily to put as much distance as reasonably possible between the federal convicts and the population of Tacoma. The fact that this distance was primarily composed of the frigid salt water of the southern extremities of Puget Sound which could not be traversed without a boat made the site of the prison ideal. It was close enough to Tacoma to be serviced by the businesses therein, but far enough from the city to allow the residents to breathe easily whenever the subject of murderers, bootleggers, and larcenous individuals was brought up.

On the island, the prison itself was a collection of buildings which housed the cells, wire fences, and watchtowers. Escape was deemed unlikely because a prisoner would not only have to break out of his cell and compound area, but would have to leap over wires and skirt watchtowers before making it to the shoreline. Then he would need a boat to cross the frigid water to the mainland.

Inside the walls, McNeil Island was a melting pot of America's criminal element. Men ranging from illegal immigrants about to be deported to murderers serving life sentences mingled with rapists, forgers, stabbers, burglars, and even a few reindeer rustlers. These men were the dregs of the courts of Pacific Northwest and the District of Alaska.

As each man entered the institution, he was logged in with his height, weight, eye color, as well as his religion – sometimes listed as "heathen" – and his property, if he had any. It was a melting pot of nationalities and criminals. Prison life was intolerable with all of the charges that could be made of an institution of those days. The cells were sweltering in the summer and freezing in the winter. The food was substandard, medical care of lamentable and sanitary conditions medieval.

Though security was tight, McNeil Island was not escape-proof. It opened for prisoners in 1887 and there had been more than a handful of escapes by 1905. Some of them were even successful. One of the first was Leo St. Cloud who was serving a 40 day sentence for sending obscene material through the mail. He arrived on September 10, 1892, and slipped out of custody 22 days later. He was never recaptured. There were several other escapes over the next decade – including two by Wade – but none quite like the mass exodus of eight prisoners on July 4, 1905.

Of all of the escapees, George Wade was the clearly most notorious. Under the alias of "Charles Smith," with his real name listed as "George Bates," he had begun his penal career by being convicted of smuggling opium into the United States in December of 1891. He was found guilty by a Port Townsend court and sentenced to a year at McNeil Island. But he didn't stay long. On March 11, 1892, he slipped out of custody and spent 11 days on the run. Recaptured, he made up for his escape, stated court documents, by working "extra hours every day" and was released on November 30, 1892.

George Wade courtesy of the National Archives

Within two years he was convicted of smuggling opium again, this time under his true name, George Wade. While in 1891 he had been sentenced for smuggling about 15 pounds of the substance in 1894, a Tacoma court found him guilty of possessing "two trunks containing about one hundred pounds" of the drug. He was sentenced to McNeil Island again on July 17, 1894. Though he was supposed to serve two years at hard labor, he didn't stay at McNeil Island nearly that long. A little more than two months later, on September 27, he escaped again. He and another prisoner were taking garbage outside the prison walls when both men made a "sudden dive for the brush" and disappeared.

Several days later, while guards were still out looking for Wade and his companion, two other prisoners poisoned the warden and were able to escape as well. The warden survived his bout with death and within a matter of days three of the four escapees were re-captured. But Wade eluded the bloodhounds and disappeared.

For seven years Wade was able to evade the law. Then in 1901 he was arrested again. But true to his reputation, again, he was able to escape. He gained his freedom before he went to trial only to be recaptured.

Sentenced to a year in jail, he escaped before the end of his term but was recaptured and forced to finish his sentence. (There is no record of what the sentence for this transgression of the law might have been or where he was incarcerated.)

Three years later he ran afoul of the law again, this time in Nome, Alaska. He was sentenced to McNeil Island for the third time, in September of 1904, for larceny. But on July 4, 1905, he was once again on the lam.

THE ESCAPE

The drama of the eight-man breakout was just as fantastic as Wade's record. McCarthy, Stickney, Wade and Malone were secured on the second floor of the prison while the other four men were locked in immediately above them on the third floor. The men on the second floor, each from his own cell, tunneled into his neighbor's cell and then into Wade's cell. Now, with their combined manpower, they bored through the ceiling of Wade's cell into Leslie's cell immediately above them.

At the same time, the four men on the third floor were separately tunneling through the brick walls dividing their cells. When all prisoners met in Leslie's cell on the night of July 3, their combined efforts allowed them to penetrate the sheet steel plates of the roof. Up through the gap, they ran across the roof of the prison and then slid down to ground level using a rope they had made of their blankets, stripped and braided.

What initially surprised the warden was the time it took for the men to break out. The prison had allegedly been thoroughly inspected on Saturday, July 1, so it was assumed that all of the digging had to have been done during the day on Sunday, Monday and Tuesday when the noise of prison routine covered the sounds of metal against brick wall. But how the eight could have escaped without being heard on the night of July 4 was a complete mystery – at least until the first escapee was caught.

Once outside the prison building, the eight men made a wide tour of the island to avoid the watchtower. Arriving at the boathouse, they forced the door and disabled the prison launch by removing a part of the boat's engine and dropping it into the inlet. Then they stole two rowboats from the shed along with eight oars and disappeared into the gloom.

Once the escape had been discovered, the most important question for the warden to ask was "In which direction will the escapees head – would they go south toward Oregon or head north toward British Columbia?" Going south was an option but not a good one. Six of the eight men were from Alaska and the other two knew the immediate area fairly well having lived there. Further, George Wade had made a living smuggling opium across the Washington/Canada border. The warden gambled that the boats would head north.

There was another good reason for the men to run north. While any run to the south would lead them to populated areas, all along the route to the north were hundreds of miles of thickly wooded shorelines where men in boats could hide out during the day. Traveling only at night, the convicts could reasonably make Canada before American authorities could catch up to them.

The route the escapees took was guaranteed to make it as difficult as possible for the local United States Marshal Hopkins and his men to follow. Once in the boats, the convicts would have to pass Fox Island, go through The Narrows and then row into Colvos Passage between Vashon Island and Olalla before coast-hopping along Puget Sound until they reached the Canadian border. But even knowing the exact route was not going to make it any easier for the forces of law and order. Time was to prove this statement correct.

Assuming that the men would have to hide out during daylight hours, the United States Marshal ordered the outskirts of Tacoma were carefully monitored. Posses of law enforcement personnel reconnoitered the countryside looking for suspicious characters wearing clothing made of prison blankets and investigating reports of chicken stealing and other crimes which suggested a convict on the run was possibly in the area.

Even with search parties beating the bushes as far north as Vashon Island, Marshal Hopkins was hard-pressed to keep track of the rumors. As more and more sightings were confirmed, Hopkins was able to develop a clear picture of where the prisoners probably were. To the best of his deductive thinking, one escapee had made it as far north as Olalla. Assuming that Wade would be the most likely candidate to have made it the farthest, Hopkins tagged this unknown escapee as Wade. If Wade were on his own, this meant that the prisoners had separated. This was good news for law enforcement because it meant that the remaining men could not collectively use Wade's genius for escape. But, on the other hand, it was bad news when it came to capturing Wade because he was so unbelievably resourceful.

Hopkins further assumed that four of the men were on Vashon Island. At least one was in the vicinity of Defiance Point Park near Tacoma because a man matching the description of Matt Moor had been seen buying a fish. This probably also meant that Takenouchi was in the vicinity as well because, in the words of the newspapers, "the ties of racial consanguinity [were] looked upon by the searchers to keep the two Japanese together during the extremities of the pursuit." But Hopkins could not account for the remaining prisoners.

It did not take long before Hopkins could start the recapture process. At around 10 pm on Friday, two days after the breakout, Ed Stickney became the first convict to be re-captured. Apprehended in Point Defiance Park where Moor and Takenouchi had been spotted, Stickney had been boldly walking up to a trolley that would take him into Tacoma when he was recognized by Deputy Marshal Tom Morris. The convict was taken without a struggle.

"Hello, Ed," Morris said as Stickney walked by the posse as if nothing was out of the ordinary.

"Well, you've got me, boys," was all Stickney replied.

Almost pleased at being re-captured, Stickney warmed up quickly. After a hot meal he was in a "good-humored and even playful mood," the newspapers reported, and talked freely about how the escape had been affected. The men had been digging for months, he confirmed, using iron spoon handles to pry the mortar free from around the bricks. This confession tore the guts out of the warden's claim that all the digging had to have been done since the previous Saturday. It was also quite embarrassing for prison officials since the supposed thorough inspection conducted the previous Saturday should have uncovered tunnels exactly like the six the prisoners were digging.

By the time of Stickney's capture, scraps of information were flooding in from all across the search front. One of the stolen boats had been recovered on Vashon Island and four of the convicts had been seen several times foraging for food on the island. But that information had not been without cost. Two posses had come upon one another unexpectedly and one group began firing before they had identified their targets. Ritter Wilkeson from Tacoma went down with a painful but not serious flesh wound in his right arm.

The posses were also using a new tool in hunting for the prisoners: photographs. McNeil Island had only started taking photos of the prisoners for identification since 1902. Now that precaution was going to become a tool of identifying the escapees. For the first time in Washington history, McNeil Island escapees would have their pictures in the paper – every paper – thus aiding the forces of law and order. Photos of the eight men were reproduced from the prison log and widely distributed to the searchers.

It was not until the next day, Saturday, that Leslie and Malone were captured. Malone was cornered on Vashon Island while Leslie was arrested as he walked into Kent. A bit of levity was added to the somberness of the search when Leslie released a copy of an epistle which the eight escapees had left for Warden Halligan on McNeil Island. It read

Dearest Happy Hooligan,

We, the undersigned, feel very happy to bid you good-bye but have just received a letter from King Edward VII, so must tear ourselves away. But do not be concerned as to our welfare and do not be concerned as to the fact of our being hungry.

The bill of fare for a while will largely consist of light summer air and mountain scenery, but liberty sauce makes good eating.

Would not leave you, but for the fact that we might fall sick here in the penitentiary and die, as in the case of Poor Richards.[sic.]

Give our cordial regards to the rest of the farmers who pass themselves off for guards and assure them of our lasting gratitude for their stupidity.

While we are admitting that we may be brought back to your hash resort at any time, we think such an event highly improbable.

We cheerfully admit that the steel plates were a tough proposition, but you know the old saw, "Where there's a will there's a way." Yours in derision.

A HARMLESS BUNCH

The fourth man to be taken was Matt Moor. Wearing a "black, slouch hat, common jumper and black pants with patches," the press reported, he was apprehended in a railyard near Ravensdale with a "sack of berries and a sack of herbs and a cabbage." Moor had crossed over from Vashon Island to the mainland in a small rowboat with Leslie and McCarthy in broad daylight. Takenouchi apparently *swam* the channel and came quite close to drowning. After he recovered from his swim, he walked into a logging camp about two miles from Olalla where he fell into a deep slumber. He awoke in chains on Wednesday, July 12th.

On the same day, W. D. McCarthy was apprehended outside Ellensburg. A posse came upon a gang of men and while a deputy was talking to a group of them, McCarthy made a break for the forest. The sheriff ran after the fleeing convict, yelling for him to stop at least six times. When McCarthy refused to halt, and appeared to be getting away, the sheriff shot McCarthy in the upper leg. McCarthy made another 20 yards before he collapsed. The wound was not fatal.

The next Friday, ten days after their escape, Malone, Leslie, Moor, Takenouchi, Castle and Stickney were back in McNeil Island and "immediately placed in chains." While they may not have been thrilled to be back in custody, they must have taken some pleasure in watching teams of 30 men work at repairing the brick walls through which they had so painstakingly dug. It was take almost a month for the prison to repair the holes in the brick walls and ceilings. The troupe of seven was as complete as was it ever going to be on August 9, 1905, when the wounded McCarthy was transported back to McNeil Island.

But George Wade never returned.

WHATEVER HAPPENED TO . . . .

Clyde C. Castle's sentence was extended to March 24, 1906. He was finally released on March 29, 1906.

Joseph H. Malone was discharged on March 6, 1909. He returned to Alaska where he was subsequently convicted of rape, the same charge for which he had been convicted the first time, under the name Herbert Flemming. He was sentenced to 8 months at McNeil Island and, upon his release, was supplied transportation to Cleveland, Ohio.

After his recovery from the rifle bullet, William D. McCarthy was relocated in Leavenworth, Kansas, on October 6, 1906. Over the next seven years he was transferred twice to the Government Hospital for the Insane in Washington state. Through some manipulation of the prison rules, he was denied all of his Good Time, that time off his sentence which he had earned for being a model prisoner, even that which he earned *after* the escape attempt. This caused him to be sullen and morose and a growing danger to those around him. He eventually wrote to legendary Alaskan judge James Wickersham, the man who had sentenced him in the first place, asking for assistance in being released. Wickersham interceded on his behalf and McCarthy was let out of prison in July of 1912. Though McCarthy may not have known it, he might have had more than fate on his side. James Wickersham's brother, George, was the Attorney General for the State of Washington, and the man who ordered McCarthy released.

Matt Moor was released December 7, 1908, while K. Takenouchi, was transferred to Leavenworth on October 6, 1906, – the same day as W. D. McCarthy. No record remains of Takenouchi's time in Leavenworth or what become of him after his release.

But there are quite a few records regarding the fate of Edward Stickney. In the McNeil Island logbook, his original release date of July 8, 1907, is scratched out with two other notations added. One reads "7-10-07" and the other "March 24, 1908." After his return to prison Stickney flooded the court with paperwork. Over the next two years his case generated over 800 pages of correspondence relating to his request for an early release. These records still reside in the National Archives in Washington D. C. The appeals must have worked as Stickney was discharged from McNeil Island on October 17, 1907.

Finally there is the matter of what happened to George Wade, ring leader and master escape artist. After his escape from McNeil Island in 1905, he disappeared from the documents of the Pacific Northwest. Assuming that he continued his life of crime, the United States Bureau of Prisons was contacted in 1992. Had a George Wade been incarcerated anywhere else in the prison system? Yes, it replied. A George Wade spent time in Leavenworth from July 5, 1927, to February 10, 1929, for violation of the drug act. This could be the same man.

As George Wade had continued to list his home of record as Burlington, Vermont, the Public Record Division of the State of Vermont was contacted for a birth certificate. This document revealed that George Franklin Wade had been born on October 27, 1858, to Jane Bradley and Luther Wade of Manchester, Vermont. On the off chance that George had returned to his home after age made his encounters with the law less desirable, the Office of Vital Statistics was asked if a death certificate for a George Wade was also registered.

Surprisingly, there was one. But was it the same man? A 90-year old George Wade died in Manchester on September 4, 1948. Though his obituary in the *Manchester Journal* indicated that Wade had been a "life-long resident," his death certificate stated that he had only been in the community for "18 days." The deceased was born on October 27,

1857 – the same month and day as the original George Wade, but the year was one digit off. The father's name for both men was the same, Luther, but the mother's name was different. The death certificate lists the woman's name as "Mary Ellen Brown."

Were these two men one and the same? Did the legendary opium smuggler and master escape artist return to his roots in Vermont? No one will ever know for sure, but the legend of George Franklin Wade is still alive today, well more than a century after he broke out of his first prison in March of 1892.

ALASKA GOLD RUSH STRANGE BUT TRUE TALES

According to Billy Moore, a steamboat captain who spent more than 40 years on the Yukon, a tried-and-true method for curing scurvy was with lice. Once, allegedly, when Moore had scurvy, he purchased two healthy lice, one male and the other female, with a plug of tobacco and soon there was a whole family of lice on his body. This got Moore and up and exercising and cured his scurvy. This, Moore claimed, was because, as everyone knows, "stagnant blood is the cause of scurvy."[283]

* * *

Quite a stir was caused in Solomon on May 15, 1908, when a team of 59 dogs pulling "big sled loads of mining equipment" came through town. What a dog team was doing pulling a sled in the middle of May was not made clear by the *Nome Pioneer Press*.

* * *

For many sourdoughs, Alaska was a blessing because the long arm of the law in the lower states often didn't reach into the last frontier. However, after these men returned to the lower states, many discovered that though they had forgotten their transgressions, no matter how small, the law had not forgotten them.

In October of 1908, Frank Manley of Tanana was arrested in Seattle on a 14-year-old warrant from Texas. Fifteen years earlier Manley had claimed his mule had been killed by the railroad. After he collected the insurance moneys, it was discovered the mule was still alive.[284]

* * *

When William A. Coghill, early cargo entrepreneur in Fairbanks, made the switch from horses-and-wagon to automobile, he found using a horseless carriage presented some logistical problems. To carry a side of beef he had to strap it to the running board of the vehicle and forced his passengers to clamber aboard through the windows. But his business was so lucrative that even in the teens, he was buying a new car every year. He sold out in 1916.[285]

* * *

At the Arctic Brotherhood Christmas Eve Smoker in 1908 in Cleary, Miss Riley and her partner won the booby prize for dancing. Her prize, the *Fairbanks Daily Times* reported, was "a pair of gentlemen's rubber boots, [and] she is looking for someone whose size will fill their vacant depths."[286]

* * *

On October 7, 1905, James Stapleton was arrested for disturbing the peace when he entered the Northern Saloon and loudly declared, "[I'm] a woolly hoses! I'm a tarantula from Bitter Creek pretty high up! I'm a yard wide and all wool! I'm a wolf and this is my night to howl!" It took the city's blacksmith, Charles Crawford, the United States Marshal and two men to get the "woolly hoses" into the Seward hoosegow.[287]

* * *

In 1900, the Reverend Peter Trimble Rowe found Circle to be a community of 800, 500 of them miners. He held a church service in Beaver's Bar which included 100 Indians squatting on the floor of the saloon.[288] Other sources state that Rowe held his service in the saloon of man named Baldwin.

"Clean this place up," Baldwin was reported to have said. "We're going to have church. Down your drinks and get the liquor out of sight." When the sermon was over, Baldwin "ordered two of his henchmen to pass the hat" and ordered the miners to "kick in or else." Then, with the collection over, business was resumed as before.[289]

* * *

Yakima Pete Norby recalled that during the rush over the White Pass in 1897, there was a hill where Argonauts dumped equipment that was considered too heavy and not important enough to carry any further. This area was known as "Lairsville" for "all the lies that were told about the trail."[290]

* * *

Michael Joseph, the *Hot Springs Echo* reported in November of 1907, "repaired to bed" during one of his infrequent visits to the city. Arriving in his hotel room, he was surprised to find no coal lamp. Instead he found a "funny looking arrangement suspended by a string from the ceiling." He blew on it and the light did not go out. He blew harder but to no avail. Thereafter he "cussed it, laughed at it and talked to it for some time, his ire steadily getting the better of him till he was completely exhausted." They he grabbed the light to throw it outside when the cord came loose. Then he just carried the arrangement out of his room and placed it in the hall where, the next morning, the electric light was still burning.

* * *

On November 10, 1898, Frank McGill is married Aggie Dalton near the mouth of the Dally River. The ceremonies, or "splicing," was done by J. Durant, also known as French Joe. The vows read

> Ten miles from the Yukon, on the banks of this lake,
> For a partner to Koyukuk, McGill is I take;
> We have no preacher, and we have no ring,
> It makes no difference, it's all the same thing.
>
> Aggie Dalton

> I swear by my get-pole, under this tree,
> A devoted husband to Aggie I always will be;
> I'll love and protect her, this maiden so frail,
> From those sour-dough bums, on the Koyukuk trail.
>
> Frank McGill is

> For two dollars apiece, in Cheechako money,
> I unite this couple in matrimony;
> He be a rancher, she be a teacher,
> I do the job up, just as well as a preacher.
>
> French Joe.[291]

* * *

Arthur A. Dietz, who would later lead a group of 18 Argonauts across the Malaysian Glacier, trained his dog team in "upper New York City." Several of men were arrested because a policeman thought they had become "unbalanced by the gold craze stories in the papers." The policeman eventually turned the men and dogs over to the humane society on a charge of "cruelty to animals." History, replete with irony, did not neglect Dietz. In 1898 he left with 18 men. When he returned, only four were left alive, two blind, and they had eaten every dog to survive.[292]

* * *

Arriving in Valdez in 1898, W. R. Abercrombie encountered what was left of the disastrous stampede over the Valdez Glacier. Hundreds were still stranded on the ice field and dying of hunger in the Copper River Valley while the lucky few who made it out were living in decrepit mining shelters "packed like sardines in a box." Deciding that "70 percent [of the derelict miners] were mentally deranged," Abercrombie reported that one Swede had talked about a "glacial demon" which had attacked he and son twice. During the second attack, the boy was strangled to death.

"When I heard this story there were some ten or twelve other me in the cabin," Abercrombie wrote, "and at that time, it would not have been safe to dispute the theory of the existence of this demon on the Valdez Glacier, as every man in there firmly believed it to be a reality."[293]

* * *

In many parts of Alaska there are humanoids which the Natives firmly believe exist. There are the "Hairy Man" of Kokako, the "Little People" of Noorvik, the **Nathan** of the Interior, the **Nuyaqpalik** or "long hair" of the Kotzebue Lagoon, and the **Kushtacah** or "water devil" of Southeast Alaska. While the white man may not have believed in any of these humanoids, the Natives did and with much trepidation. (A graphic discussion of what a **Kushtacah** can do, allegedly, can be found in Harry D. Colp's book THE STRANGEST STORY EVERY TOLD. {Exposition Press, New York, 1953.)

In the early years of the century, a ship went down outside of Katella. As the water was only 15 feet deep and the submerged close to shore, the insurance company decided to salvage the wreck and sent a diver north to inspect the wreck. Soon after he had submerged for the first time a group of Natives paddled alongside the scow handling the air hoses and asked what the whites were doing. As a joke, the whites said that a **Kushtacah** had capsized a boat and they were fishing for the water devil – and would kill him if they caught him.

The Natives hovered around the scow so the whites decided to pull a practical joke. As soon as the diver indicated he was coming up, the whites went into a frenzy explaining to the Natives that they had caught the **Kushtacah**. As soon as the diver's hard hat broke the surface of the water, the Natives "all jumped overboard and swam to shore."[294]

* * *

Missionaries were not always successful in translating the meaning of the Bible to the Eskimo. Sometimes the words of the Bible were taken a little too literally. In Kotzebue, a group of Eskimo "declined to hunt or fish or attempt to lay in their usual supply of winter provisions" because they were convinced that the Lord was going to provide for them. In Nome, an old Native woman waited day after day for "a big, good white man with a team of dogs to come along with a great supply of food. This was her conception of Christ."[295]

* * *

In January of 1908, mail carrier George Blain was caught in a storm on Kotzebue Sound. To save his life, he quickly built an ice igloo and crawled inside with his dogs. For three days they all huddled together to stay warm. On the fourth day, when Blain was able to crawl up of the igloo, he discovered that the warm bodies of the dogs had caused the ice on the igloo walls to melt and refreeze thus

> binding the dogs so tightly [to the walls of the igloo] that there were unable to extricate themselves. A party of men is now hastening to the rescue of the animals. They will have to be chopped out.[296]

* * *

Archie Shiels, author of SEWARD'S ICEBOX, told how he and a friend had been called to an Indian camp to assist a man who had taken a bullet in his shoulder. They were able to extract the bullet but the man was in terrible pain so Shiels and his partner sent an Indian to a local shopkeeper with a note for something to quiet the injured man down. The shopkeeper, who did not like Indians – or "savages," as he called them – sent back a note stating that he could nothing of value in his medicine chest but was sending something back that was "the best thing he knew of to put an Indian to sleep." It was a pick handle.[297]

* * *

Truth is often stranger than fiction and sometimes court cases sounded more like Hollywood movies or Saturday Night Live skits than legal tangles. For instance, on May 14, 1893, the Grand Jury in Juneau heard the case of Whiskey Jim who was accused of selling whiskey to an Indian, Broken Nose Jake. In Seward in October of 1915, there was a civil case over the failure of the defendant, the Seldovia Salmon Company, to pay for labor. The Plaintiffs were Goon Dip and H. K. Mar Dong doing business as Goon Dip & Company. The case was listed in the National Archives as "Dip & Dong." [298]

* * *

In February of 1908, Tommy McCartney of Moses Lake went crazy. Believing that all the members of his party had been "transformed into huge mosquitoes which were continually trying to suck his life's blood," he seized all the weapons in camp and forced everyone to walk ahead of him for 12 miles. They all bedded down for the night and the next morning discovered by McCartney was gone. The firearms were later found but McCartney never was.[299]

* * *

The two men most associated with the literature of Alaska, Jack London and Robert Service, never wrote of Alaska. Both men wrote tales of the Klondike. Jack London did spend about three weeks in Alaska, but he was traveling down the Yukon River to St. Michaels so he could catch a steamer for San Francisco. Robert Service, on the other hand, did not even arrive in Dawson until years after the strike. He also visited Alaska, but it was late in his life and he came on an author's tour to sell books.

* * *

Jefferson Randolph "Soapy" Smith of Skagway fame liked to imbibe a bit and one of his favorite drinks was called "giggle soup."[300]

* * *

One of the early dances in Alaska was the "Hoochinoo Club Hop"[301]

* * *

According to Arthur Dietz, in a lagoon behind Yakutat there were so many fish that when a spiked pole was stuck into the water, "at least twenty fat herring and smelts" were on the spikes. Dietz reported that there were so many fish in the water that he believed it would be possible for a man with snowshoes to walk across the stream.[302]

* * *

For years, a spring ritual in Fairbanks was to watch the Turner Street Bridge, a wooden structure, be pummeled to splinters by the tons of ice coursing down the Chena River. During the summer, debris would collect on the bridge's footings and once, in 1905, it created a dam that flooded the city. The Turner Bridge was demolished in 1917 to make way for a steel structure which was, in turn, demolished in 1959 for the concrete bridge which still stands.[303]

* * *

The first conviction for gambling in Fairbanks came in November of 1908, and only after the court dropped charges against nine other men who were gambling at the same table in exchange for their testimony.[304]

* * *

In November of 1910, A. Preston of Hot Springs was arrested for burglarizing his own cabin. In spite of the fact that several witnesses attested to the fact that Preston was renting the cabin, Preston was bound over for trial.[305]

* * *

Diamond Jim Wilson of Nome was celebrating with great enthusiasm on Christmas Eve, 1900, when he suffered a stroke and died mid-party. His good friends dragged him upstairs to his bed and, in circle, toasted their dead comrade. Then they fell to dividing his possessions. Such was the way inheritance was handing in Nome.[306]

* * *

Most miners lived on a staple diet of "Alaskan strawberries," better known as beans.

* * *

In the early days of Fairbanks there was a miner from White River whose feet were frostbitten so badly they had to be amputated at the instep. He had a pair of bear's feet made into moccasins so he could use the bear's claws as toes.[307]

* * *

Perhaps the most important of the Argonaut 's supplies was his Yukon Stove, an ingenious device that was light, durable, and functional. It was all that kept many a 98er from freezing to death along the trail. It was invented by an Alaskan, Dan Walker of Juneau, a tinner by trade. Life was not kind to Walker and he had to be sent south to Portland in 1915 where he finished his life in an insane asylum.[308]

* * *

In 1905 Vuko Perovich was sentenced to death in Fairbanks for the murder of a Greek fisherman. The fisherman had been murdered on the bank of a slough which thereafter became known as "Deadman's Slough." Perovich was held in a small log jail awaiting execution and a scaffold was built immediately adjoining the jail. It was supposed to have been a temporary structure but Perovich's appeals took so long that the scaffold stood for two years and became known in Fairbanks as Perovich's "Two-Story House."

When Perovich's case made it to the United States Supreme Court, his death penalty was upheld. Two years later Perovich was still alive – and the scaffold still standing – when President Taft changed his sentence to life imprisonment in Leavenworth. Only then did the scaffold come down.[309] Perovich was later released and spent the last two years of his life as a barber in Rochester, New York.

* * *

In Fairbanks, the dwellings of the prostitutes were separated from the rest of town by a "high solid board" fence which was known as "The Line" or "The Row." Over the years the residents of "The Line" changed and in the 1950s the entire area was razed during a stint of urban renewal. When the dust settled, "The Line" was replaced with a Safeway and Woolworth's.[310]

* * *

According to Jed Jordan, Reverend Sheldon Jackson was once talked into having a bit of "Monangahela rye" which had been falsely labeled as "Sherry." Sheldon Jackson filled a water tumbler of the medicinal and "swallowed the whole dose, without a murmur." Returning to his church in Nome in high spirits, he "preached such an inspiring sermon that 20 people marched down the aisle and saved their souls." Truly, Jordan noted in his memoirs, this "must have been a powerful talk because two of these converts took it seriously and stayed with the church for a month or so."[311]

* * *

In January of 1908, Nome had a number of men training for a 100 mile race. "Most of the runners take a run of twenty to thirty miles outside," the *Nome Pioneer Press* reported, and finished with a "few hours" inside the Eagle Hall. This is rather surprising considering the **average** daily temperature in Nome in January is 5.8 degrees![312]

* * *

Taking census data from Natives in 1910 proved to be difficult since many of the Natives did not know in which year they were born, much less what month. In the Juneau area, one enumerator developed a "calendar" by which the Natives could estimate the month of birth of their children by what they were doing at the time. Equating months with these events, some of the calendar was as follows

April	"sea otter hunting"
May	"make gardens"
June	"salmon first run in bay"
July	"seal babies come" or "berries first ripen"
August	"plenty berries"
October	"first snow"

In the same year in Valdez, many foreigners working on the railroad feared that the census was nothing more than "a canvas preliminary to the assessment of some tax" and avoided the enumerators by "shifting from one lodging house to another." In two instances, foreigners had to be arrested so the enumerator could collect the required information.

But these problems were a minor inconvenience compared to the travails of Enumerator 12 whose saga, probably in the Aleutians, is reproduced verbatim from the ABSTRACT OF THE CENSUS for 1910:

> Enumerator No. 12 was caught in one of those severe storms which occasionally sweep the passes from the Pacific to the Bering Sea. In this treeless coast region there was no shelter, and no wood available for fuel. After three days, during which a blinding snowstorm continued, a start was determined upon, since the supply of food for the dogs had been exhausted and it was feared that the dogs would freeze in their state of exhaustion and hunger. On the way to the nearest camp the party was blown off a slope into an open mountain creek. The sled had to be rolled over to get it out of the stream and to free the baggage of water. Some of the baggage was spilled in the upset, and since life depended upon speed in the race to make a distant camp before freezing, the lost baggage, which included the census pouch, was not missed until the sled was unpacked. With clothing frozen stiff and various parts of the body frosted the little party succeeded in reaching the isolated camp for which they had set out. Three attempts were made subsequently to retrace their steps in order to recover the pouch but the storm was too severe to face. The agent enumerated the camp on some waste paper and returned about 200 miles for more census supplies.

The agent's next experience was in the mountain where he found one of the survivors of the wrecked **Farallon** who had been living on Native food, had frozen his fingers, and had himself cut off one gangrenous member with his knife. The enumerator could not leave a fellow being in this condition and conveyed him to the nearest settlement, which was fully 60 miles away. At another locale, one of the men in his party stepped into the water and froze his foot, which turned black, but afterward recovered without serious consequences. The agent making this circuit had been over all of the route before, but had never encountered such severe storms. His first landing was delayed 10 days, and he was driven 300 miles in the storms.[313]

* * *

On the Copper River, a work crew was faced with a problem. Oats which had come up the railway from Cordova for the horses had been transported in a rail car which had previously hauled coal oil. There was enough of a taint of the coal oil in the oats that the horses would not eat their food.

No one knew how to get the horses to eat the coal oil-tainted oats until Stikine Bill Robinson came up with a solution. He rubbed some coal oil on the horses "being careful to get it on their nostrils." With the smell on the horses, they did not know that the oats were tainted and thus ate their food.[314]

* * *

On the front page of the defunct *Yukon Valley News,* published in Hot Springs, a community that no longer exists, is the announcement that the boomtown of "7 Up," not on any current map, which boasted of "one saloon, two restaurants and two stores" and a **daily** stage line to Fairbanks "during the winter" was being rename Gates City in honor of Swiftwater Bill Gates, a Klondike hero who died in Peru.[315]

* * *

In 1903, Wickersham heard one of the great Alaskan stories which, unlike most others, turned out to be both amazing and true. A group of prospectors dammed a small stream and then constructed a canvas channel which about 18 inches wide that fed into a four-inch nozzle. A wire mesh was attached at the upper end of the channel to keep twigs and debris from clogging the nozzle. Then, using the power of the water from the 200-foot canvas tube, they were able to hose down their digging. The nozzle was raised a few feet off the ground and it sprayed all day and all night.

One morning, several of the men were amazed to find four grayling, each approaching 20 inches, lying on the ground by the nozzle. Examining the canvas channel, they found it full of grayling that could not exit because of the wire mesh on the upper end. The fish had come upriver and when they came to the spot where the nozzle was blasting water, the fish, true to their instinct, jumped. As a tribute to their accuracy, Wickersham noted that "only four of the hundred or more attempting this ascent had failed" to leap from the stream into the canvas channel.[316]

* * *

According to the *Skaguay News,* "miners in the Yukon district require strong and rich food and they will drink bacon grease like so much water."[317]

* * *

In a sarcastic news item in July of 1906, the *Fairbanks Daily Times* reported how Dr. Joseph Weyerhorst had proven himself to be adept in "decorating his wife's face with lasting remembrances of the impressionist." Mrs. Weyerhorst had become disenchanted with her husband and moved out of their home to take a room in a local hostelry.[318] Her husband had tracked her down and when he could not convince her to return, had beaten her and then, in "a playful mood" had tried to "induce her to swallow a small towel."

Rather than face trial, Dr. Weyerhorst jumped bail – to the annoyance of two local men who had posted his bail because his trunk of "surgical equipment" left as security was found to empty.[319] The doctor had then fled on the steamer **Sarah** to St. Michael where he was apprehended and returned to Fairbanks. (The cost of his attempt to flee justice, $400 according to the November 11, 1906, *Fairbanks Times,* was later paid by the doctor.)

There was reason for the doctor to flee justice. Though he had only been in Fairbanks a short time, he had raised enough suspicion that the law enforcement officials had run a check on him, such as they were in 1906. The results of that background investigation revealed that a "careful eye" should be kept on him "where there was any substantial evidence he would have bumped against an indictment." His crime in that previous local is not stated plainly. Rather, the *Fairbanks Times* stated cryptically, "He was not a fellow Roosevelt's belief in race perpetuation."[320] [Author's note: This might be taken to mean that he was an abortionist.]

Additionally, in June of 1906 he was charged with malpractice for the death of F. G. Brose who apparently died while undergoing surgery. Weyerhorst claimed that Brose had died of "fatty degeneration of the heart and to congested lungs" which had nothing to do with his surgical skills. He also produced a certificate to prove that he had graduated from a medical school in Belgium. When asked about his incisions, Weyerhorst admitted to two. One was for the operation while the man was alive. The second, Weyerhorst claimed, had been performed "after death and said this was done for scientific purpose."[321]

At the time of his arrest and subsequent flight from justice, he had left at least one patient in his sanitarium. Her name was Mrs. Minnie Robinson. She had fallen down her stairs weeks before and had gone to a local doctor who wired her broken jaw shut and stated that was all he could do. Then "along came Dr. Joseph Weyerhorst with a blaze of trumpeters, himself playing solo bugle" and convinced the woman to part with $250. He wrote out a guarantee and had the woman transferred to his sanitarium across the river where he "performed the operation of putting sundry bandages on the jaw to hold it in place – and keeping her from crying for help." Claiming that he had a patient on "Ester Creek suffering from gas," Dr. Weyerhorst left Fairbanks with her $250 in his pocket. Two days later, Mrs. Robinson was released from her bandages and taken to a local hospital.[322]

At his trial for assaulting his wife, a "letter of introduction" for Weyerhorst was then presented to Judge Erwin by Fairbanks Chief of Police Hagan. At his trial, Weyerhorst stated, "I life my vife und hev lofed her for – let me see – yoost 12 years und six months day before yesterday." When it was the

Judge's turn, he waxed eloquently on Cicero, the Ceasars, "the Appian Way and other pikes traveled by progress," Christianity and concluded

> I regret, sah, that youh wife was not heah to testify against you, sah. But sah, I understand she is afraid you will kill hur. I am convinced that huh absence is due to huh feah that she will suffuh great bodily hawm in the futuah.

After he had completed his statement, Judge Erwin ordered Dr. Weyerhorst to pay a fine of $100. Before the Judge had even completed the sentence, Weyerhorst "swung his arm over the chair as if he was about to spring the old gag about having that much in his hip pocket." Then the judge finished the sentence, ". . . and fifty days in jail."

Weyerhorst's brushes with the law were newspaper grist. He had been accused of removing a healthy appendix and causing a patient to die earlier that year. This fact was used by the newspaper as part of its humorous reporting of the case. "Having fully diagnosed the doctor's case, [Fairbanks Chief of Police Hagan] decided that instead of removing the appendix he would take the whole thing away." Weyerhorst was then taken to jail.[323]

The next report on the elusive doctor was two years later, May of 1908 when he was charged with practicing medicine without a license – and filed for divorce in Nome. Dr. Weyerhorst charged his wife with "intoxication, unfaithfulness and desertion" among "many other reasons." Apparently his wife was still living in Fairbanks where she had become a "habitue of the Flora Dora dance hall" where she made her living as "dance hall girl."[324]

Weyerhorst was then able to stay out of the public eye until 1911 when he was charged with practicing medicine without a license in Douglas. The next year he was back in the news, this time for removing a woman's ovaries and, in the process, maiming her. On April 27, 1918, he was charged with obstructing recruitment during the First World War because he would not perform a physical. There was also a second count. He was alleged to have said to a potential inductee, "I could remove your eye and then you wouldn't have to go." His trial resulted in a hung jury on June 5, 1918. He was tried a second time and found Not Guilty on June 9, 1918. (Ironically, Weyerhorst had been appointed to the Selective Service Exemption Board for Douglas in August of 1917.)[325]

Weyerhorst died in October of 1921 in Great Falls, Montana where he was working as a physician for miners and was running a small hospital. His wife – not the one of Fairbanks infamy – claimed his estate of $875, unusual in that his death certificate lists him as "single."[326]

* * *

In 1898, Will R. Newland recalled a preacher who "had a nice little wife back in Indiana" but had acquired a "mining pal" whom he described as "a fine looking 'blond.'" The relationship didn't last as the couple's boat capsized and they lost all their equipment whereupon the preacher's "gold digger" abandoned the man of God.[327]

* * *

No one was immune from the long arm of the law in Alaska, regardless of how trifling the matter was. On May 13, 1888, J. G. Brady of Sitka was cited for "creating and maintaining a public nuisance" because he allowed a "large heap of manure and other refuse" from his cows to build on his property which created drainage problems and thus did "grossly disturb the public health." At that time, J. G. Brady was the Governor of the District of Alaska.[328]

* * *

In Nome, because glass was so expensive, some of the windows were made of beer bottles.[329]

* * *

Commenting on the mosquitoes in the interior, Arthur Dietz reported that there were so many of them it impossible to hide. Bread could not be kneaded without becoming black with the insects and the bottom of cups of coffee was layered with their corpses. "At first we were fearful of eating the insects and attempted to pick them out of our food," Dietz reported, "but within a very short time we abandoned this plan. Everything we ate was flavored with mosquitoes."[330]

Other parts of Alaska were not much better. In 1898, Charles Goodyear Hubbard noted that the mosquitoes of the Cordova area were so powerful that they "pierced the leather of [a] boot" and some of the men were "bitten through heavy buckskin gloves."[331]

* * *

In Nome, in 1900, Reverend S. H. Young, was having trouble with Yupik, one of the languages of the Eskimo. He was particularly having difficulty with the 23th Psalm which reads "The Lord is my Shepherd; I shall not want. He maketh me to lie down in green pastures; He leadeth me beside the still waters." To facilitate translation he hired an interpreter who did not know what a "sheep" was and therefore could not understand the terms "shepherd" and "green pastures." After considerable explanation, the interpreter seemed to get the idea. But the congregation was unimpressed. It was only after Young learned Yupik that he understood how the translator had butchered the Psalm to "The white man is a mountain goat. The Lord is a goat hunter. The Lord is no good. He shoots me down on the mountain and drags me to the beach."[332]

* * *

According to the *Nome Chronicle,* August 16, 1900, Albert Hoepner, on trial for attempting to kill his partner in the "drugstore on Front Street," claimed that his intended victim, Isaac Abramson, "exerted a certain hypnotic influence over him." Hoepner claimed that he found it "impossible to resist" this power of hypnotism and that Abramson could also hypnotize inanimate objects. One of these alleged objects, claimed Hoepner, was a cash register from which his nefarious partner took 75 or 80 dollars to "rent the store vacated by Kelly & Co." The two men had gone into partnership, according to Hoepner, because Abramson had "waved his hand majestically over Hoepner's eyes, emitted a few seductive hypnotic volts into the latter's brain" and hypnotized him into a partnership.

But the partnership did not proceed without altercation. Abramson power over Hoepner appeared to fade, as the *Nome Chronicle* reported, for Abramson could not rouse Hoepner to "his duty in the culinary department or perform light upstairs work of some sort." Abramson resolved his dilemma by using a 2 by 4 to rouse Hoepner to do his fair share of work about the shop.[333]

* * *

In 1905, "Mysterious" Yannert from "Cold Storage and Purgatory" was incensed that someone had stolen his only – and therefore favorite – pair of red socks. He chased after the villains never catching them – although he did meet one man who had "never heard of such an article of apparel." Yannert asked for police protection if he bought a new pair and was turned down. So he swore never to buy socks again. Two months later, Yannert discovered that he had been wearing his socks the entire time.[334]

* * *

Perhaps the seed for Jack London's THE CALL OF THE WILD came from the hundreds of dogs that were shipped to Seattle to be trained as sled dogs. Collected from pounds around the country, the dogs tore at each other when they first arrive until "nearly every dog has one or more wounds." One of the handlers noted the dogs in Seattle would not be as strong as the Eskimo dogs. The "cur from the states" would have to be heavier to pull an equivalent load, an interesting comment considering that some of the dogs in the pen were included hounds, mastiffs and "some not much larger than pugs."

Half the dogs that were in the Seattle-Yukon Dog Company in November of 1897 were black, while the rest were "yellow and red dogs." This was about to change, noted the *Seattle Times,* for in a few days the company was expecting 200 more dogs that would be thrown into the pens with the 200 already there. "The people in charge of the dogs are wondering what a dog fight with four hundred dogs engaged will be like."[335]

* * *

When Charles Harding left Council City in late August of 1902, he left with "long piece of rope belonging to Tom Dwyer." Rope wasn't particularly valuable but what made the scenario noteworthy was that "the rope was attached to a horse also owned by Mr. Dwyer."[336]

* * *

The gold fever appears to have struck everyone, often with fatal effect. Three sailors from the Revenue Cutter **Perry** were so infected by the gold bug in August of 1897 that they deserted. They stole a small sloop in Dutch Harbor and attempted to cross 600 miles of the Bering Sea to reach St. Michaels expecting to go to the gold fields from there. They never made it. Buffeted by storms they were driven onto a deserted island where two of the men starved to death. The third was rescued in a "deplorable state, nothing but skin and bones and so dazed he took no interest in his surroundings." Two hours after being rescued, he died.[337]

* * *

In October of 1908, two well-known drinking men, A. B. Ferguson and Captain Donovan, were on their way to "Quail Creek in the Troublesome [C]reek [C]ountry" when they discovered they had neglected to pack enough provisions for the trip. Stopping at Tolovana they wired Bill McPhee of the Washington Saloon in Tanana: "Trail bum. Send mustang liniment. Out of booze." McPhee immediately sent the men "a few bottles of his choicest brands."[338]

* * *

In 1904, Sam Archer, running for the Nome City Council, hit upon an unusual method of advertising. He offered to decorate the parkas of Eskimos in Nome free of charge. The Eskimos flocked to his establishment and he embroidered their parkas to read "VOTE FOR **SAM ARCHER** FOR COUNCILMAN." As the Eskimos walked around Nome, Sam Archer got advertising. The photo of one of the Eskimos in an embroidered parka was published in *Worldwide* in 1904.[339]

* * *

Before the coming of the white man, an Eskimo soothsayer by the name of Maniilaq made a number of startling predictions. Among those which came true were

1) fire-powered boats on the water and in the sky,
2) fire that could be contained in houses,
3) thin birch bark on which one could write,
4) coming of a people with light skin and hair,
5) light that will come in the form of the word.
6) famine

Considering that Maniilaq came from the Upper Kobuk, where the Kotzebue Strike was to draw thousands of men in 1898, his predictions were hauntingly accurate.[340]

* * *

In December of 1899, Oliver Lawson rode a bicycle from Dawson to Skagway using the frozen trails and lakes as his roadway, He made the trip in 14 days.[341]

* * *

In 1899, fire insurance was available in Skagway through a fire insurance agent by the name of Colonel Fry.[342]

* * *

In 1902, an Indian woman sued her husband for divorce and filed for alimony at the rate of "six moose a year."[343]

* * *

In the early days of Fairbanks, "drinks" usually meant whiskey and it was served straight up, I.E., with no mixer. Those who wanted to cut their whiskey used water, often taken from the fire buckets which hung on the walls about the room. One night a man by the name of Oscar Nordale and his friends were in a brothel drinking straight whiskey. Drinking whiskey straight wasn't unusual for Alaskans, but usually one did not go to a brothel to drink.

"What's the matter with you stupid bums," the Madam demanded of the gay dogs when she realized they were not mixing their whiskey with water. "Trying to get drunk you can't do right by my girls?" she asked with an entrepreneurial interest.

Not exactly, the men said. Oscar had urinated in the fire bucket and the men were damned if they were going to "drink out of Oscar's urinal."[344]

* * *

In July of 1897, P. B. Weare of the Alaska Transportation Company telegraphed the Treasury Department and requested the services of a

Revenue cutter to protect his steamships carrying gold because " a band of Chinese pirates ha[d] been organized for the express purpose of intercepting and looting any of the treasure craft which are expected to leave the gold region [between] August 5 and September 15."[345]

* * *

In September of 1909, an attorney was arguing a legal point with Judge Cushman in a Juneau courtroom. Suddenly a man in the audience stood up and addressed the court in "unintelligible language." The offending individuals was hustled out of the court room and in the hallway, was asked by a deputy what he meant by disturbing the court. The man declared that he had become incensed by listening to the attorney drone on and say nothing. "I was tired was tired of listening to him and I wanted the judge to shut him up."[346]

* * *

In an interview with the Victoria, B. C. *Daily Colonist*, C. Fred LaMont of crystallized egg fame noted that his factory checked every one of the 360,000 egg which arrived every day. If an egg was not fresh, it was put in a vat full of "oil which tanners use on leather." If the egg was decayed, it was made into a "lubricating oil" of the same variety as that sold in Russia "for healing purposes."[347]

* * *

On July 8, 1908, Governor Wilford B. Hoggatt wrote the President of the United States, Theodore Roosevelt (a Republican) that "it affords me much pleasure to inform you that the last dancehall and gambling house in Alaska has been closed." Crediting the "Hoggatt Delegates to the Republican National Convention," the Governor stated with assurance that "the gamblers and dancehall men have given up."[348]

* * *

The *Mining and Industrial Reporter* of Denver in 1898 editorialized an endorsement of the "Klondike and Cuba Ice Towing and Anti-Yellow Fever Company." The company planned to capture icebergs in the North Pacific and then barge them "in a gigantic fine mesh net" around South America and sold in cities "along the ocean route, such as Calcutta, Valparaiso, and Tokio." Once the iceberg arrived in Cuba, it would be parceled out to patients at the "Yellow Fever Cold Storage Hospitals." The charge would be $1,000 per patient it was estimated that each iceberg would cure 419 patients.

But the news for this "sure money maker" got better. The icebergs the company was planning on exploiting would only be those calves which came from glaciers in which there was gold. This would allow the company to extract the gold as the iceberg melted and thus pay the towing expense. The company had already located a number of likely icebergs which it had assayed "from $1.27 to $628.19 per cubic yard."[349]

* * *

Though not as popular as sled dogs, goats were sometimes used as dray animals. The *Seattle Times* reprinted a communiqué from D. H. Sanborn who claimed that goats were so efficient that the Hudson Bay Company was "discarding the dogs and using goats." While a dog required four pounds of food per day on the trail, the goats could browse thus saving the Argonaut valuable cash as well as space in the sled. Goats would also provide "milk, butter, food and clothing. [They] will drag one-half more than a dog, will go up a steeper grade [and] can carry a pack of fifty pounds." Further, Sanborn contended, "goats can stand more cold than dogs."[350] In spite of these obvious advantages, dogs were still the preferred means of travel in the northland.

* * *

The Reverend Jules Prevost was on his way to Rampart when his horse became lame and he had to shoot it. Shortly thereafter an Argonaut came upon the still-warm body of the animal and butchered it. Overtaking the reverend, the Argonaut sold the man of the cloth his own horse as "moose."[351]

* * *

In December of 1910, the hottest sale item in Chitna was a cat. There was a virtual plague of mice and every cabin in town had its fair share.[352]

* * *

In 1899, Custom Inspectors in Seattle became suspicious of a coffin being sent to Unga. Upon opening the coffin they discovered it was packed with whiskey. The coffin and liquor was confiscated leaving the dead man on Unga Island to "pine many a long day yet for his coffin."[353]

* * *

In the first edition of the Skagway *Interloper* in May of 1908, the paper editorialized with sarcasm how commendable it was that one of its competitors, the *Juneau Record*, had come out for the "abolishment of dance halls." Such dance halls as those to which the *Juneau Record* referred were "notoriously places of the lowest order" which robbed men of their hard-earned dollars. It was about time, the *Interloper* editorialized, that the federal authorities in Juneau got busy in Juneau stop "chasing rainbows that result when senseless suits are brought against alleged sellers of whiskey and *Siwashes*."[354] (A *siwash* is a man married to an Native woman or a man living with Natives – or like a Native.)

* * *

Abe Smith, described as "the notorious," "the unclean," was so filthy that he was novelty in 1909 Fairbanks. To attract customers, Abe Smith was paid to sit in the front window of the Tanana Club where he attracted quite a bit of attention. "Like a vampire he sits," noted the *Miner's Union*

Bulletin," more animal like than human" with a "vacuous expression on his inexpressibly loathsome countenance." Since Smith was well known to do anything for money, the *Miner's Union Bulletin*, suggested that he be paid to "get into a sewer or some other fitting place, so that his congenial surroundings will make him unnoticed."[355]

* * *

Erik Lindblom, one of the "Three Lucky Swedes" who had discovered the Nome strike, took his wealth to San Francisco where he set up the Liberty Film Company of San Mateo to satisfy his wife's urgings to become a movie picture queen. In February of 1917, Mrs. Hannah Sadie Urika Sparman Lindblom had contracted with the Dunhem Motion Picture Manufacturing Company to develop and print a motion picture. After a small down payment, the Lindbloms paid no more.

Victor Duhem and his son Ray then went to Lindblom's office in San Francisco to ask for payment. A "fierce encounter" ensued "which raged for nearly twenty minutes and which created a near panic among hundreds of tenants in the building [after which] the Lindblom offices resembled a shambles."

When the police arrived, the battle was in "full swing." Lindblom and his secretary, Charles Anderson, had been beaten by "heavy pieces of gold quarts seized off Lindblom's desk." After the battle, Anderson's face was described as "swollen and discolored." Lindblom had an injury on his cheek and leg while the two Dunhem's had cuts and bruises and at least one broken bone.

The Dunhems were charged with assault with a deadly weapon and disturbing the peace. The quartz was booked as evidence.[356]

* * *

In Nome in 1900, Crad reported a case of "grave jumping." The Arctic Brotherhood raised money to bury one of their members, an expensive proposition during the winter as the ground was frozen solid. However, when the funeral procession arrived at the grave they found it occupied. The intruding body was dug up and "dumped on the frozen shore" of the Bering Sea before the "dearly departed Brother" was interred.[357]

* * *

Life for the troops at Fort Egbert, all 150 of them, was austere. Other than hunting, fishing and mining during the summer, there wasn't much else to do. Though it was established in 1900, it did not have a library until 1908. But the library must have been an unusual place to read for, according to the Quartermaster General, it had to be "liberally equipped with spittoons."[358]

* * *

Anthony "Tony" Dimond, Alaska's lone delegate to the United States Congress from 1933 to 1944, was a master at selecting juries when he was a private practice in Valdez in the 1920s. In one particular suit against the Kennecott Copper Corporation in which a worker was maimed, Dimond managed to have the jury packed with men who had lost legs, arms, fingers or eyes. Even the judge was crippled. When it came time to address the jury, Dimond, who had himself been crippled during the Gold Rush when he nearly blew his leg off, limped before the jury to plead the case of his client. The jury found for Dimond's client "without leaving their seats."

Later, the attorney for the Kennecott Copper Corporation remarked to a friend, "Justice is not only blind, but she's lame also, in Valdez anyhow. Next time I try a damage case against Dimond I'll take care to have every maimed man in Valdez kidnapped [sic] in advance of the trial."[359]

* * *

Building material was at such a premium in Nome that when steamships were no longer useable, they were dragged above the high tide line and used as structures. The **Minneapolis**, for instance, became a hospital and boarding house while the **Quickstep** and **City of Chicago** become hotels. The **City of Chicago** boasted a capacity of 175. Rooms went for a $1 a night a spring beds were 50 cents a night. There was also a restaurant and beer garden and, while they lasted, 10-year old whiskey and Key West cigars were available for the well-heeled.[360]

* * *

One Argonaut on the White Pass tried to dissuade thieves from stealing his food by having it packed in sticks like dynamite and labeled "Pigs Ears Soup." A box of the cargo apparently fell off his sled and was discovered in the trail. Argonaut Mont Hawthorne discovered the truth of the mixture when he examined a stick closely and "had a lot of good eating that winter out of my box of dynamite." [361]

* * *

The whaling station six miles east of Point Hope at the confluence of the Arctic Ocean and the Chukchi Sea was known as "Jabbertown." This was because the community was truly polyglot. In 1900 there were over 200 Eskimos from numerous communities, many speaking different dialects, along with more than 20 whalers, white and black along with "Cape Verdeans, Portugese, Japanese, German, and Irish" seamen.[362]

* * *

At the turn of the century, one aspect of the Arctic Ocean that whalers quickly learned was that the weather was unpredictable, even in the summer. On Hershel Island, a collection of whalers from three ships decided to stage a game of baseball on an unseasonably warm Saturday, March 7, 1897. Even at 20 F, the game was well attended. At the bottom of the second inning, a storm hit the island with no warning.

Within moments the temperature had dropped to -20 and the snow was driving so hard that it was impossible to see more than a few feet in any direction. Everyone stumbled for whatever shelter they could find. When the storm lifted the next morning, five men -three whalers and two Eskimos - were found frozen to death.[363]

* * *

Like many miners of the era, Slim Carlson, a miner on Slippery Creek in what is now Denali National Park, lived in poverty. One day Joe Quigley from Kantishna offered him some coffee but Slim turned the refreshment down. He couldn't afford coffee or tea, Slim told Joe, and he didn't want to be unhappy not having it later.

Though he may have been poor, Slim was quite adept at living off the land. He drank "Hudson Bay Tea" he fashioned from local herbs and survived on the meat the land provided. But sometimes he had to fight for Nature's bounty. Once he killed several caribou and then went back to his cabin to retrieve his dog team. When he returned to the site of the kill, he found a big grizzly dinning on his caribou. He didn't want to tangle with the grizzly, but then again, he didn't want to lose his meat either so he set his dogs to harass the bear. As the bear was snapping at the dogs and stumbling through the forest, Slim fashioned a temporary 12-foot high cache and slung the meat aloft. After it froze, the bear wouldn't be as interested in eating it.[364]

* * *

In 1909, a group of miners in Tanana were faced with the prospect of dealing with a claim jumper who was an ex-policeman. They did not have the money to hire an attorney so they asked the claim jumper to leave. When he did not, they threw a parka over his head and began beating him with switches of green birch. When he had had quite enough, he was given an axe and, with a rope knotted about his neck as a reminder of what could happen, he was ordered to cut down his own location notices. Very soon thereafter, the claim jumper left the area. None of the miners were identified so no charges could be filed.[365]

* * *

For many miners, cooking was an art they never learned well. One day a man from Boston by the name of Holt asked his friend Tom how to cook rice. Tom didn't know for certain and gave Holt the wrong recipe. As food was dear, Holt followed Tom's recipe exactly. Unfortunately Tom didn't know what he was talking about and the rice boiled over and Holt had to use several pans to hold all the rice. After that, he chased Tom around Rampart with a double-barrel shotgun.[366]

* * *

During the Kantishna Rush in 1905, a party of miners came across a four-mile stretch of water near Mt. McKinley and said among themselves, "I wonder how we missed this [stretch of water] before?" Thereafter the lake became known as "I Wonder Lake." When it was finally written on a map, the "I" was thought to be a typo and dropped.

* * *

In the 1920s, when Denali first became a National Park, Bobby Sheldon ran the transportation concession including the Savage River tourist camp. One of his campers, a hardware store owner, complained that Sheldon's hotcakes tasted like asbestos stove pads from his hardware store. Sheldon decided to play a practical joke on the merchant and cooked a hotcake so slowly that it was rock hard. But the hardware store camper turned the table on Bobby. He got some medicine bottle stickers and stuck them on the hotcake. On one he put a Fairbanks address and on the other the message "Bob Sheldon is our cook, the food is fine, here is a sample." They he sent it through the mail. It arrived in Fairbanks, so the story goes, "without a nick on it."

* * *

After Fannie McKenzie and Joe Quigley had lived together for years, they were finally married by Commissioner Brooker whom they apparently caught by surprise. Since Brooker did not have a Bible handy, he used a Montgomery Ward catalog.[367]

* * *

Alaskans have always been famous for their practical jokes. In the 1920s on Slate Creek near Kantishna, John Bowman, a notorious drunk, was having a birthday party. Bowman had made some money in the Klondike Strike but had drunk his way through his fortune in Dawson. Though he was not a successful miner, he always seemed to have enough to buy booze. On his birthday, sometime in midwinter, one of his buddies decided to play a practical joke on Bowman. The friend constructed a birthday cake out of wood and then covered it with frosting. After a birthday dinner, Bowman, well-greased, was presented the cake. After vainly attempted to cut the cake, to the merriment of his friends, he laid down his knife and, with swimming fisheyes, said to the gathered revelers, "It musht be froshen."[368]

* * *

One of the more dependable whaleboats turned passenger craft of the Alaska Gold Rush era – and well into the 1920s as well – was the **Dora**. In about 1910, the **Dora** was anchored at Cold Bay, near Unalaska in the Aleutians, when her anchor pulled loose. The crew bumbled too long and lost control of the vessel. Out into the North Pacific she floated, her compass broke, a prisoner of the tide and current. She went as far as Japan where she became caught on a reef and remained lodged for several hours before a wave set her free. Back she came across the Pacific until she ended where she had begun her life: Cape Flattery off Port Townsend. Once he recognized the coastline, the captain ordered everyone to heft an axe and find what fuel they could to bring the **Dora** home. Out of food and exhausted by their ordeal, the 21 men and one woman finally set foot on land after 92 days at sea. But the **Dora** had one more surprise for them. When the ship was hauled out at a dry dock, it was discovered that a rock from the Japanese reef had become lodged in her hull. The **Dora** had thus floated across the North Pacific with this natural plug in her hull. The rock was removed and until as late as 1956, the rock sat on a dock in Seattle.[369]

* * *

About 1910, Kenneth Gilbert and three of his friends were lured into a poker game in Ketchikan. After about an hour it was apparent that the men against whom they were playing was cheating. One of Gilbert's friends, Joe, examined the back of the cards and noticed some strange splotches.

"What are those?" Joe said indicating the splotches.

"Them marks?" The hustler asked. "Why, they're nothing more than dried stain of salmon eggs."

"Then they must have been the smartest salmon that ever swum," Joe replied, "because I notice that they laid their eggs only on the aces and kings."[370]

* * *

Preacher Brown in the Fairbanks area was known for his dedication to God. Trying to collect contributions one evening from Billy Miles, the man of God was lured to a gaming table in the hopes of raising enough money for the construction of his church. After lengthy play, the Preacher walked away with $1,000 of Miles money. Only later did Miles find out that before he got religion, Preacher Brown has been "one of the slickest card-dealers in Nevada."[371]

* * *

When the *Stikeen River Journal* asked a miner by the name of Frost about the quality of diggings in the Windham Bay District, the miner replied, "There is gold there, but there is a powerful lot of dirt mixed with it."[372]

* * *

In the 1700s, a naturalist writing about the walrus, which he called a *morse,* stated that the walrus used his tusks for pulling himself up icy mountains. The Eskimos would seek out these walrus, presumably while they were asleep, cut holes in their flippers – which were "impervious to sensation"—and pass ropes through the holes. When the ropes were secured to giant rocks, the Eskimos would then create a great din which would awaken the walrus. In fright, the great beast would charge downhill and, in the process, jerk himself out of his skin. Reverend S. Hall Young also reported that he was asked by a Californian if walrus "brought forth their young alive or laid eggs and hatched them."[373]

* * *

Mrs. Schwatka, wife of the famed explorer, was quoted in THE ALASKA AND KLONDIKE GOLD FIELDS as stating that "I have known persons to die merely from the bite of the mosquitoes."[374] She also noted that "Alaska was a poor place for women and no place at all for children."[375]

* * *

With the exception of Nome, Alaska appeared to be a calm setting for a Gold Rush. This could have been, as Miss Anna Fulcomer noted, because "'lawyers and other disturbers of the peace' are kept out."[376]

* * *

On December 5, 1905, world famous Norwegian Arctic explorer Roald Amundsen, suddenly appeared in Eagle. He had mushed from Hershel Island, 1,000 miles to the north, where his sloop, the **Gjoa**, had become frozen in the ice pack. He came to Eagle because it was the closest community that had a telegraph and, from Eagle, he broadcast the news to the world that he had discovered the fabled Northwest Passage. Of course, he had had to sail through the passage at the speed of the ice pack. The first large ship to navigate the Northwest Passage under its own power was the **SS Manhattan**. It left Chester, PA on August 24, 1969 and was in Point Barrow on September 21. Its voyage was an exercise sponsored by three oil companies to see if it would be possible to ship Alaskan oil across the Arctic Ocean during the winter. This little experiment in polar transportation cost the three oil companies $40 million.[377] The first ship to reach the North Pole was the **USS Nautilus**. The ship, a nuclear submarine, left Point Barrow on August 1, 1958 and was under the North Pole at the top of the world two days later. On August 4, she was in Atlantic, for a trip of 1830, the bulk of it under the polar ice pack.[378]

* * *

Noted Alaskan writer Rex Beach was once in a storm so bad that he had to lash his wrists to the handle bars of his sled to keep from losing touch with the sled.[379]

* * *

Paul Makinson, deckhand on the steamer **Ida May**, reported that the Indians along the Yukon River traded for soap, in this case, oxydol. "It seems they melt it down and coat their fish with it," he wrote. "It evidently was quite a delicacy."[380]

Rex Beach

* * *

One Argonaut was pooh-poohed by his partners for carrying a grind stone up the 1,200, three footsteps of the Chilkoot Pass ice staircase. When he got to the top of the pass he set up shop and charged $.25 apiece to sharpen Argonaut 's picks. Then he "sat back and watched the men who had guyed him on the trail stand in line for him while he hauled in the dollars."[381]

* * *

In the early years of mining on the Seward Peninsula, some miners were impressed by the hoar frost that coated the willow tree twigs along the creek in which they were prospecting. Since the twigs looked like candles, they named their community Candle.[382]

* * *

At one time it was speculated that Alaska would be the ideal place for the development of an Arian Race. According to an article that appeared in the *Alaska Capital* on January 2, 1910, Alaska and the "northwest coast" was a wonderful location for health resorts for "neuroaesthenics." (Webster's defines "neuroaesthenia" as "an emotional and psychic disorder that is characterized by easy fatigability and often by lack of motivation, feelings of inadequacy and psychosomatic symptoms.") Even more important, or so claimed the *Alaska Capital,* these areas were ideal "as a breeding ground for people who by their great brain power should continue to dominate civilization."

* * *

Sightings of Noah's ark seem to have been the rage during the Alaska Gold Rush. In July of 1902, the *Valdez News* ran an article on the discovery of a "petrified ship lying high up on the side of a mountain" on the Porcupine River to the north of Rampart. Indians from the area claimed the boat to be about 1,200 feet in length. The Indians, the paper noted, were "convinced that the ship is none other than Noah's Ark." Unexplained in the article was how the Indians accounted for the petrified "safe or chest" they found in the vicinity of this mysterious vessel. In spite of their efforts, they were unable to open the safe.

Then, in August of 1902, another "Noah's Ark" was discovered 300 miles from Coldfoot. The vessel, about half a mile long, was apparently in such good condition that a Dr. Cleveland was considering opening "a roadhouse in the mythical vessel."

Four years later, in May of 1906, yet another "Noah's Ark" was discovered "on a high hill overlooking a string of lakes, 30 or 40 miles from the head of the Chandalar River. This craft was 14 feet high and 100 yards long "made with copper nails, bolts and washers." The fact that there were Russian words on this structure tended to put a hole in the theory that this truly Noah's Ark.[383]

Casey Moran, the newspaper editor who generated the rush to Barnette's cache in the dead of winter in 1903, was also responsible for a story on the discovery of Noah's Ark on a mountain top in the Koyukuk region. For a while the story did "considerable damage" to the "Mt. Ararat tradition."[384]

* * *

Early on the morning of June 15, 1902, W. B. Koon successfully escaped from the Valdez jail for the second time in five days. Charged with assault and battery against Mrs. Barrett, Koon had jumped bail and had been discovered hiding in a coal bunker aboard the **Perry**. Re-arrested on Wednesday, June 11, he was escorted back to jail. Several hours later, someone stopped at the Marshal's office and asked why Koon was still at liberty. Marshal Hasey made quick check of jail and discovered that one of the bars in the jail and been wrenched loose. Koon was lose for a number of days and then re-arrested. Then came the second break

Immediately after escaping, Koon awoke Reverend Cram and escorted the cleric to the home of Mrs. Barrett where he, Koon, married Mrs. Barrett. The marriage, not under duress, solved Koon's legal problems "as the bride was the only witness against Koon he could not be tried on the charge for which he was arrested as a wife cannot be forced to testify against her husband." But he was charged with defacing a building, I.E., the jail, and was re-arrested. However, as there was "little or no damage," the jury acquitted him. But the jury did deliver a letter to the Commissioner stating:

> Sir: The undersigned jurors in the aforementioned case are of the opinion that the present condition of the United States jail at this place presents a constant menace to the peace and security of the community and affords a standing invitation to prisoners to make an easy and hasty escape therefrom.[385]

* * *

Cannibalism was not unknown in the harsh conditions of Alaska's winters. In May of 1899, the bodies of three men were found near Circle. The three men, Michael Daly (Providence, R.I.), Victor Edair (Woonsocket, R.I.) and M. Provost (Brockton, MA) had been on their way to Jimtown when they became disoriented and starved to death. After the bodies of Edair and Provost were discovered, a search was made for the third man. "Daly's partially eaten body was found on the stove in the tent just as it was left when death overtook the others."[386]

A case of almost-cannibalism took place in August of 1901, when two men with food stumbled upon two men preparing to make a repast of their former partner. Jack Huston and Joseph C. Thiery were found with the remains of their partner, George Dean, after they spent 23 days without food. Marooned on the Aqiapuk River near Teller, the men were described as "living skeletons" by their rescuers, Louis Reich and

George Woods. The men had been hiking cross country and lost their way, barely making it to the *barabara* where they were found.

The men had tried to make a small boat to cross the Aqiapuk but the canvas they were using leaked too badly. They abandoned the craft and this was what attracted the attention of the rescuers. As they were examining the craft "they heard the unfortunate men in a weak voice crying to them for God's sake to come into the *barabara* and rescue them." Dean had died some six hours earlier and the two remaining men were "preparing a stew of flesh cut from his thigh."[387]

There is also a highly speculative story of how an Indian who had been reduced to cannibalism during a famine. When asked if it was true that he had eaten his wife and child, the Indian replied, probably tongue in cheek, that this was not true. He had only eaten the child. [388] The *Nome Nugget* also published a story of cannibalism in the Dawson area but the story was only from one person. Supposedly the Indian, name not revealed, had killed and eaten his wife and when hunger again returned, he devoured his two children as well. Then, adding more speculation as to the veracity of the story, the Indian "made his way to the camp of some other Indians where he told of his crime" and was being shunned.[389] Why the Indian did not go the neighboring village when he go hungry in the first place was not stated in the article.

* * *

One's religious belief have very little to do with honesty. In June of 1899, W. H. Leamon, a Methodist preacher in Skaguay, salted a claim by adding some quartz with gold filings into a sample being pounded out. The claim was bought by three other Methodists from Leamon's congregation. After the fake was discovered, Leamon "took advantage of the timely arrival of the **City of Seattle** and left for Everett, (Washington.)" Leamon apparently made good his escape – with $500 for his share of the salting deal.[390]

* * *

In June of 1906, Joe Cook, "a professional claim jumper," took possession of one claim too many. The property in question had been staked by Joe Voegler and his partner and the men had dropped an 80 foot shaft. Voegler's partner had become sick and, while the two were at the hospital in Fairbanks, Cook and his partner staked over the 80 foot shaft. When Voegler returned and complained about the trespass, Cook replied that if he didn't like it they could go to court but to keep in mind that he, Cook, had the backing of a silent partner who would "see him through." Voegler, broke, tried to talk Cook out of it but to no avail. Local miners heard of the dispute and gathered at McGuire's Roadhouse when Cook happened by. "A rope was brought out, and Cook was given to understand that when a mosquito bites a man it is crushed, when a dog is so vicious that it becomes dangerous it is killed, and that he, being considered in the same light, his time had come." Cook was that given the "choice of dangling at the end of a rope or leaving the country." Needless to say, Cook decided to "hit the trail immediately."[391]

* * *

In the summer of 1905, a decision was made to fill the numerous potholes in the Fairbanks street with whatever debris was available – and free. One of the items dumped was hay, bales of it that had been scorched in a fire and then wetted, presumably by the fire department. The owner of the hay filled holes and spread the rest of it over the street. For a short period of time Third Street appeared level. Then stray horses began eating the "pavement." Though the outside of the bales had been inedible, the inside "was a sweet as a hickory nut." The Mayor was furious but all he could do was frighten off the horses and "pray for the next meeting of the [City] Council when the ordinance preventing horses from running at large will become a law."[392]

* * *

Chief Jack, one of the oldest (115) and most respected Natives in Alaska died in his home in Killisnoo in September of 1908. He had been present at the lowering of the Russian flag at Sitka and was considered an old man then.

He was well known to travelers for he met every steamer that docked in Killisnoo for more than 40 years dressed elaborately in one of his many stately uniforms. Once he turned up in Salvation Army Officer's [outfit], another time he wore the uniform of a Russian rear-admiral, while his chief's costume, which was worn many times, he varied with all kinds of decorations. Once he covered his [Native] dress with some thousand poker chips in various colors, while another time he [was] asserted to have worn attached to his dress, a set of church collection plates.

The Chief stored all of his uniforms in an ebony coffin which he had shipped to Alaska. He was deathly afraid of being buried alive and left "most explicit instructions" to make certain that he was indeed dead. There were several tests involved, including the "discharging of a cannon near his ear."[393]

* * *

Rivalry between Alaskan cities at the turn of the century was not unusual. In October of 1905, the *Seward Daily Gateway* cheerfully described the fate of 14 workers for the Alaska Central Railway that had gotten off the steamer **Santa Clara** in Valdez:. [The **Santa Clara**] started with 70 [workers] but at Valdez fourteen misguided creatures fell victims to the alternating currents of hot and cold air generated by the boomers and the glacier, or [were] overcome by the coffin varnish dispensed there as whiskey, and dropped by the wayside. From some cause they are now classified on the books as "lost, strayed or stolen."[394]

* * *

In August of 1905, when a dam outside of Valdez broke and flooded the city, the *Seward Daily Gateway* remarked that the bowling alley and several saloons were flooded. In the case of the former it was temporarily impossible to "set 'em up" in any alley. In the saloons, barkeeps could "set up for a little while and no glasses were required. It has not yet been learned whether any whiskey was injured by mixing with the fluid abhorred by all Kentuckians."[395]

* * *

In December of 1900, S. L. Colwell of Nome was walking home when he was accosted by a thug with a mask holding a revolver. The bandit demanded that Colwell throw up his hands, which Colwell did. "But in throwing them up he took special care to throw his right hand, tightly clenched, under the thug's jaw." The criminal fell to the ground whereupon Colwell "administered a kick or two with heavy overshoes" and continued his promenade.[396]

* * *

Mt. McKinley was originally known as "Denali," the "Great One" by the local Natives. The Russians named it "Bolshaya," the "Great One," and later it was known as "Densmore's Mountain" for a local prospector. It was not until 1896 when W. Dickey of Montesano, Washington , named it "McKinley" did the name stick. But the name stuck because, as legend has it, because Dickey was a Princeton man, and his tales of Alaska were given great credence in the America press. Today, "Denali" is both the name of the Mountain and the National Park.[397]

* * *

As of September 15th, 1900, "all parties employing females in saloons or permitting them to drink at the bar of saloons" were in violation of the law.[398]

* * *

Wyatt Earp accepted the job as Deputy Marshal of Wrangell for ten days. His name "was a big help," reported his wife, in a town so rough that Wyatt referred to it as "Hell-on-wheels." On one of those ten days Wyatt was called upon to disarm a man waving a pistol about in a saloon. After the man had given up his pistol, he realized that he recognized the aging lawman.

"By Gawd, y'all're Wyatt Earp ain't you?"

After Earp nodded in the affirmative the man replied, "By damn if this don't beat all! Here I go to the end of the earth, and the first man I run into when I let off a little steam is Wyatt Earp. Y'all threw me and a bunch of the boys in the pokey in Dodge City for the same thing twenty years ago!"[399]

Of more dubious authenticity is the claim that while in Alaska, Wyatt Earp met Butch Cassidy. And, on the same trip, allegedly, was the Sundance Kid. But there are some holes in this supposition – setting aside the generally-held belief that both Butch Cassidy and the Sundance Kid had been killed in Boliva in 1908. Supposedly the two former members of the Hole-in-the-Wall Gang met with Wyatt at his "gambling joint" in Anchorage in 1912. Doubt is cast on this allegation as Wyatt left Alaska in 1901 and was never in Anchorage because the city did not exist at that time. Further, in 1901, the whereabouts of Butch Cassidy were well known to the law enforcement community and his haunts did not include Alaska. The only reason this account should be given some credence is that Butch Cassidy's sister, Lula Parker Betenson, confirmed that Cassidy under the name of William T. Phillips made a trip to Alaska, possibly in 1912.[400] But then again, Wyatt Earp was not in Alaska in 1912.

* * *

The mainstay of most stampeders was beans and beans and more beans which was not particularly appetizing. When men had the money to order good food, they went for the American fare of meat and potatoes. But the memory of beans and beans was hard to forget. Reverend

Rowe reported watching a sourdough who made big order a hearty meal of steak and potatoes. Then, at the last moment, the man ordered a plate of beans. When the beans came, the sourdough set the plate on his water glass and addressed the vegetables: "There, damn you, watch me enjoy a feast."[401]

* * *

Since men outnumbered women by a factor of nine to one, it wasn't hard for the women to dip into the miners' pockets with ease. It was infinitely easier than standing hip-deep in any icy stream and dumping gravel into a sluice box. Thousands of women worked as dancehall girls, prostitutes, "actresses," cardsharps and salon shills adding spice to the reputation of Alaska. Sometimes their names told all, like Ethel the Moose, Nellie the Pig, Three-Way Annie, Fewclothes Molly, Short and Dirty, Passionate Annie, May the Cow, Kitty the Bitch and others. Brothels were common and were usually open around the clock. But just like the miners, a few prostitutes left Alaska wealthy but most simply slipped into the pages of history as colorful vignettes of the wild and woolly north.

* * *

Many of the missionaries suffered scurvy, a disease the Natives somehow avoided. Some of the results of scurvy were open sores on the body and receding gums to the extent that teeth would fall out. One of the cures was the consumption of a raw, grated potato mixed with vinegar.[402]

* * *

In August of 1900, Barney Durand of Nome started the first shelter for "homeless and destitute canines." A venture of the private sector, Durand would gather up stray dogs and charge the owners two dollars per animal and 50 cents per day to redeem the animal. By his third month in business he had gathered 160 dogs which created such a sanitation nightmare that to find the establishment all one had to do was "follow your nose." Those dogs which died were buried on the grassy slope above the pound where they were dug up and eaten by derelict prospectors some of whom "got as high as one hind leg and a lobe of liver to the pan."[403]

* * *

Sometimes the news coming from the Interior was spotty. The *Seattle Times*, in April of 1899, reported that in Circle on a date unknown "Bruce Lloyd, well known on the inside, married somebody and the result was a great celebration."[404]

* * *

A uniquely Alaskan remedy for frostbitten fingers and toes was to immerse them in port wine.[405]

* * *

Even in the winter there was a way to make a dollar honestly. During the winter of 1901-1902, Dell Clark of Council City cut 30 tons of ice and packed them in sawdust anticipating that ice would be in great demand the next summer. This monopoly, the *Council City News* reported, was "probably why [Clark] has of late talked so much about the rights of trusts and monopolists, and walked around whistling, 'Wouldn't You Like to be an Iceman Now?'"[406]

* * *

Freida Goodwin, an Eskimo in Kotzebue who remembered the coming of the miners in 1898, recalled that they "put up lots of tents" to the east of what is now the city of Kotzebue. As a humorous aside, when the missionaries came to Kotzebue that year the women wore long dresses, something the Eskimos had never seen. The dresses hung all the way to the ground and covered the women's feet. When the Eskimo children first heard the stomping of shoes they "wondered what kind of feet those women had since they always made noise. We tried to see their feet when they were wearing, but we couldn't because of the long skirts. We wanted to see what kind of feet they had."[407]

* * *

There are many tales, a great many of them apocryphal, of the re-action of Eskimos to the white man's culture. One story, possibly true, relates how an Eskimo woman feared she would be unable to find her hotel room in the ten-story, San Francisco establishment and "blazed a trail with a jackknife on the banister all the way down the stairway."[408] Other stories have Eskimos referring to a phonograph as "Canned White Man."[409]

* * *

The *Skaguay News* ran a special on what women should be bring on the trek to Dawson. Written by a woman, Annie Hall Strong, the article emphasized that it took "strong, healthy courageous women to stand the terrible hardships that must necessarily be endured." Only those women who were willing to subject themselves to such conditions should con-sider the trip, a journey that was ill-suited for "delicate women" or those who "love luxury, comfort and ease." With the exception of the clothing, the list is nearly identical to that which a man should bring, which is understandable, but some of the unusual items suggested by Ms. Strong include "house slippers" and "knitted slippers." She also suggested that the best footwear would be a "tall bicycle shoe with extra sole."[410]

* * *

The mystique of Alaskan men also permeated to the lower states. In July of 1906, the *Fairbanks Times* reported that an article in a Seattle paper had informed matrimonially-minded single women in the contiguous states that there were "4,000 husky and well-fixed miners in the Fairbanks district that are pining for married happiness." This brought a number of letters to the *Fairbanks Times* which were published. As could be expected, most of them seemed too good to be true. One woman asked for a husband who had a "pocketbook that holds enough for two." Another woman, perhaps not sure how to approach to dating game, listed herself as "a healthy young woman, weight 180 pounds." Some sent photos[411]

Not all communities welcomed the civilizing influence of women that easily. A few months later, in Wrangell, a Bachelor's Club was established and a real war of the sexes began. In the vein of humor, the *Fort Wrangell News* printed a column entitled "Reflections of a Bachelor" with such classic tidbits as:

Reasonable women are about as rare as peaches without fuzz.

No girl has any idea how much she cares for a man till she begins to have an idea how little he cares for her.

A woman's opinions on politics are just about as pronounced and reliable as her opinions on the women her husband knows but she doesn't.

A woman is pretty sure to see that the whole family hears her when she tells her husband he ought to be ashamed to talk so to her before the children.[412]

A Bachelor's Club was soon formed in Fort Wrangell and then the war of the sexes erupted. The meetings were well publicized, and members of the Bachelor's Club objected and speeches were made which "roasted to a fine brown" newspaper reporters. The meeting was adjourned to another location to avoid the prying eyes of the press and at that meeting, covered by the press, J. F. Collins did an oration on "The Death of Ceasar."[413]

A week later the Club met again. Even though the location of the meeting was changed to prevent the news media from discovering its whereabouts – and the password was changed as well – the newspaper carried an article on the gathering. Then the president read a letter of protest from the "grass widows, genuine widows and maids" of Wrangell – 17 of whom signed the petition – to become an auxiliary. Now the fuse was lit. Col. Crittenden, who was hosting the secret meeting that everyone seemed to know about, immediately protested. Collins, who had given "The Death of Cesar Oration" the previous week, gave a ten minute speech in which he said he "had no use for women" and at that comment, "everybody commenced to snicker." One of the bachelors present "nearly burst his sides with laughter" while Colonel Crittendon "crammed a rag into his mouth to suppress his mirth." Several other men made statements, many of which were met with a horse laugh. When the mirth had subsided, the petition of the women was rejected.[414]

There were several secret meetings the next week and at one of them, the President read an anonymous letter he had just received:

You Old Sausage Cover:

> You think you have did a bright thing in not lettin us women come to the club and jine it. You think you is smart don't you? You are nothing but a lot of pumpkin rollers and gum chewers anyhow. I once though you was kinder nice, but this letter will let you know how I have changed my mind up.

HATEFULLY YOURS, AN OLD MAID

Then he gave a short speech about how he had "never been called such names before" and that he wasn't against women, just against them in the club. Other speeches were made regarding the depressing nature of the letter and the president concluded that being called a pumpkin roller "was not to be passed over lightly" and suggested that a future meeting look into the matter.

As the speeches were winding down, a knock on the door attracted everyone's attention. Though the stranger had the proper password, the doorkeeper was sure it was a woman. Three men were chosen to investigate the sex of the intruder. It was concluded that it was indeed a man and he was admitted. Shortly thereafter the meeting was adjourned.[415]

For several weeks thereafter, the antics of the secret meeting of the Bachelor's Club were published the paper, including a satirical eye-witness account of a woman who swore she had attended one of the meetings dressed as a man. Eventually the Club passed from the scene, but it did serve to illustrate that in the more established communities – Wrangell having its birth in the 1830s – the refining influences of a feminine presence were not so highly prized.

* * *

While the demand for women, and particularly single women, was high, marital bliss was not universal. In Nome, Captain and Mrs. Banks had a parting of the ways in November of 1900, according a front page article in the *Nome Chronicle*. Mrs. Banks "picked up her doll rags and flew" from the room of her husband leaving him to "wrestle with a lot of wine bills and an angry creditor or two." Mrs. Banks had married the Captain under the impression that he was a wealthy man. When it appeared he could not even pay the $500 for their drinks and the honeymoon apartment over the Nevada Saloon, she "flew the coop" leaving him to pay the bills.[416]

What makes this particular story memorable was that the Banks marriage had been headline catching. On September 24 of that year, Lillian Dale – the future Mrs. Banks – was seeing two men at the same time, Banks and a gambler named Riess. She apparently gave both men cause to believe that they were favored in her eyes. When Banks went to get a minister, Riess locked himself in the woman's boudoir and refused to let Banks in or the woman out. Harsh words were said on both sides of the portal with curses that would have crinkled paint. Curses were followed by each party threatening to fire through the flimsy door. Neither party relented until the United States Deputy Marshal arrived and demanded that the door be opened. The door was opened and a few minutes later, Lillan Dale became Lillian Banks.[417]

* * *

Because there were so many Scandinavians in Fairbanks it was said that "Swedes were cheaper than timber."[418] (At that time, the terms Scandinavian and Swedish were synonymous.)

* * *

In 1898 there was a brief fling at a colony of Finlanders to be established in the Yukon Valley. J. A. Nordenskeld of Helsingfors, Finland, and eight other Finlanders arrived in the Yukon Valley to prospect for land. As the Yukon Valley was at a similar latitude as their country, they felt they could raise crops as well in Alaska as Finland. These crops included oats, potatoes, rutabagas and beets. While wheat was not a viable possibility, Nordenskeld said, barley was, a fact taken by heart by the State of Alaska in the 1980s when the Delta Barley Project was established in the Fairbanks area.[419]

In 1903, there was still talk of settling Finns on an agricultural colony in Alaska. The Alaska Colony Company had been established to bring "shiploads of hardy immigrants of the agricultural class." The draw of Alaska on the Finns was strong because "the people of Finland are, as a rule, tillers of the soil and nothing else." Further, the Finns had no love for their sovereign who, at that time, was the Czar of Russia. (Finland would not declare its independence from Russian until December 6, 1917.) Therefore, "the bird of freedom holds a much higher place in the minds of these humble people than does the Russian bear."[420]

Sheldon Jackson also convinced the United States government to contract with some individuals to choose the best place for a colony of Lapps in Alaska. After more than 1,500 miles of exploring up the Yukon and Kuskokwim watersheds, the Lapps chose Unalaska as the most likely spot for the colony.[421]

* * *

There was quite a bit of myth in the early writers when it came to the Alaska Native. Since readers were expecting igloos, naturally, the diarist provided just that. Dietz, who survived the trek across the Malaspina Glacier reported that the Natives of Yakutat had "ice huts" and it was "like solving a Chinese puzzle to get into one of them without a guide."[422] There may be some truth to this because the snow in Yakutat can get so deep that getting into a structure requires, quite literally, tunnels through the snow.

* * *

While Sheldon Jackson looked upon the establishment of reindeer stations as a success, many other Alaskans did not. These individuals looked upon the reindeer stations as "experimental" and did little good for too many Natives lived where the stations were not.[423] Mortality among the reindeer being transported from Siberia to Alaska was high. In November of 1901, it was reported that of the 425 reindeer that left Siberia, only 254 made it ashore alive. Some of the mortality was due to natural causes, like "being constantly thrown down by the action of the ship." But other reasons for deaths of reindeer was the result of human stupidity. When the transport ships were assembled, the feeding troughs were built too high for many of the animals to reach."[424]

* * *

Drunken Indians were treated by the press either as sad characters or comical for their antics. For instance, the death of "Humpy Stephen," a well-known drunk around at the turn of the century, was treated with humor. Humpy, so named for a physical deformity, was officially a resident of "Tyoonok, but his habitat embraced the entire Cook Inlet region, especially the localities where the white man's hooch grew rankest."

Humpy had been a "sort of assistant priest or servitor in the Greek church" but was better known for his conniving skills which he practiced upon the religious brethren. When his con games left his short of cash, Humpy "would induce the lambs of his flock to join him in a poker game, in which he usually sheared them." Inevitably, "all the Indian money came his way, but he always put it into circulation again and it gravitated rapidly to the white man." Humpy came to sad end reported the *Seward Daily Gateway*, when he, under the influence of "Cook Inlet Vodka," fell into the waters of Resurrection Creek. When his body was recovered, "it was found that his spirit had flown to the happy hunting ground."[425]

* * *

As could be expected, the Natives were none too pleased with the miners and anyone of the white persuasion after the plague of 1900. Dr. Romig, a doctor in Bethel, reported that a missionary he had sent into the Arctic, a Native named Neck, found that at first the Natives of the north "would not let him talk" and when he tried to conduct religious ceremonies, the Natives "blew out the candles he tried to use in the ceremony."[426]

* * *

When E. T. Barnette's wife filed for divorce in San Francisco in September of 1918, she released two letters which her husband had written to his mistress, Mrs. Dorothy Pullen of New York. Mrs. Pullen apparently liked Alaskans for she had had affairs with both Barnette and his good friend and well-known womanizer, Leroy Tozier. Tozier had such a satyrific appetite that even Swiftwater Bill, legendary for his peccadilloes, noted that in Nome, Leroy Tozier was such a ladies man that "if I wanted to locate him at once, do you know what I would do? I'd go outside and make a noise like a woman's skirt rustling."[427]

* * *

By 1905, the concept of Alaska as being the wild and wooly north had changed substantially. When a stampede occurred on the Bearpaw River near Kantishna, old time Argonauts from Dawson "almost balked at the sight of women and children on the trail so close to the diggings," reported the *Fairbanks Weekly News*. One of the Argonauts was quoted as saying that this strike was not

> natural. It's too tame like. You ride almost to the digging in up-holstered seats on a steamer and find petticoats all along the line. I kept looking for the telegraph line, and it was hard to realize I was on a real stampede such as we used to follow in the old days. I suppose electric cars will be soon whirring up the canyon.[428]

* * *

Not everyone who invested in Barnette's bank lost their savings. Legend has it that a man by the name of Frank Goan chased E. T. Barnette down the Circle Trail and caught up with him near Twelve Mile Summit. "You've got $30,000 of my money," said Goan as he leveled a rifle at the fleeing banker. "Give me my money." Apparently Barnette did.[429]

There have always been speculation as to E. T. Barnette's money. Quite a bit of it went into land in Mexico. He bought a tract of land ten miles long by three and a half wide less than five miles from the ocean. His 20,000 acres cost him $2,000,000. Immediately after he bought the land he hired "the best white manager he could find" and ordered land cleared for 1,000 acres of bananas, 1,000 acres of tobacco, 2,000 acres of sugar cane and room enough for 25,000 coconut palms. He hired 150 Mexican workers and bought 1,400 head of cattle, 100 mules, 100 brood mares, 80 yoke of unbroken oxen, 40 yoke of broken oxen, and 40 saddle horses. The main house was built around a Mexican courtyard with a fountain and contained 36 rooms.[430]

* * *

At Holy Cross, the nuns didn't help much with their attempted cure of the disease with "coal oil, flour and water, carbolic acid and whiskey."[431]

* * *

If there was any doubt as to the existence of the Klondike Strike, it was extinguished when the **Portland** docked in Seattle carrying more gold dust-laden prospectors. Though it was only carrying $700,000 in gold, according to the *Post-Intelligencer,* the Chicago *Tribune* jumped the quantity to "a ton." There was so much gold on board, a Seattle paper noted, that some gold had been smuggled aboard the **Portland** to avoid the freight charge.

Interestingly, the vessel that brought the news of the Klondike Strike to Seattle, the **Portland**, made only two trips to Alaska during the Klondike era. She had been built in 1885 as the **Haitian Republic** and began her career as a gun runner for rebels in Haiti. Four years later she was working as a cannery ship – until Federal authorities caught her smuggling Chinese and opium. She was bought at auction by the Alaska Commercial Company and renamed the **Portland** to be used in the passenger trade.

Adding to her fame, on her second trip back from Alaska, she was escorted by an American revenue cutter to protect her from "Chinese pirates" allegedly interested in the $2 million in gold award. The rumor that "Mongolians" had been recruited in San Francisco raised such a furor that the United States Revenue Cutter **Bear** was sent to look for these alleged brigands. There were, of course, none to be found.[432]

But the owners were taking no chances. A 37-mm Maxim rapid-fire gun was installed on the starboard side of the forward deck to fight off any pirates the ship might encounter. Newspapers captivated readers with tales of the romance of a treasure ship fighting off swarms of brigands of the North. Such sensational accounts turned out to be bad publicity for the **Portland**. She was reclaimed by her original owners and transferred to San Francisco. Thus she did not partake in the frenzied gold rush she had initiated.[433] After the enthusiasm for the Klondike

Strike had ebbed, the **Portland** returned to Alaskan waters and sank at Katella in 1910.

* * *

Arriving in Eagle, a Dawson sourdough noted, "I haven't sent my wife a letter with an American stamp for three years," one ex-Dawson-ite not an Eagle-ite reported. "Gosh, but she'll be glad to see this!"[434]

* * *

Occasionally the steamboat inspectors did order a ship to unload because it was dangerously top heavy. In August of 1897, the **Moonlight** was so loaded that Inspector W. J. Bryant objected to the "several thousand feet of lumber, piled high over the rail" and ordered the lumber removed before the ship was allowed to leave port. [435] The next year, on May 30, 1898, the Captain of the **Rock Island** became concerned that his ship "was loaded too deep for the ocean trip" from Seattle and he ordered coal taken off the boat. Enough coal was taken off to raise the ship ten inches.[436]

* * *

In Nome, prices were so high that a quarter ($10.20 in 2020 dollars) was the smallest denomination of change used.[437]

* * *

In March of 1899, Horace S. Conger noted that the Copper River Indians were hostile – all one of them –"for he was afraid," but Conger was able to overcome this murderous intent of the one Indian with "a little tobacco."[438]

* * *

All manner of locomotion devices for use in northern climes were invented as well. In September of 1897, A. W. Charleston of Seattle invented a dogsled that had a mast and sail attached. Dogs would be used to pull the sled uphill and then, on the down side, the dogsled would sail. Steering would be by a "small rudder or block of wood under the front part of the sled." What would happen to the dogs on the downhill side of the trail was never made clear.[439]

Another invention was the "snow locomotive." The machine had sprinklers attached to its engine which wet the snow ahead of the vehicle thus making it hard and slick. The locomotive would drag cars built like sleds behind it. Invented by Powers & Simpson and first used in northern Minnesota, the snow locomotive was alleged to have the ability to carry up to 50,000 feet of logs at a speed of up to eight miles an hour. This ability made it a "Klondike Possibility."[440]

For smaller loads there was Palmtag's Moving House, a house trailer with treads instead of wheels. Invented by M. Palmtage of New Whatcom, Wisconsin, the vehicle had wooden cleats for deep snow and cleats for travel over ice. As designed it was seven feet wide and 24 feet wide and would weigh three and a half tons and could carry eight passengers – and would require a contingent of 10 men to clear the ice of impediments as the Moving House cleated its way along the frozen surface of the river. (It was not made clear if the 10 men were passengers as well.)[441]

Another invention of dubious reliability was the Yukon "Go-Devil," a stern-wheel bobsled. The vehicle was 30 feet in length of which four feet was composed of the drive wheel, a large drum which had steel spikes in which to drive into the ice for traction. A seven-horse power engine would drive it over the snow and, when the ice broke, a hull could be built around the vehicle to turn it into a boat. Invented by Col. R. H. Ballinger, the contraption had the added benefit of being worth a small fortune to a large mining operation for "a well-equipped machine shop goes with the outfit."[442]

* * *

One Argonaut , Will R. Newland, came north on the **Noyo** and was sleeping among the timbers on an upper deck. A great lurch threw him from his bunk onto a fellow passenger's pet skunk. The skunk thereupon "opened fire with his machine gun and poured hard and fast volley after volley" forcing the men to take themselves and their bed clothing outside.[443]

* * *

Several West Coast cities claimed they were the "Gateway to the Klondike." Not the least of these was Seattle whose businesses struck it even richer than the miners on Bonanza Creek. All this was thanks to the unsung and unheralded Erastus Brainerd.[444] Born and raised on the East Coast, Brainerd began his career as a journalist. He wrote for the *Atlanta Constitution* and *Philadelphia Press* and was working for the *New York World* when he received an unexpected offer. In 1890, a friend, W. A. Bailey, bought a struggling newspaper, the *Seattle Press*, and urged Brainerd to run it. Brainerd accepted the offer and came to Seattle. But his tenure was not long. He resigned shortly after arriving in Seattle to become a state land commissioner. His stay at this job was also brief. With the next election, he was out of a job.

Brainerd then served in a number of capacities, one as the Paraguayan consulate in Seattle, and was looking for other means of employment when the news of the Klondike Strike reached Seattle. Brainerd's moment of opportunity rode the same tide as the gold ships. The Seattle Chamber of Commerce, attempting to secure its slice of the Klondike outfitting pie, named him to head a committee to look into the matter.

Brainerd was perfect for the job. A master of innovation, his journalistic background was put to good use in producing a stream of press releases and magazine articles. Further, as he knew quite a few East Coast editors on a first-name basis he would have no trouble getting Seattle news into the nation's presses. With a fat expense account and a pen, Brainerd helped change the face of the Pacific Northwest forever.

He began his campaign conventionally: he advertised. But he did more than just place a few newspaper ads in a handful of papers. He blitzed the nation. Seattle was advertised in more newspapers, journals, magazines, tabloids and periodicals than all the other West Coast ports combined. From Hearst's *New York Journal* to the myriad of smaller, regional and rural papers, he beat the drum for Seattle. Ads praising Seattle's unique qualities and its proximity to the Klondike also appeared in such magazines as *McClure's, Century, Cosmopolitan, Munsey's, Scribner's and Review of Review's.*[445]

Brainerd pioneered techniques that would be used so effectively in the future. One of his innovative techniques was to pair civic-minded individuals and recent arrivals to Seattle with their home towns. Then, subscribing to a clipping service, every time Seattle was mentioned in any newspaper across the country, Brainerd had someone who could write to their home town paper and demand a correction, if necessary, or send a follow-up letter to the editor about the wonders of Seattle as the gateway to Alaska and the Klondike Strike. Usually the people "sending" the letter just signed their names to pre-written letters of which Brainerd had many. This duplicity did not diminish the value of the correspondence. Letters were published by the hundreds and Brainerd's campaign for free publicity was off to a running start.

He also coordinated a letter-writing campaign to mayors across America offering advice and information for Argonauts and trumpeting the virtues of Seattle as a Klondike way-station. Pictures of Seattle were sent out gratis and Brainerd persuaded the State of Washington to produce a guidebook – which, of course, advertised Seattle as the gateway to Alaska and the Klondike – and sent it out as a promotional item. If there were any questions, he stated in the correspondence, please feel free to contact me in Seattle. He was flooded with responses. To each correspondent, he continued to preach the virtues of Seattle.

Brainerd would also mine new articles from old ones. He generated magazine articles from news stories and then wrote news stories from the magazine articles he had just written ad infinitum. This Niagara of words poured out-of-state to the armies of journalists hungry for Klondike News.

With an eye to convincing Argonauts to spend their equipment dollars in Seattle, he published a document called "Distance, Dangers and Probable Expenses" discussing the nuts-and-bolts and dollars-and-cents of Klondike travel. When the *Post-Intelligencer* printed a special Klondike insert, Brainerd bought 100,000 copies and sent them to every postmaster, library and mayor across the United States.[446] So great was Brainerd's impact on the United States that in March of 1898, Seattle formed a Bureau of Information to handle the increasing number of letters seeking information on transportation and outfitting for the Klondike Strike.[447]

Business in Seattle boomed. In August of 1897, the income of its businesses doubled.[448] But even this was not enough. The city's merchants wanted to make every cent off the trade they could. Thus, in the Spring of 1898, Brainerd was given another assignment – again with an unlimited budget. His instructions were simple: arrange to have the United States assay office for Klondike gold established in Seattle.[449] With the assay office located in Seattle, merchants could take advantage of both ends of the gold rush. They could sell supplies to miners on their way north and then providing the luxury items after the successful Argonaut had converted his yellow metal to cash.

Brainerd's legacy was visible even in his lifetime. The push by Brainerd and the Seattle Chamber of Commerce to make Seattle the leading West Coast shipping port was stunningly successful. By October of 1898, Seattle had doubled the output of San Francisco in the St. Michael trade and dwarfed that of Vancouver, Victoria and Portland as well. In the race for mercantile supremacy, Portland failed to even make an honorably showing. In the 1898 shipping season, only two ships left Portland for St. Michael as opposed to 34 from Seattle. Portland tonnage for the entire season was 688 tons while Seattle's was 22,000.[450]

* * *

Paul Makinson, working as a deck hand on the **Ida May** as she made her way up the Yukon, reported that the meat used for feeding the passengers was hardly kept in sanitary condition.

The meat was stored on the afterdeck; it was kept under a heavy canvas tarpaulin, which ran over a wooden frame and was fastened down at the four corners. This meat consisted of a couple sides of beef, about three whole hams, and a couple of sides of pork. We had no means of refrigeration on board, so the meat was hung where it would remain the coolest. I had the job of sweeping out the pilot house, which was up on the top of the Texas deck. And I went there and swept worms and maggots out of the wheel house; it sickened me. The captain said, 'Do it early in the morning before the passengers are awake so that they won't know.'"[451]

* * *

One of the nagging incidents which took place at the border was the brother of the California Gold Rush poet Joaquin Miller who "cut the halyards and pulled down the British Custom House flat which was flying over the place where British officials were transacting business connected with the Custom House. He kicked it contemptuously and threatened to do the same every time it was hauled up."[452]

* * *

Just before Klondike Fever infected the world, many predicted that the strike would amount to very little. William M. Sauers of Gray's Harbor, Washington, reported that Skagway was a ghost town in October of 1897. "A deserted village composed of disheartened men without money and without prospects," he told the *Seattle Times*, "Skaguay is certainly a 'busted' town."

There is no record of Mr. Sauer's comments a year later.[453]

* * *

Skagway also had its novelties, including the blind Italian accordion player, an enterprising Italian from Naples who made a fortune selling balloons to the Argonauts, "Peter the Apostle" who patrolled the White Pass giving assistance and spiritual guidance to the flood of humanity, and the Kilkenny Wildcat, a boxer from Seattle. The Kilkenny Wildcat, it should be mentioned, went into a rage whenever he heard the sound of bagpipes. Fighting "The Platteville Terror," a bartender in Skagway, bets were running heavily against the Wildcat. Midway through the fight it was apparent why. At a critical juncture in the fisticuffs, the plaintiff moan of bagpipes broke out. As the Wildcat looked around in a frenzy for the purveyor of such music, the Platteville Terror knocked him out.[454]

* * *

Skagway is Alaska's windy city. The town gets its name from the local Indian word "Skagus," meaning "Home of the North Wind" while Dyea originally meant the "carrying place" in Tlingit.[455] Skagway certainly lived up to its reputation as one Argonaut noted. The wind blows like the "mill tails of hell," B. E. Axe reported.[456]

* * *

Mail was also important to the Argonauts and the postman was an important part of the rush. In Dyea, for instance, the post office was open Monday through Saturday and "a line of people anywhere from a couple of dozen to 300 to 400" would be waiting to check for mail. Further, since the postmaster would not allow any man to take mail for more than two people, men who came into town for ten people had to wait in line 5 times to get all the mail for their party. Because of the waiting time, it was not unreasonable for a man to spend a day and a half in line only to find that there was no mail for him or any of his party. The Postmaster at Dyea, Clara H. Richards, claimed that if she allowed men to ask for mail for more than 2 persons, she would have ended up with a line "several hundred feet long" in front of the Post Office every day.

The mail coming into Alaska at the start of the gold rush was no less voluminous. In February of 1898, the United States Post Office reported that it had received 135 sacks of mail in three and a half days – about a three and a half tons. Outgoing letters were being sent at the rate of 600 per day, the highest in the United States since 1884.[457] Postmaster was paid 10 cents a letter. Some men coming down from Dawson were charging a dollar a letter for delivery in Skagway. C. W. Watts reported that a man came from Dawson with 100 letters for which he was charging a dollar apiece. "He said he could just as well have brought 1000 – think of that," Watts declared.[458]

There were so many Argonauts that the mail was backlogged, often sitting in port for weeks, victims of both the weather and too many recipients. Often the mail was taken to Dawson by enterprising individuals who charged a dollar a letter for the service. Wilson Mizner reported that he once received 26 letters in this manner – and 11 of them were bills.[459]

* * *

For a party of five, the recommended food list included:

350 pounds of flour
150 pounds of bacon
100 pounds of beans
15 pounds of tea
25 pounds of rice
50 pounds of dry salt pork
100 pounds of dried fruits
50 pounds of salt
2 pounds of evaporated vinegar
20 pounds of condensed milk
50 pounds of corn meal
50 pounds of rolled oats
50 pounds of coffee
100 pounds of sugar

25 pounds of dried beef
25 pounds of evaporated potatoes
10 pounds of evaporated onions
10 pounds of baking powder
2 pounds of condensed soup[460]

Were these foods adequate? In April of 1995, Sandra C. Burnham, M.P.H., R. D., a chronic disease nutritionist working for the State of Alaska, Department of Health and Social Services, Division of Public Health, examined the Argonaut 's list of food for its nutritional value. Basically, and to her surprise, she found that the foods were adequate.

"Considering what we know today and they didn't know then, the foods as listed would support someone for a year." If these foods were all someone ate, Burnham estimated that an Argonaut would consume about 5,000 calories a day, twice what an adult is eating today. But, she noted, "The [Argonauts] were probably doing much more physical labor/activity than your average 1990s kind of guy so they needed a lot of calories." Additionally, "there aren't any fresh fruits and vegetables" she noted, "and [the list is] a little low on Vitamin A, and calcium while the sodium and phosphorous content is a bit high."

But was it healthy? "Yes," stated Burnham, "but it's not a very exciting diet."

* * *

Wilson Mizner, a dubious character in his own right, reported that in Soapy Smith's saloon he had an "accommodate" in the table where he played poker. This accommodate was in the form of "an almost invisible slit" in the felt of the table from which Soapy would "improve his hand."[461]

* * *

A family by the name of Finnegan figured to cash in on the men flooding north and built a small, rickety bridge just outside of Skagway.

Then they tried to collect tolls. That only worked until so many Argonauts were crossing the bridge that there was no way to enforce payment. So the Finnegan's stopped asking for the toll and set up a saloon.[462] In the end, the family probably prospered more from the saloon than the toll road.

* * *

Though Alaska was not even a Territory in 1904, it discovered that often international events where played out on the streets of its cities. In August of 1904, while the Japanese-Russian War was raging in the Far East, a fight broke out between Japanese and Russian miners in Douglas. It began as a quarrel between "a son of the Mikado" and a "former soldier of the Czar." When the fight erupted, more than 100 Japanese and Russians were involved and "staves and clubs and hob-nailed boots were used to effect." One man had an eye put out and another a leg broken but, as quickly as the trouble stated, it ended. By the time the Marshal got to Douglas the next morning, all was calm.[463]

* * *

A little known fact of the Alaska Gold Rush is that the man responsible for the building of the Valdez to Eagle section of the telegraph line that was to link Alaska with the rest of the country was young Lieutenant by the name of William "Billy" Mitchell. Mitchell was appalled at the rush into Barnette's cache in the middle of the winter but there was little he could do about it. "People like this should not be allowed to proceed," he said the rushers who were afoot in the Alaskan winter with inadequate clothing and scant supplies of food. But there was nothing he could do about it as he was in the military and the rush was a "civil matter and I had no jurisdiction."[464]

* * *

For more than six decades there has been a battle going over who was the first to climb Mt. McKinley. Frederick Cook claimed that honor and even had the photographs to prove his claim. However, careful examination of the photographs reveals that he probably did not reach the summit of the mountain. As late as 1996, the dispute was carried to a mock courtroom where Bradford Washburn showed documentary evidence that proved Cook could not possibly have done that he claimed to have done. Cook, *in absentia* because he had been dead for five decades, was represented by a court appointed attorney because the Cook Society refused to participate.[465]

The first party to reach what was believed to be summit was the so-called Sourdough Expedition. There were originally four men in the party – Charlie McGonagle, Tom Lloyd, Peter Anderson, and Billy Taylor but only two of them, Taylor and Anderson, made it to the crest of the north peak. There they planted their flag pole on the 18,470 foot level and claimed their place in mountaineering history. Only later was it discovered that they had not put it on the highest elevation, the south peak, which is officially 20,320 feet.

* * *

John Sidney Webb, writing in *The Century Magazine* in 1898, noted that "Alaska is a country of more square miles than square meals."[466]

* * *

While there may have been men a plenty in Nome, some jobs were so unpleasant that manpower had to be gathered in an unusual manner. In June of 1908, the first case of land shanghaiing occurred when Otto Zoeckler and D. B. Patterson "were fallen upon by a band of fierce walrus hunters, taken from their beds and forced to drink drugs which made resistance on their part useless."

However, it soon became evident that the crew of shanghaied walrus hunters were worse than no crew at all. Though the captain was cruel, the moment his back was turned shanghaied crew members would dash for the galley or the warm fur robes which were lying on the deck. Then the crew proceeded to eat until all of the provisions were gone and drink until all of the drinkables were consumed. In two days the ship was back and the shanghaied men beached outside of Nome.[467]

* * *

When a merchant could corner a market, he did. In October of 1902, two Nome merchants cornered the market on beer and, in a single day, jumped the price from $17.50 to $23.50 a barrel. Other prices were rising as well leading some to speculate that a winter of "famine prices" reminiscent of Nome's recent history would prevail.[468]

* * *

In December of 1900, Tom Stevens and his partner Bill Lawson had a shootout over a woman in Teller. Lawson got the worst of the deal. He took three .41 slugs and his chances for recovery were "about even." The two had been partners for years and Lawson, on what could very well have been his deathbed, insisted that nothing be done to Stevens as the fracas in which he took the four slugs was "only a family quarrel."

* * *

In March of 1908, two Greek prospectors, Andrew Carllis and Rossetos Bortolis, were found frozen stiff. They had apparently been on the trail to the camp in Sinrock when they became lost in the storm. They had been missing 19 days when their sled was found, complete with their dogs still tied to the traces. The dogs, weak from hunger, "had been feeding upon the bodies of the dead. Two thirds of the flesh [was] eaten from both and in a number of instances the bones [were] bare."[469]

* * *

According to the affidavit of Reimond Matlayo, a "Native of Austria," he estimated that 200 men had been killed in the Treadwell Mine and that he had personally seen 20 men killed and over 50 men injured by blasts or falling rocks. The Imperial and Royal Austro-Hungarian Embassy wrote a letter of protest to the Governor of Alaska on May 3, 1910, protesting treatment of its subjects in the Treadwell Mine strike.[470]

* * *

While gold rushers would rush just about anywhere there was alleged to be a strike, the individuals most interested in a strike were the merchants. The real money wasn't made in finding gold; it was made in selling merchandise to the miners. Thus it was in the interest of the merchants to get to a rush site quickly and the encourage other miners to join in the rush. This was called "boosting."

In August of 1900, Charley Suter of the Cabinet Saloon in Nome reported that there was a "host of real estate boomers" at Port Clarence, 100 miles north of Nome on the coast, claiming "mild weather, good climate and everything under the sun that is desirable for a boost." Wind, however, was not being mentioned by any of the boosters. Suter reported that while he was in Port Clarence, "the wind blew so hard . . . that front doors had to be fastened permanently and an entrance made at the back or leah side of the tent or building."[471]

Today, Port Clarence is an abandoned United States Coast Guard LORAN station and those who have been stationed there will attest that the conditions described by the boomers do exist – for about a week-and-a-half each year.

* * *

As a young lawyer working as an Assistant United States Attorney, George Grisby – later a legend in Anchorage legal circles until as late as the 1960s – was infamous for his practical jokes. In Nome about 1900 he dared a lawyer to call the new judge, Alfred S. Moore, a "red headed sonova$%^&*." The lawyer took up the challenge and told the judge "There are people at the bar who call you a red headed sonova$%^&*." I, of course, defended you."[472]

* * *

Robert Dey reported that Siberians wore "white man's underwear" and had seen the Natives "stripping the fat off the entrails of a seal and eating it while it [was still] steam[ing] with animal heat." As to personal hygiene, "their filthiness is most too horrible to describe and I dare say they never in their lives had a bath. Nevertheless, the passengers eagerly bought their lousy furs off their backs and expect to use them. I say lousy because I have seen them crawling over them thicker than mice in a corncrib."[473]

* * *

Joe Carroll, a mail carrier of Nome, decided that there was an easier way of making a living. On December 31, 1900, he collected $2,000 for the delivery of letters to Dawson, and then ran up his debt in Nome buying a sled and provisions by promising to pay for them the next day. That night "got drunk, stole six dogs, left his letters and pulled out on the trail before daylight." When the decamp of Carroll was discovered, those he had swindled grabbed rifles and "went in pursuit of the man with orders to shoot him on sight." But Carroll's lead was substantial and he escaped, probably into the Kotzebue area."[474]

* * *

Rex Beach described Ramparts as a community that was "a mile long and eighteen inches wide, consisting of saloons, dance halls [and] trading posts." He spent the winter there and, come spring, had the grand total of six dollars pass through his hands.[475]

* * *

James Herdman, in the Tyonek area near Anchorage, reported the liquor there was known as "Hoocheru," which he made from "three gallons of crude 'Island' sugar and 50 pounds of graham flour." This batch made five bottles which were quite potent. After draining the five bottles in a Christmas celebration, one of the distillers had to be dragged home by his arms.

"The next day," Herdman reported, "the Indians were out pointing and laughing at the snaky groove in the snow."[476] How the Indians knew what tracks a snake would make is not clear.

* * *

"Dutch Mike" Max Gottschalk was a notorious bootlegger during the Alaska Gold Rush in the Nome area. To cover his tracks, confuse authorities, and upset a competitor, Gottschalk once painted his boat so it would like that of his competitor, and sold liquor to the Eskimo. Then, before he returned to Nome, he repainted his craft.[477]

* * *

In May of 1909, the *Fairbanks News Miner* reported a story that was so bizarre that the paper even checked the facts. Supposedly a flock of 1,300 sheep was moving up the trail from Valdez. Some of the old timers who knew the ways of sheep were skeptical because, in addition to the swamps, flies and mosquitoes, the flock would have to cross many streams. While a cow could swim a stream, "it [would be] up to the herders to pack or throw sheep across a ford one by one." While other Alaskan papers commented on the existence of the sheep, there is no evidence in the *Fairbanks News Miner* that the flock ever arrived in Fairbanks.[478]

* * *

According to the By-Laws of the Circle Miners, membership was limited to anyone who was a "white male, of the full age of eighteen, years,

of good moral character in sound health and a miner by occupation."
With regard to good moral character, members using "profane, obscene
or abusive language in the hall of the Association" were to be fined $5.[479]

* * *

According to the sourdoughs,

> You can always determine a camp's age and stage of develop-
> ment by the price charged for drinks. Four-bit whiskey means
> recent occupation, unsettled conditions and the presence of one
> half barrel which some fellow has brought over the trail. Two-bit
> whiskey indicates that the regulation boom is on, that tenderfeet
> are plenty and regular communication with the outside world has
> been established. The next drop to three for a half is not a sign
> of a slump but merely shows that the first excitement has passed
> and the town is getting down to what they call a "business basis."
> Fifteen cent drinks mean that the business basis is reached, courts
> have been established, claim-jumping has become bad form, plug
> hats are tolerated, and faro banks have moved upstairs. Any further
> decline is a danger signal. Two-for-a-quarter whiskey is a sure sign
> of Deterioration, and five-cent beer means that a stampede has
> set in for the next diggings.[480]

* * *

On July 4, 1900, Clarence Warner and "Tarantula Jack" Smith staked
the area which is now Kennecott, the "World Largest Ghost Town."
Eventually bought out by the Guggenheims, the Kennecott copper strike
produced as much as $300 million in copper before it closed in 1938.[481]

* * *

In Fairbanks in 1904, a young Irishman, probably drunk, was brought into a hospital with a broken leg. He revealed that he believed that the walking stick he was carrying was the "invincible shillelagh" and with such he had attacked a moose. There is no reference to any damage to the moose from this ancient and feared weapon.[482]

* * *

Smuggling was common and frequent. A. H. Brown, who claimed to be an "innocent smuggler" reported how "Windy," the bartender at the Herrington Saloon in Circle got his whiskey. Windy and an unsuspecting Brown mushed into a community unnamed and went to an unnamed company store.

Windy tried to buy whiskey with $1,600 in gold but the company agent refused saying, "You see it's against the law for us to break the seals [on the whiskey kegs.] The stuff is bonded through to Dawson, so I can't sell it to you." Then, reported Brown, the clerk gave Windy a "very knowing look" and said, "You know we're going to move the whiskey out of that old warehouse. Maybe the men will leave eight ten-gallon kegs outside tonight. But, I say [Windy], you'd better leave that $1,600 sack of dust with me if you're afraid to carry it back to Circle City." Thus was the transaction completed, Brown stated, as "both men were on their honor."

Clearly the law took a different view. On the trail back to Circle, Windy took out his pistol and began cleaning it. "Officer Holmes has declared that if he ever catches me with a load of whiskey he will send me to Sitka and he swears he'll shoot [my favorite dog] too." Windy squinted along the barrel of his pistol and then said, "I guess he won't be any too anxious to meet us when we get [into Circle.]."

Fortunately they didn't. But they did get a scare at the edge of town. As they came to the custom house, the door suddenly opened and Windy snapped his revolver to the ready. Then he relaxed as a Native woman with a "guilty little laugh" ran past them. Windy's only comment was "Durn if I didn't really plug a hole through that squaw." [483]

* * *

Cultural clashes between Native and non-Native were frequent. Though both ethnic groups could leave in peace side-by-side, some Native customs caused incredulity. Sorcery and shamanism, for instance, raised eyebrows when it was mentioned. Sickness was supposedly caused by evil spirits that had to be exorcised, sometimes in a painful manner. The treatment, overseen by the shaman, was considered vulgar at the very least by Americans and steps were taken to break the power of the Indian medicine doctors.

In December of 1898, for example, Captain Glass of the **Jamestown**, arrived in Sitka to destroy all the Native stills he could find because the Natives who were drinking hoochinoo became "veritable brutes" under the influence of the "vile beverage." (The newspaper made no mention of destroying stills owned by non-Natives.) Additionally, to break the power of the shaman in the area, Glass "shaved off the hair of every Indian doctor he could find." Since the Natives believed that the long hair allowed the shaman to communicate with the spirits, known as "Yek," a shaman without long hair was like Sampson without his locks. Glass was clearly successful in his attempts to drive the shaman from Sitka for his actions precipitated the death of some of the shaman and the "remained left Sitka."[484]

* * *

Accusing someone of being a witch was an odious charge and it has surfaced more than once in Alaskan history. John Panter was probably the first to actually be indicted. On October 19, 1898, Panter was indicted for accusing a Native woman, An-Ki-Lat with being a witch with the intent of having her driven from the Native village of Sitka. The Grand Jury charged him with "disturbing the public peace."[485]

On March 10, 1905, Scundoo, (possibly Scumdo), an Indian in Haines, convinced an Indian couple, Mr. and Mrs. Joe Whiskers, that he could tell them who was bewitching their daughter, Carrie Joel. Carrie was "very sick with consumption" so the Whiskers paid Scundoo "twenty three dollars and fifty cents, in money and Blankets[sic.]"

After he received the money, Scundoo claimed that "Kitty Jones, and Mrs. Joe Tagcook were the witches that had bewitched the sick woman, and said that the witches must be tried for witchcraft." After the Whiskers paid the money and blankets and the daughter did not get better, Scundoo was reported to the authorities who charged him with "intent to defraud."[486]

This was not the only case of witchcraft to reach the courts. In December of 1909, Shorty Johnson and his wife, Mrs. Shorty Johnson, went to the home of Mrs. Phillips in Angoon and accused her of being a witch and that she was "bewitching their daughters and bringing sickness upon them which would result in death." Mrs. Phillips was concerned for Shorty and his wife threatened to have her pronounced a witch. She had reason to be concerned for if a person were declared a witch, it was

> the practice of the [N]atives to tie the witch by the hands and hair to a tree for a period of seven or eight days without food or drink and then, if the [Indian] doctor does not find that the vile spirits have been driven out of the victim, death is inflicted."

After the United States Commissioner, Sidney E. Flower, heard the case, he had "good reason to fear the commission of a crime" and fined Shorty and his wife $100 apiece.[487]

* * *

In Nome, circa 1900 a sheepherder claimed that the dog of lawyer Albert Fink had killed 28 of his sheep. Fink turned the courtroom upside down by declaring that his dog had not killed those sheep in malice but had "repelled the attack of these bloodthirsty ship, which disfigured [his dog, Dick] forever and nearly killed him." The sheep, Fink declared, had clearly been gored by their neighbors in the mad pandemonium. Just after the case was remitted to the jury, the offending herd of sheep came thundering down the street and Fink had to tackle his malamute to keep it from leaping in the herd to slaughter more sheep.

"Poor old Dick," Fink said in a calming tone as the courtroom erupted into laugher. "Don't be afraid. I won't let those wild sheep hurt you." The jury found for Fink.[488]

* * *

In 1906, trials were often as animated as the crimes themselves. In January of 1906, two lawyers in Nome – Albert Fink and A. J. Daly – "engaged in a fist fight" during a murder trial. The judge had called a recess so that Daly could interview two witnesses but Daly objected to Fink's "sticking around" and the fisticuffs broke forth. "During the melee the Court sought refuge in the Marshal's office."[489]

* * *

On May 22, 1906, the city of Fairbanks appeared doomed. A massive fire was threatening to burn down the entire city and all that stood between the roaring flames and extinction were the fire hoses. But there were too many fire mains opened and the pressure was dropping critically low. When word was sent to the power station for more pressure but the man operating the boilers had no more wood.

Had that man not been Volney Richmond, Fairbanks manager of the Northern Commercial Company, the city of Fairbanks would have been, quite literally, wiped off the map of Alaska. Resourcefully, Richmond ordered the larder of the Northern Commercial Company opened and 2,000 pounds of bacon removed. Slab by slab the bacon was tossed into the city's boilers and the pressure of the fire hoses went up. Fairbanks was saved and the Northern Commercial Company was in the odd position of saving its own bacon by consuming it.[490]

* * *

Alaska writer Rex Beach noted that there were three basic commandments of the north whose violation could mean instant death:

Thou shalt not steal they neighbor's grub.
Thou shalt not refuse him when "up against it."
Thou shalt not send him on fake stampedes. [491]

* * *

Alaska did not have vigilante groups that would compare with the famous Committees of Vigilance of San Francisco. While there certainly were groups that gathered to deal with intolerable situations, as in the case of Skagway with Soapy Smith and Nome with Judge Noyes, in most cases the vigilantes were more of a one-time organization. In June of 1906, Joe Cook, "a professional claim jumper," was given a choice. Leave the vicinity or be hung. Cook chose to leave.[492] A vigilante committee of 100 was established in Chena to help the police department.[493]

* * *

As most Hollywood productions revealed accurately, drunks were treated as comical characters rather than sad individuals with no self-control. A classic example of the hilarity with which drunks were treated was the McGinley vs. Cleary. In August of 1904, Judge James Wickersham was asked to make a ruling as to the legality of contract drawn up between two drunks over a gambling debt which had been written when both were in a state of advanced inebriation.[494]

Wickersham's decision, written officially with tongue in cheek, revealed that on November 30, 1903, McGinley, the owner and bartender of the Fairbanks Hotel, had been "engaged on his regular night shift as barkeeper in dispensing whiskey by leave of this court on a Territorial license to those of his customer who had not been able, through undesired or the benumbing influence of the liquor, to retire to their cabins." At 3 am, he and Cleary, a miner, were "mutually enjoying the hardships of Alaska by pouring into their respective interiors unnumbered four-bit drinks, recklessly expending undug pokes, and blowing into the next spring cleanup" when the men decided to "tempt the fickle goddess of fortune by shaking the [McGinley's] dicebox." McGinley lost badly and later claimed that his "brains were so benumbed by the fumes or the force of his own whiskey" that he was mentally incompetent in the matter of signing any IOU. His opponent, however, swore otherwise and even produced a witness. However, at the time of the dice game in question, the witness, Tupper Thompson, was as drunk as the gamblers. He had been sleeping "bibulously behind the oil tank stove" when he was rudely awakened to witness the IOU. Later, when asked of the sobriety of McGinley, Tupper replied that he, Tupper, was more sober than the barkeeper because he, Tupper, "could stand without holding to the bar." Judge Wickersham concluded that Tupper's testimony was not credible for, in addition to being drunk at the time of the incident in questions, "it is quite evident that [Tupper] had a rock in his sluice box."

Cleary, the miner, then had the good sense to encourage McGinley, the barkeeper, have the IOU legally recognized. In spite of the two men's "temporary intellectual eclipse" they did stagger to the cabin of Commissioner Cowles, about a block away. Cowles, however, was less than thrilled to see two drunks on his doorstep at three in the morning and told them to come back in the morning. When the men did return the next day, there was dispute as to whether the IOU had said that McGinley had lost 1/2 of the Fairbanks Hotel or 1/4 of the establishment, whether Clearly had agreed to give 1/2 of his mining claim to McGinley, and how the alleged loss of $1,800 in gambling debt was to be resolved. The men subsequently settled on 1/4 of the Fairbanks Hotel being given to the miner for one dollar. Both men signed the IOU.

But the tale was not over. McGinley had a change of heart soon after and brought suit to set aside the IOU "upon the ground of fraud (1) because he was so drunk at the time he signed the deed as to be unable to comprehend the nature of the contract, and (2) for want of consideration." The "want of consideration" meant he had not received the single dollar state in the contract.

"It is currently believed that the Lord cares for and protects idiots and drunken men," Wickersham wrote and decided in favor of Cleary. "Equity will not become a gambler's insurance company, to stand by while the gamester secures the winnings of the drunken, unsuspecting, or weak-minded in violation of the law, ready to stretch forth its arm to recapture his looses when another as un[s]crupulous or more lucky than he wins his money or property."

* * *

The trip home from Alaska after prospecting was not a piece of cake. In addition to the problems of being captured by the Bering Sea ice, weather was just as much a factor going south as it was going north. Though the ships were not as packed with cargo going south, they were still overloaded from a safety point of view. Food was limited and space at a premium.

In June of 1900, Deputy Collector Hatch in Sitka reported assessing fines on two ships, the barge **New York** and the steamer which was hauling it, **John C. Barr**. The duo had a passenger list of 170 but inspectors counted "100 in excess of that number." Further, the **New York** had no license to carry passengers and no licensed mate on board. The barge was fined $600, which Hatch declared was appropriate as "if ever there was a just fine imposed on a vessel this is one."[495]

The schooner **Hera**, which left Nome September 26, 1900, was at sea for almost a month before it docked in Seattle. During the trip the passengers were "treated like dogs," survivors were quoted as saying, and two passengers died of "starvation and exposure" while another dozen were "too weak and famished to take care of themselves." At least one man "dropped from sheer hunger." Another, "crazed from lack of food," ironically, "was kept lying on the dining room table until meal time when he was placed somewhere else."[496]

* * *

Being a literary genius does not necessarily mean that one must know how to read. This was proven by Uyaquq (Neck) of Bethel at the turn of the century. Though he could not read or write English or Yup'ik, this Eskimo developed a phonetic system for writing the Yup'ik language.

While some cultures took thousands of years to master a phonetic writing system, Uyaquq did it in less than a decade and ranks as one of the few individuals in the history of mankind to have "invented" writing.[497]

* * *

So many ships using so much coal and wood necessarily stripped the forests along the Pacific Coast and Yukon River. In 1901, even after the collapse of the Klondike Strike, steamers were still using "no less than 1,000 cords of wood a day," according to Special Agent Dixon of the Department of the Interior. [498]

* * *

Not everyone was intent on making their money in Kotzebue Country from gold in the ground. Because there was more money to be made in transportation, chicanery was sometimes involved. Captain Jens B. Neilson of the **General McPherson** arrived at St. Michael from Seattle with a ship full of "coal, lumber and hardware." Because the cargo was so valuable, he imprisoned the owner's representative, James Poole, and sold part of the cargo in St. Michael. Then he left for Kotzebue Sound – with James Poole still under lock and key below deck – where he sold another portion of the cargo and took on passengers at $500 apiece. (Quite a steep price but then again, it was the right time of year.)

Neilson made it back to Kotzebue a second time where he sold more supplies and spent the winter – Poole still being under lock and key. In January of 1899, the **McPherson** was still in Kotzebue – and Poole under boat arrest – when the owners heard a rumor that Neilson was going to make a run for Manila when the ice broke. Assistance of the United States Attorney General of Alaska was requested for one of the owners to go onboard the **Bear** to witness the arrest of Neilson. (Neilson had done this before in Mexico where he had served time.)[499]

* * *

Infrequently the death of a Native made the news. Akpak was an exception. When he died in Council City in August of 1902, his passing made the front page of the *Council City News.* There was good reason for Akpak's death from pneumonia to be publicized as it was the "first death from natural causes in the history of this section since the advent of the white man." Though Akpak had only been 18 when he died, his funeral was attended by many residents.[500]

* * *

Some whalers, in this case the notorious James McKenna, regularly took on liquor for the specific purpose of debauchery. In June of 1904, for instance, the *Nome Nugget* published the apparent fact that McKenna was in Unalaska with two whaling ships and schooners which were loaded with "40 tierces (1680 gallons) of alcohol on board for Native debauching purposes."[501]

This news story appears to have been misleading. The Revenue Cutter Service investigated the claim and found it to be in error. In fact, Captain Hamlet stated that the total amount of liquor on board was actually 12 cases. Hamlet's investigation also revealed that McKenna had tried to trade liquor in Siberia and he had been "ordered off by a Cossack at the point of a gun." Apparently the Russians were as displeased with the liquor traffic as the Americans. Hamlet could also find no evidence of the debauch as reported in the *Nome Nugget.* However, Hamlet did concede that illegal liquor was an ongoing problem as was the problem of how to keep Native women away from the men on the whaling vessels.[502]

McKenna did not drink or smoke but it was said that he would "feed whiskey to a baby." He is best remembered as the man who traded for all the furs, seal oil and blubber on St. Lawrence Island in 1879, leaving the Natives to starve that winter. Death rates in the village of Kukulook were recorded at about 90 percent. When missionaries went to the village two years later, skeletons littered the village. Notably missing were any skeletons of children "the supposition being that they had been eaten by starving adults."

When McKenna was appraised of the disaster, he took it as a joke. "Tut, tut, man," he said. "I just sell them Snake River. There is so much water in the stuff it would not harm an infant." This was little consolation for the village of Kukulook.[503]

As an interesting tidbit of history, one of the few to better McKenna was his second in command, Charles Klengenberg. Placed in command of McKenna's second schooners, the **Olga**, Klengenberg gave McKenna the slip in a dense fog and absconded with the ship. When he reappeared, only five of the original nine men on board were still alive. It was the loss of the four that generated his trial in San Francisco.[504]

* * *

The wind blowing down the trail near Yost's Roadhouse, (Mile 208 on the old Fairbanks-Valdez Military Trail, just beyond Summit Lake on the Delta River), was so strong that during the winter that some people actually died within sight of the structure. To alleviate the situation, the owner, Charlie Yost, constructed a fence where the trail crossed the Delta River. This prevented travelers who fell on the ice from being blown down the river. He also installed a bell and an outside light so that travelers could locate the roadhouse even on windy, stormy nights.[505]

* * *

The feeling was that the gold on the beach in Nome was part of a geologic belt that extended under the Bering Sea all the way to Siberia.[506] Though nothing was to come of it, in March of 1898, the Russian Ambassador in Washington D. C. told the United States government that certain areas of Siberia would be open to mining. Specifically, the area open to claim ran from Marcia to Indian Point, a distance of about 150 miles, and mining was allowed no further than 30 miles from the coast. For all gold extracted from Russia, a tax of 10 percent would be levied.[507]

With the opening of Siberia, there was also a push for one of the great pipe dreams of the era: an Alaskan-Siberian railway. Supposedly this railway would be like Skagway and Dyea in the south and Vladivostock in Siberia. In October of 1899, Captain Siem, an agent of the Kimball Company, was in Nome to make arrangements for the railway. Anticipating the opening of Siberia to mining the next year, he was in the Nome area getting the right of way for the railway – and talking about a tunnel beneath the Bering Straits. One of the touchy questions which he tip-toed around was what would happen to the claims of miners who were on the beach when right of way was granted. While Siem claimed that the Alaskan-Siberian railway "was not a scheme to gobble up the beach diggings" he did say that the rights of individual miners "would be worked out." At the same time, he did concede that a railroad in Alaska would receive, gratis, a 200 foot wide right of way from the Secretary of the Interior, as well as land for stations and other railway yards and buildings.[508]

* * *

Men with money would often hire "bummers" for "$15 a day and expenses" to stake claims for them. This, however, was not a sterling idea as many of the bummers would drink their pay and then "appear with fictitious claim notices on mythical creeks" which were then duly recorded. Some men held as many as 6,000 acres of bogus claims.[509]

* * *

No ground was sacred to the Argonauts in Nome. When it was discovered that the graveyard had a shroud of gold covering it, the graves themselves were tunneled out.[510]

* * *

There was a lot of money to be made in the liquor business in Nome and everyone was trying to get a "piece of the action." Wise to the ways of the world, Jed Jordan was quick to pay a $100 "clearance charge" assessed by the ship to insure himself "against breakage."[511] Moving quickly, he bought a lot on Front Street and erected tent, naming his business the Ophir Saloon. Jed Jordan's "bar" was a 20-foot plank laid on barrels. There was also a shortage of bottle. Miners liked to break whiskey bottles when they were through with them, and this led to a shortage of bottles.

Jordan also reported watching the drinking customs of the "Loblocks," a derogatory term for the Laplanders who had been imported along with the reindeer from Lapland by Sheldon Jackson. One Loblock would order a drink, take a sip and pass it down the line of his friends. When the drink was finished, the second man in line ordered a drink and the sequential imbibing was repeated. Hour after hour it continued, each man taking a sip and passing it along to his neighbor.[512]

* * *

In 1898, the United States Post Office flirted with the idea of using reindeer to carry mail. The idea went as far as buying more than 500 and establishing reindeer mail stations in Haines and Chilkat. John Clum, Alaska's first Postmaster, examined the herds in March of 1898 but the idea never took off.[513]

* * *

A saloon in Alaska, one *cheechako* noted was nothing more than "a tent, a board counter a foot wide and six feet long, a long fellow in a Mackinaw coat, and a bottle of whiskey."[514] Even Tex Rickard's Northern was "bare and barnlike" with the exception of "a long mirrored bar and a few crystal chandeliers" and, true the traditions of the Old West when you walked into the establishment, "somebody was playing an upright piano that was on a platform, but you could hardly hear it over the noise and confusion at the bar."[515]

* * *

Even though James Wickersham brought some semblance of law and order to Nome, the city was slow to change its irresponsible ways. As late as 1903, Governor James G. Brady wrote to the Secretary of the Interior, his superior in Washington D. C., that law and order was a sham in many parts of Alaska. As one instance, he wrote of a United States Marshal in Nome who was found guilty of fixing juries and fined $300. He appealed the case and was still on duty enforcing the law. Further stalling law and order in Nome, the District Attorney had "left his post of duty and was absent all winter." How can we expect Alaskans to feel secure," he asked the Secretary, "if there is such law and order in Alaska?[516]

* * *

Stowaways on northbound ships were not uncommon but they were hard to spot with so many people milling around on deck and in the dining rooms. One passenger, Mont Hawthorne, on the **George W. Elder** reported a search by troops for four stowaways on board. Hawthorne was rooting for the stowaways and fearing what would happen when they were caught. Then he caught sight of one of the stowaways. "He was dressed up in an army uniform, and was going all around looking for himself." The other three stowaways were also dressed like soldiers and, of course, they did not find themselves.[517]

While this story is very fanciful, it might not be true. Depending the date when Hawthorne made his trip, the troops may very well have been black and the majority of the passengers and stowaways white. But then again, the stowaways could have been black as well.

* * *

John Clum, Alaska's first Postmaster noted in St. Michaels that one of the vessels on its way to Kotzebue had "a full blown brass band which discoursed sweet music as the setting sun gilded the sky and sea with a glorious blending of most exquisite tints."[518]

* * *

Tales of evil-doers flaunting the court system are as old as America and the Alaska Gold Rush was no different. In the early days of Nome, a rich pimp was brought before a judge on the charge of running a brothel. At that time the established fine was $1,000 – $31,000 in 2020 dollars – and the pimp decided to flaunt the court. So he set about to collect every dollar bill he could find. When he was able to find 1,000 one dollar bills, he made a great show of dumping the thousand dollar bills onto a table in front of the judge.

The judge sat back in his chair and said, ". . . and one year in prison. Do you have that in the grip?"[519]

* * *

The firewood shortage in Nome was so severe in the winter of 1899 that every source of the substance was exploited – including Native burial caches. Frances Fitz reported seeing a burial cache with a sign that read "Please do not use this grave for firewood."[520]

* * *

On August 20, 1900, Edward C. Hasey, United States Marshal for Ketchikan, wrote to United States Attorney General for Alaska, James M. Shoup, in Juneau regarding a death in Ketchikan. The report, in its entirety, stated:

August 13, I received a warrant to arrest one Daniel Robinson for assault and after several unsuccessful chases, I at last came up to him and placed him under arrest. He resisted and in the scuffle that ensured, he being armed with an oar, I received some injuries, arm and ribs broken and a few other small ones. He succeeded in getting away. He then armed himself with a rifle and a revolver and announced his intentions to kill me and leave the country. Learning he was coming, I took a rifle and went out in front of the jail, and when he came I fired first. Attached please find copy of coroner's jury inquest. I am still doing the business of this office.

* * *

In 1912, the President of the First National Bank of Juneau, C. M. Summer, was charged with embezzling over $1.6 million. That's about $45 million in 2020 dollars! Considering that Juneau only had a population of about 2,200 in 1910, it is hard to understand how Summers could have spent that much money in Juneau in so short a period of time and not have alerted the residents that something was amiss. Eventually they did and in May of 1912, Summers went on trial for 56 counts of embezzlement. Found guilty he was sentenced to five years per violation at McNeil Island, the penitentiary in Washington where Alaskan felons were sent. In spite of the evidence against him, he was able to get the conviction reversed! Even more surprising, when the case was brought up again in January of 1914, the judge ruled that Summers had "already suffered enough" and dismissed it. Summers died in Washington in 1919 a free man.

PHOTOGRAPHS II

James McCain Shoup who was the first United States
Marshal in Alaska, 1897 to 1909. Shoup was born in
Pennsylvania and left home at 16 to serve in the United
States Navy during the last year of the Civil War. After the war he moved to Idaho where he established a
law practice and served in the first Idaho State Senate,
1889-1892. He moved to Alaska in 1897 to become
the first United States Marshal in the Territory, 1897-1909. After he
left the Marshal's office he returned to the practice of law and opened
an office in Ketchikan. He died in Ketchikan in 1927. [James Shoup.
Photograph courtesy of the J. Simpson MacKinnon Photo Collection
at the Alaska State Library, ASL-P14-021.]

Emory Valentine

Emory Valentine was born in Michigan in 1858 and at 10 years of age he left Colorado on a horse using his overcoat as a saddle and rope for stirrups. He lost a leg in the mines in Colorado and became a jeweler. He moved to Juneau where he opened a jewelry store and became heavily involved in real estate and the lumber industry. He organized the Juneau Wharf Company and built the first Juneau docks in 1886. Later he went to Skagway during the Klondike Rush where he built the Skagway docks and was involved in the wholesale lumber business. He organized the Juneau Fire Department and the Juneau water utility. He served one term as a city councilman and six terms as Mayor. He also served as the Japanese Vice Counsel in Juneau and was awarded the Order of the Rising Sun. He died in 1930. Photograph courtesy of the J. Simpson MacKinnon Photo Collection at the Alaska State Library, ASL-P14-071.

Bartlett Thane

At 33 years of age Bartlett Thane was the Manager of the Alaska Gastineau Mine, one of the most successful mining operations in the history of mining. In his time he was, quite literally, the king of Juneau. He was also making Juneau, quite literally again, a ton at a time. The overburden from the Alaska Juneau Mine was dumped at the foot of the mountain from which it had been extracted and, foot-by-foot the city of Juneau extended out from the shore. Thane's reign lasted until the ore ran out. He tried to turn the bankrupt Alaska Gastineau Mining properties into a pulp mill. He failed and died a broken man at age 49. Photograph courtesy of the Winter and Pond Collection at the Alaska State Library, ASL-PCA-87-2356.

Center Juneau

Juneau in 1905. Note how close the city is to the steep slope of the mountains. Also note how the city extends outwards courtesy of the overburden from the Alaska-Juneau Mine. Photograph courtesy of the Ocha Potter Papers, UAF-2003-163-4m.

The **City of Seattle**, one of the vessels of the Alaska Steamship Line. The crowd on the dock is in Juneau to welcome the new Governor of Alaska, W. B. Hoggatt. Historically interesting, during the Alaska Gold Rush undesirables were given a "blue ticket." This meant they were provided transportation out of town in any direction on the first available means of transportation. It was called a "blue ticket" because the practice was first used in Nome in about 1900. The only way out of Nome was the Alaska Steamship Lines whose tickets were blue. This photograph is courtesy of the Case and Draper Collection at the Alaska State Library, ASL-PCA-39-0363.

In the first decade of the 20th Century the 'top of the line' steamship that served Juneau was the *Queen*. This photograph is courtesy of the Frank LaRoche Collection at the Alaska State Library, ASL-130-003.

The Mendenhall Glacier which sits on the outskirts of Juneau. Photograph courtesy of Robert A. Kinzie Collection at the Alaska State Library, ASL-PCA-13-30.

Alaska's ghost ship, the **Clara Nevada**. It sinks on February 5, 1898 and resurfaces on February 25, 1908, almost exactly ten years later. It was carrying 110,000 ounces of gold, about $20 million in 2015 dollars, that has never been found – even though the ship only sank in 24

feet of water. The best book on the *Clara Nevada* is GOLD, GREED, MURDER AND ALASKA'S INSIDE PASSAGE. The photograph is courtesy of the Winter and Pond Collection at the Alaska State Library, ASL-P87-1594.

Today a teamster is someone who drives a truck. The name originates from the days when goods were moved by horse and wagon by men who drove teams of horses, thus the name *teamsters*. This photograph was taken in Nome in 1907 and is courtesy of the University of Washington Nowell Collection 5885.

Downtown Juneau, 1910. Note the wooden planks for the street. The photograph is courtesy for the Winter and Pond Collection at the Alaska State Library, ASL-PCA-87-0958.

BARGE TRAFFIC

To this day Alaska cannot sustain its population with in-state food and supplies. Everything consumed or used in Alaska has to come from the lower states, today called the Lower 48. Today, lighter cargo and food usually comes north on airplanes or trucks but the heaviest supplies still come on barges. North of the Aleutian Islands, and specifically into the Yukon and Kuskokwim river shed, barge traffic can only come when the rivers and Bering Sea are ice-free. This means that the first barge into the area cannot come until about the first of June and must be out of the river sheds and Bering Sea by the middle of October. Everything large and heavy that has to be sent "Outside," leaves on the barge. Above is a photograph of **Annie W.** in April of 1919 with 800 tons of freight for Alaska Engineering Commission.

Saloon in Juneau about 1910. Photograph courtesy of the Skinner Foundation Collection at the Alaska State Library, ASL-PCA-44-178. Compare this saloon to the boomtown saloon below.

An authentic Alaska Gold Rush boomtown saloon. This one was in Koyukuk about 1900. Note the pin-ups of the day on the wall behind the bar. The photograph is courtesy of the Art Wyman Collection at the Anchorage Museum of History and Art, 201.

* * *

To fully appreciate the Alaska Gold Rush, you need an on-the ground understanding. This is particularly true of the Nome Rush. To fully comprehend what happened in Nome, you have to know the lay of the land. When you examine a map of Alaska you will see a string of 300 islands extending west from the mainland. This archipelago stretches for 1,200 miles, about the same distance as from Los Angeles to Austin, and extends so far west it becomes east. That is, the last island on the Aleutians is Attu, the site of the bloodiest battle during the Second World War. Attu is 6 degrees into the Eastern Hemisphere. Thus Alaska is the most northern, western and eastern of the states of the United States.

In a state of oddities, the Aleutians are an anomaly. The southern shores of the Aleutian islands are washed by the Japanese Current, the *Kuroshio*. It is this current which keeps the North Pacific ice-free. But there is no complementary current on the northern shores of the Aleutian Islands. There the mantle of ice on the Bering Sea can be 15 feet thick and stops all marine traffic from mid-September to the beginning of June.

Every year.

Because the distance between the warm southern shore of the Aleutians and the ice-cold northern waters of the Bering Sea is so close – in some cases zero feet – the Aleutians have the worst weather in the world. Warm air from the south mixes with frigid winds from the north making weather patterns that are not only unpredictable; but deadly. As Alaskans say, in the Aleutians there are no atmospheric patterns: weather just arrives. The sky can be clear at 10 a.m. and be socked in at 10:05 a.m. And it can stay socked in for ten days.

Even today, flying in the Aleutians is, under the best of conditions, treacherous. There are few places to land and like bear stories, every Alaskan who has flown in the Aleutian has a tale to make you want to stay in the big city. In Cold Bay, for instance, it is not unusual for a bush plane to crab to port on takeoff and then, midway down the runway, crab to starboard because there are two, 50-mile-an-hour winds blowing 180 degrees from each other with the winds interfacing halfway down the runway. "Every time I think I about flying in the Aleutians," is a favorite bush pilot expression, "I don't." As Alaskan humorist Warren Sitka notes, "In Alaska, wild animals, children and weather in the Aleutians are predictably unpredictable."

Why is this important to understand the Nome rush? Because Nome, 143 miles south of the Arctic Circle, is 736 air miles north of the Aleutians. Across the Bering Sea. Which freezes with a mantle of ice 15 feet thick every winter. Today, and during the Alaska Gold Rush, the last ship to leave Nome had/s to be out of the Bering Sea by about September 15th. After that, no ship can make it into Nome until the next June. During the Gold Rush, if you were in Nome on September 16th, you were there until June. And you'd better have the money to make it through the winter. Just before that last steamship of the season left, all of the derelicts, homeless and destitute were rounded up and put onboard an outgoing steamer. This was called 'getting a Blue Ticket' because the color of the Alaska Steamship Company tickets was blue.

The Nome rush was unusual for three reasons. First, you could arrive by steamship. To get to Nome, all you had to do was buy a ticket. There was no hiking involved. Because the Nome harbor was so shallow, the Argonauts had to be lightered ashore. In the background of this photograph of a cargo barge coming ashore, you can see the sailing ships anchored offshore.

Wyatt Earp, on the left, with John Clum, in Nome

Second, while there were mines well back from the city, the bulk of the Argonauts were on the beach. The beach was federal land so you could not stake a claim. But you could dig for gold on the sand beach.

When the tide was low.

So, every 12 hours from June to September, like an army of ants, gold seekers swarmed onto the beach with pots, pans, cradles along with a wide range of gold extraction contraptions and separated the gold nuggets and flakes from tons of sand. But only from the sand where you were standing, an area which extended on all sides as far as your shovel could reach. Third, everything Nome needed had to come in by ship: food, clothing, whiskey, medical supplies, horses, mules, tables, chairs, pipes, stools, bar counters, et cetera. Further, Nome had no nearby forest so all wood for homes and coal for heat had to come in by ship. This photo is of 10,000 tons of coal in burlap sacks to take Nome through the winter of 1902.

For those who enjoy trivia, many residents and gold seekers in Nome would shape American history. Wyatt Earp was in Nome but left in 1901. His combination saloon and brothel, DEXTER, here on the left-hand side of the street, can be seen in some of the photographs of Nome's Front Street.

Jimmy Doolittle, later of THIRTY SECONDS OVER TOKYO fame, spent his early years in Nome – and earned a reputation as a boxer.. Billy Mitchell, later to be court-martialed for browbeating the United States Navy to spend on airplanes rather than battleships, spent four years in Alaska stretching the telegraph wire that would connect Nome with the lower 45 states at that time.

General James Doolittle

Then there was Wilson Mizner, a loveable scoundrel. Mizner was involved with gambling and prize fighting in Nome and it was said he was probably the only man with the reputation of being able to "borrow money from a lamppost and is said to be the only man who ever hired the Nome brass band on credit." In addition to these northern distinctions, in the course of Mizner's life he was also a mining engineer, actor, playwright, a Fifth Avenue art dealer, husband of the "second richest woman in the world," proprietor of the legendary Brown Derby in Los Angeles and, with his brother Addison, a founder and promoter of Boca Raton, Florida.

Brigadier General William L. Mitchell, United States Army Air Service

In Nome, Mizer was known as the Yellow Kid. He earned this sobriquet by putting syrup in his hair every night when he worked as a bartender. In those days whiskey was bought with gold dust. Mizner's fingers, sticky from the syrup in his hair, would pick up few grains of gold dust every time he weighed out a drink. He would run his fingers through his hair frequently thus transferring those gold dust grains onto the strands of his hair. After his shift, he would shampoo his hair and pan for the flakes. This was a true scram.

In 1902, Mizner was involved in a badger game in which he was to play the "damaged husband." He drank too heavily the night before and when he awoke, late for his appointment to break in on the love birds, he discovered his pistol had been stolen. Looking for a prop, he found a can of tomatoes and stripped off its label. Thus armed he crashed into the lover's nest and threatened to blow up the two lovers. The man paid for his life with his money belt which yielded $10,000 in gold. After the man had fled in terror, Mizner's partner asked for her share of the boodle. Mizner handed her the tomato can. When she asked what good the can was going to do her, Mizner calmly stated, "It just got me $10,000."

True, as well was the theft of $40,000 from the Gold Commissioner's office in Dawson in "Marshal Jew Bob." Depending on the source, the thieves were either Scurvy Bill and Two Tooth Mike or Mit, Half-Kid and Two-Tooth Mike. Mizner listed himself as the "Deputy Sheriff" at the time but he probably meant "Deputy United States Marshal." By his own admission, just after Mizner had hidden Scurvy Bill in his own attic, Mizner was called to join the posse in looking for the very criminal he had just hidden. The posse then followed blood to a cabin where they assumed the criminals were hiding. Mizner astonished the posse by "rolling a cigarette in one hand and holding a revolver in the other" and kicking in the cabin door. History does not record what happened to the $40,000. Additionally, possibly true, according to Mizner he once robbed a restaurant in Nome for chocolate for his girlfriend "Nellie the

Pig" with the words "Your chocolates or life" and grubstaked the future owner of Grauman's Chinese Theater in Los Angeles. ("Nellie the Pig" got her name for biting off the ear of a bartender.)

At the height of the Alaska Gold Rush in Nome, about 1906, Nome had a population of about 15,000 people and stretched along 20 miles of the Bering Sea coast. At the southern end of the Nome strike was Solomon which had a railroad. The locomotive and cars – originally owned by New York City – were transported to Nome in 1903. A huge storm washed out the rails in 1913 and the train was left where it was. It can still be seen today both physically and virtually as "The Last Train to Nowhere."

Technically – and legally – a *cord* is a pile of wood four feet by four feet by eight feet. In real life terms, a *cord* of wood is a lot of cutting and hauling. During the Alaska Gold Rush it took thousands of cords of wood to keep steamboats plowing their way up the Yukon and Kuskokwim rivers. But the steamships could only use the river systems for about 130 days a year, roughly the middle of June to the end of September. The rest of the time the rivers were covered with six feet of ice. Woodcutters like these men would fell trees and split wood all winter and stack it in piles by the river's edge. Then they would earn a year's income in 130 days. To the modern eye, this is just a photograph of a large pile of wood. To these woodcutters it was solid gold.

APPENDIX

IN THE UNITED STATES DISTRICT COURT OF THE SECOND DIVISION OF THE DISTRICT OF ALASKA

IN THE MATTER OF THE FINAL REPORT OF THE
GRAND JURY, April, 1905 TERM:

ESQUIMAUX

We recommend that the United States Government take immediate steps for the relief of the Esquimaux and to that end suggest the following:

1. A relief fund for the relief of the sick and indigent [N]atives, to purchase medicines and the necessaries of life;
2. Government hospital for [N]atives is an absolute necessity from the standpoint of charity as well as the consideration for the health of the white population.
3. Some measures should be secured to prohibit [N]ative families from living in Nome, and the government should build small comfortable cabins at the larger villages and such places as the Quartz Creek Colony, and offer each [N]ative family a little home as an inducement to move away from this camp and other undesirable localities, where they cannot obtain liquors and become demoralized.

4. An Alaskan law which absolutely prohibits individuals form taking Esquimaux to the states for any purpose whatsoever, excepting in the case of taking such [N]ative boys and girls out as may be trained for education or missionary work among their own people.
5. Making the giving or selling of liquor to [N]atives a felony.
6. Vigorous prosecution of unlawful cohabitation with[N]ative women.
7. Requesting the business men of Nome to not give the [N]atives any articles of food or clothing or in any way encourage them to become beggars and vagrants.
8. Introduction of industrial training in all the Esquimaux schools even if it be only in a very moderate degree.[521]

COPPER CENTER, ALASKA, MAY 8, 1906

We the undersigned declare, from personal observation, that the condition of the Copper River Indians is most pitiable. Fully 25% of them have died in the past two weeks, and those that are left are emaciated and unable to work or hunt. They have not been able to care for their sick or bury their dead. Without immediate special assistance the mortality among them will be greater.

Their condition has been brought about by the lack of food and clothing. Since the rabbits perished during the extreme cold weather they have been short of food. They have no footwear but moccasins or old cast off shoes and when the snow began to melt[,] their feet were wet and cold. They have made a special effort to hunt and work when work can be obtained.

They have taken heavy colds and because of lack of nourishment and clothing the colds have resulted in grippe and pneumonia. It is our conviction that unless some new policy is adopted by the government to aid these Indians they will become extinct in the not distant future.

John McCrary	Ralph McCrary
Frances McCrary	Nelson McCrary
Oscar Expert	Walter T. Neal
Otto H. Strappe	Lydia S. Neal
F. S. Coleman	J. W. Neal
Fred Sherman	J. M. Jule

Mrs C. S. Horsfall
Charles W. Rodeen
G. E. Simpson
G. Asplmel
Henry C. Hempe
H. R. Clevenger
G. B. Rorere
W. T. Soule

R. Blix
Mrs. G. E. Simpson
G. Parker Smith
Victor Olson
Henry Buck
Paul Hansel
Charles G. Horsfall
J. V. Donahue[522]

CONSTITUTION OF THE CAMP OF VALDEZ

Whereas the citizens of the United States on their way into the Copper River country, Alaska, realizing that we have no protection under the law of the land, deem it necessary to enact a code of laws to govern our conduct during our journey to and our stay in Alaska:

Therefore be it resolved:

1. That any person guilty of murder shall be punished as a jury of twelve men may decide;
2. That any person guilty of assault, assault and battery, aggravated assault, or assault with intent to kill, shall be punished as a jury of twelve men may decide.
3. That any person stealing any property whatever shall be tried by a jury of twelve men and, upon conviction, shall be sentenced to restore the property stolen and to pay the injured party all damages sustained directly or indirectly in consequence of the theft. In case the guilty party shall not restore or make good all damages aforesaid, the injured party make take sufficient property of the defendant to satisfy all damages, and dispose of it in any way he deem fit and proper.

    The defendant shall also be banished forever from the country, and failing to leave immediately upon notice, shall receive not less than ten or more than 50 lashes: and failing to leave within ten days after such punishment, he shall abide by the consequence of his temerity.

Should the value of the property stolen exceed $100 in money, punishment shall be the same as in the case of murder.

4. Any person charged with crimes as described above shall be tried by a jury of twelve men in the district, and in all trials shall be entitled to three peremptory challenges. Before a person shall be adjudged guilty not less than ten of the jury shall be agreed upon his guilt.

The officers elected to enforce these laws shall consist of a judge, a sheriff and a clerk of the court.

[Author's note: C. A. King was the "unanimous choice for judge." Dalbert Stevens was the sheriff and Frank P. Reid was chosen district clerk. All men assumed office on February 9, 1898.][523]

DEPARTMENT OF THE INTERIOR

Indian School Service
Office of Superintendent

U.S. Indian Training School,
Chairman, Oregon. Dec 30,1898

To Whom it may concern:

The bearer of this letter is Chief Johnson of the Taku Tribe near Juneau Alaska. He was elected by the Chiefs of several Alaskan Tribes to go to Washington in the interests of the Alaska Indians, and has stopped off at this school where he could use some of the Alaska pupils who talk his language, in interpreting in English the object of his mission, and the great needs of his people.

I have written down the words as spoken by him through a reliable interpreter for your information and consideration.

Very respectfully,
Tess Potter

Superintendent

* * *

Gentlemen:

I have come a long way from my home in Alaska to see you and tell you of the condition of my people. I was sent here by the Chiefs of the principal tribes to represent them, and have brought with me a petition signed by them

We find our country Alaska over run by white men who have crowded or driven the Indians from their fishing grounds, hunting grounds, and the places where their fathers and grandfathers have lived and been buried.

Russia came and took possession of our land without consulting the natives of Alaska, the real owners of the country, and later on sold it to the United States. The Indians never knew anything about this sale until years afterwards, altho' it was our land and country which was sold. We have never tried to make any trouble over it, and this is the first time we have ever brought the matter to the Washington Government to consider, altho' Russia stole our country and sold it to [the U.S.]

We do not ask anything unreasonable of the U.S. government. We do not ask to be paid for the lands which were ours by rights. We do not ask that the whites be prevented from coming to Alaska.

We do ask and pray that the good white people who have true and kind and just hearts will listen to our words and assist us in protecting us by good laws, and requiring the same to be enforced.

There [are four] principal things which the Indians desire the help of the government viz:

1st. That the fishing and hunting grounds of their Fathers be reserved for them and their children, and that the whites who have driven them of off the same be ordered by the government to leave them. The Indians chief method of support is by fishing and hunting and that is the only way the most of them can live, as only a small number are educated sufficiently to go out in the towns of the land and compete with the whites.

2nd. The Indians of Alaska pray that the U.S. government will set apart certain reservations for them and their children where they and their children can each have a home allotted to them, the same privileges as Indians of the United States enjoy. We ask this in return for all of Alaska which has passed into the hands of the whites, without a murmur from us. We have given up a great deal and now only ask the great and good Father at Washington to give us back a little of the land, in return for the much we gave him, and protect us from the encroachments of greedy white men who would drive us into the Sea in order to advance their own interests.

3rd. Many of the Alaska Indians are poor and destitute, and have to beg from their friends in order to live. We ask the government to help the old and destitute, and to establish Industrial Boarding schools among the Indians of Alaska so as to fit them for citizenship and self support. We need schools and education as much as the Indians of the U.S. We are now apart of the United States, and we want to learn how to live like the good white men and adopt their laws and customs. There are hundreds of Indian boys and girls in Alaska who never saw a school. Only a few are able to attend the mission schools, and the one small government school at Sitka, and the most of the children must grow up in ignorance, superstition, and poverty. We ask that the United States will help the Alaska Indians just as it helps the South Dakota Indians, and those of other parts of the country. We have never gone on the war-path or given the government any trouble, and we feel we can appeal justly for help and protection as we belong to Washington just as much as any other Indians living in the States.

4th. We ask that laws will be made and enforced which will compel the Indians of Alaska to give up their heathenism and superstitious customs among themselves as we want to live like white people and be governed by white men's laws. One evil custom (as well as many others) I desire to speak about. That is in the case of death, of a husband or wife, the parents of the one dead seizes all the property, as the imme-diate sur- viving members of the family, including the children are left destitute and beggers. This is a very unjust custom and works hardship and misery among the Indians.

There are many other evil and superstitious customs still in existence among our people, and we the Chiefs want the white man's law to help us stop them.

Therefore I have come to Washington to speak and to lay our case before the Congressmen of the government, to implore their aid in giving the Alaska Indians homes and schools, and protecting them by law from the encroachment of avaricious white men.

Signed, Chief Johnson [His + Mark]

Interpreter
Joshua Johnson
John Dennis

Witness to the above
        Tless. Potter
           Supr. Salem Indian (?)

SIGNIFICANT GOLD DISCOVERIES

Russian River	1849
Stikine	1862
Windham Bay	1869
Sumdum Bay	1870
Cassiar, B. C.	1871
Juneau	1880
Fortymile	1886
Yakutat	1887
Lituya	1887
Resurrection	1888
Rampart	1893
Birch Creek	1893 (Also known as Circle)
Seventymile	1895
Klondike, Y. T.	1896
Atlin, B. C.	1898
Chistochina	1898
Porcupine	1898
Nome	1898
Yakutaga	1898
Shungnak	1898
Manly Hot Springs	1898
Council City	1898
Port Clarence	1899

Bonanza	1899 (Also known as Ungalik)
Solomon	1899
Bluff	1899
Kougarok	1899
Fairhaven	1899
Koyukuk	1899
Goodnews Bay	1900-1928
Nizina	1902
Koyuk	1902-1915
Fairbanks	1902
Valdez Creek	1903
Bonnifield	1903
Kantishna	1905
Yentna	1905
Richardson	1906
Chandalar	1906
Innoko	1906
Ruby	1907 (Also known as Poorman)
Aniak	1907
Melozitna	1907
Iditarod	1909
Kiana	1909
Hughes	1910 (Also known as Indian River)
Nelchina	1912
Chisana	1912 (Also known as Shushana)
Marshall	1913
Livengood	1914 (Also known as Tolovana)

ALASKA GOLD RUSH ERA PUBLIC OFFICIALS GOVERNORS

John G. Brady, appointed by President Theodore Roosevelt, June 23, 1897 to March 2, 1906

Wilford B. Hoggatt, appointed by President Theodore Roosevelt, March 2, 1906 to May 20, 1909

Walter E. Clark, appointed by President William Howard Taft, May 20, 1909 to April 18, 1913

SECRETARIES OF ALASKA (Lieutenant Governors)

Albert D. Elliot	July to August, 1897
William Langmead Diston	1897 to 1913

SECRETARIES OF THE TREASURY

W. J. Mills	1897 to 1901
William L. Diston	1902 to 1912

DELEGATES TO CONGRESS

Frank W. Waskey	1906 to 1907
Thomas Cale	1907 to 1909
James A. Wickersham	1909 to 1917

FEDERAL JUDGES

First District (Juneau)

Charles S. Johnson	Appointed July 28, 1897
Melville C. Brown	Appointed April 1, 1900
Royal A. Gunnison	December 3, 1904
Thomas R. Lyons	May 4, 1909

Second District (St. Michaels and later moved Nome)

Alfred H. Noyes   Appointed June 6, 1900
Alfred S. Moore   Appointed April 27, 1902
Cornelius D. Murane   Appointed July 5, 1910

Third District (Eagle and later moved to Fairbanks)

James Wickersham   Appointed June 6, 1900
Silas H. Reed   Appointed November 6, 1907
Edward E. Cushman   Appointed May 18, 1909

Fourth District (Valdez and later moved to Anchorage)

Peter D. Overfield Appointed March 3, 1909

District Attorneys

Sitka Headquarters – prior to June 6, 1900

Burton E. Bennett   1895 to 1898
General Robert A. Frederick   1898 to 1902

First Judicial District, Juneau

General Robert A. Frederick   1898 to 1902; moved to
                                Juneau in 1900
Thomas R. Lyons   1902 to 1903
John J. Boyce   1903 to 1910

Second Judicial District, (St. Michaels and later moved Nome)

Joseph K. Wood   1900 to 1902

John L. McGinn	January to May, 1902; 1903 to 1904
Melvin Grigsby	1902 to 1904
Henry M. Hoyt	1904 to 1907
George B. Grisby	1908 to 1910
Bernard S. Rodey	1910 to 1913

Third Judicial District, (Eagle and later moved to Fairbanks)

Alfred M. Post	1900 to 1901
Nathan V. Harlan	1901 to 1918
James J. Crossley	1908 to 1909; transferred to 4th District
Cornelius D. Murane	1909 to 1910

Four Judicial District, (Valdez and later moved to Anchorage)

James J. Crossley	1909 to 1914

UNITED STATES MARSHALS

Sitka Headquarters – prior to June 6, 1900

James McCain Shoup	1897 to 1900

First Judicial District, Juneau

James McCain Shoup	1900 to 1909
Dan Sutherland	1909 to 1910

Second Judicial District, (St. Michaels and later moved Nome)

Cornelius L. Vawter	1900 to 1901
Frank H. Richards	1901 to 1904

Steve Levi

| John H. Dunn | 1904 to 1905 |
| Thomas Calder Powell | 1905 to 1913 |

Third Judicial District, (Eagle and later moved to Fairbanks)

George C. Perry	1900 to 1908
Henry K. Love	1908 to 1909
Harvey P. Sullivan	1909 to 1913; 1921 to 1933

Four Judicial District, (Valdez and later moved to Anchorage)

| Henry K. Love | 1909 to 1913 |

TERRITORIAL DELEGATES

Frank H. Waskey, Nome	1906 to 1907
Thomas Cale	1907 to 1909
James Wickersham	1909 to 1921

ALASKA ROAD COMMISSION PRESIDENT

| Wilds P. Richardson | 1905 to 1917 |

COLLECTORS OF THE CUSTOMS

Captain Joseph W. Ivey	1897 to 1902
Captain David H. Jarvis	1902 to 1905
Clarence L. Hobart	1905 to 1908
John R. Willis	1908 to 1913

NATIONAL COMMITTEEMEN

Democrat

Arthur K. Delaney, Juneau	1897 to 1904
Louis L. Williams, Sitka	1905 to 1908
William W. Casey, Juneau	1908 to 1909
Alfred J. Daly, Nome and Fairbanks	1909 to 1912

Republican

Miner W. Bruce, Juneau	1889 to 1900
John G. Heid, Juneau	1900 to 1908
Louis P. Shackleford, Juneau	1908 to 1912

GOLD OUTPUT OF ALASKA FROM 1880 TO 1906

Year	Total Output
1880	$20,000
1881	40,000
1882	150,000
1883	301,000
1884	201,000
1885	300,000
1886	446,000
1887	675,000
1888	850,000
1889	900,000
1890	762,000
1891	900,000
1894	1,282,000
1895	2,328,000
1896	2,861,000
1897	2,439,500
1898	2,517,000
1899	5,602,000
1900	8,166,000
1901	6,932,700
1902	8,283,400
1903	8,683,600
1904	9,160,400
1905	14,600,000
1906	17,000,000 (est.)

Gold Output of the Seward Peninsula, 1897-1904

Year	Output
1897	$15,000
1898	75,000
1899	2,800,000
1900	4,750,000
1901	4,130,000
1902	4,561,000
1903	4,465,000
1904	4,164,600524

Official Populations for 1900

Juneau	1,864
Kenai	290
Ketchikan	459
Kodiak	341
Nome	12,488
Sitka	1,396
Valdez	315
Wrangell	868

BIBLIOGRAPHY

Secondary Sources

Abercrombie, Captain W. R. COPPER RIVER EXPLORING EXPE-DITION. United States Government Printing Office, 1900.

Alaska State Troopers. 50 YEARS OF HISTORY. 1991.

Anderson, Ph. D., Eva Greenslit. DOG-TEAM DOCTOR, THE STO-RY OF DR. ROMIG. Caxton Printers, Ltd., 1940.

Anderson, Thayne I. ALASKAN HOOCH. Hoo-Che-Noo, 1988.

Anzer, Richard C. "Dixie." KLONDIKE GOLD RUSH. Pageant Books, 1959.

Atwood, Evangeline. FRONTIER POLITICS: Alaska's James Wicker-sham. Binford & Mort, Portland, Oregon, 1979.

Atwood, Evangeline and Robert N. DeArmond. WHO'S WHO IN ALASKAN POLITICS. Alaska Historical Commission, 1977.

Austin, Basil. THE DIARY OF A NINETY-EIGHTER. John Cumming, Mount Pleasant, Michigan, 1968.

Badlam, Alexander. WONDERS OF ALASKA. Bancroft Company, 1890.

Barry, Mary J. A HISTORY OF MINING ON THE KENAI PENIN-SULA. Alaska Northwest Books, 1973.

_____. SEWARD, ALASKA. Self-published, 1986.

Beach, Rex. PERSONAL EXPOSURES. Harper & Brothers, 1940.

Beattie, Ed. "China Joe," Alaska Sportsman, September, 1949.

Bebbe, Iola. THE TRUE LIFE STORY OF SWIFTWATER BILL GATES. Self-published, 1908.

Becker, Ethel Anderson. HERE COMES THE **POLLY**. Superior Publishing, 1971.

_____. KLONDIKE '98. Binfords & Mort, 1949.

Berton, Pierre. KLONDIKE FEVER. Carroll & Graf, 1958.

Black, Martha Louise. MY NINETY YEARS. Alaska Northwest Books, 1976.

Bockstoce, John R. STEAM WHALING IN THE WESTERN ARCTIC. Old Dartmouth Historical Society, 1977.

_____. WHALES, ICE AND MEN. University of Washington, 1986.

Bowen, Robert. O. AN ALASKAN DICTIONARY. Nooshnik Press, Spenard, Alaska, 1965.

Brooks, Alfred Hulse. BLAZING ALASKA'S TRAILS. University of Alaska, 1953.

Brown, William E. A HISTORY OF THE DENALI - MOUNT MCKINLEY REGION, ALASKA. National Park Service, 1991.

Buranelli, Vincent. GOLD: AN ILLUSTRATED HISTORY. Hammond, Inc., Maplewood, New Jersey, 1979.

Burke, John. ROUGUE'S PROGRESS. G. P. Putnam's, 1975.

Burnham, John B. THE RIM OF MYSTERY. G. P. Putnam's Sons, 1929.

Burroughs, Polly. THE GREAT ICE SHIP BEAR. Van Nordstrand Reinhold Company, 1970.

Calasanctius, Sister Mary Joseph. THE VOICE OF ALASKA. Sisters of St.Anne, Lachine, Quebec, 1947.

Campbell, J. L. CAPE NOME, ALASKA, THE POOR MAN'S DIGGINGS. Self-published, 1900.

Cantwell, R. C. S., First Lieut. J. C. REPORT OF THE OPERATIONS OF THE U.S. REVENUE STEAMER NUNIVAK. Government Printing Office, l902.

Carlson, Leland H. AN ALASKAN GOLD MINE. Northwestern University Press, 1951.

Carpenter, Frank G. ALASKA, OUR NORTHERN WONDERLAND. Doubleday, & Company, New York, 1925.

Carpenter, Herman. THREE YEARS IN ALASKA. Howard Company, 1901.

Cashen, William R. A BRIEF HISTORY OF FAIRBANKS. Self-published, 1971.

Chase, Will H. THE SOURDOUGH POT. Burton Publishing, Kansas City, 1943.

Choate, Glenda J. SKAGWAY ALASKA, GOLD RUSH CEMETERY. Lynn Canal Publishing, 1996.

CHURCH IN ALASKA'S PAST. State of Alaska, Office of History and Archaelogy Miscellaneous Publication 23, 1979.

Clark, Henry W. BUCK CHOQUETTE, STAMPEDER. Self-published, 1960.

_____. HISTORY OF ALASKA. Books for Libraries Press, New York, 1972.

Clifford, Howard. RAILS NORTH. Superior Publishing, 1981.

_____. THE SKAGWAY STORY. Alaska Northwest Publishing Company, 1975.

Cohen, Stan. GOLD RUSH GATEWAY. Pictoral Histories, Missoula, 1986.

Cole, Terrance. E. T. BARNETTE. Alaska Northwest Publishing Company, 1981.

_. GHOSTS OF THE GOLD RUSH. Tanana-Yukon Historical Society, 1977.

_. NOME, "CITY OF THE GOLDEN BEACHES," Alaska Geographic, 1984.

Collier, William Ross and Edwin Victor Westrate. THE REIGN OF SOAPY SMITH. Sun Dial, New York, 1937.

Colp, Harry D. THE STRANGEST STORY EVER TOLD. Exposition Press, 1953.

CORDOVA TO KENNECOTT, ALASKA. Cordova Historical Society, 1988.

Couch, Jim. "The Wizard of Eagle," Alaska Sportsman, February, 1957.

Crad, Joseph. WHITE HELL OF THE NORTH. Sampson Low, Marston & Company, London, 1900.

Crane, Water R. GOLD AND SILVER. John Wiley & Sons, 1908.

Curtin, Walter R. YUKON VOYAGE. Caxton Printers, Idaho, 1938.

Curtis, Edward S. "The Rush to the Klondike Over the Mountain Passes," The Century Magazine, March 1898.

Davis, Mary Lee. SOURDOUGH GOLD. W. A. Wilde Co., Boston, 1933.

Davis, Phyllis and Evangeline Atwood. A GUIDE TO ALASKA'S NEWSPAPERS.

Gastineau Channel Centennial Association and Alaska Division of State Libraries and Museums, 1976.

Davis, Trevor M. LOOKING BACK ON JUNEAU, THE FIRST HUNDRED YEARS. Self-published, 1979.

Dean, David M. BREAKING TRAIL: HUDSON STUCK OF TEXAS AND ALASKA. Ohio University Press, 1988.

DeArmond, Robert N. "Fortunes Misfortunes," Fairbanks Daily News Miner, March 11, 1990.

_____. THE FOUNDING OF JUNEAU. Gastineau Channel Centennial Association, 1967.

_. A SITKA CHRONOLOGY. Sitka Historical Society, 1993.

Dietz, Arthur Arnold. MAD RUSH FOR GOLD IN FROZEN NORTH. Times-Mirror Printing and Binding House, 1914.

Ducker, James H. "Gold Rushers North," Pacific Northwest Quarterly, July, 1994.

Dunham, Sam C. THE ALASKAN GOLD FIELDS. Alaska Northwest Publishing Company, 1983.

Earp, Josephine Sarah Marcus. I MARRIED WYATT EARP. University of Arizona Press, 1976.

Easton, Robert. GUNS, GOLD AND CARAVANS. Capra Press, 1978.

ENCYCLOPEDIA OF AMERICAN FACTS & DATES. Harper & Row, 1987.

Engstrom, Emil. JOHN ENGSTROM, THE LAST FRONTIERSMAN. Vantage Press, 1956.

Ferrell, Ed. BIOGRAPHIES OF ALASKA-YUKON PIONEERS, 1850-1950. Heritage Books, 1994.

Fitz, Frances Ella. LADY SOURDOUGH. Macmillan, 1941.

Forselles, Charles af. COUNT OF ALASKA. Self-published, 1994.

FORT EGBERT AND EAGLE, ALASKA, A PRESERVATION PLAN. National Trust for Historic Preservation in the United States, 1975.

FORT EGBERT AND THE EAGLE HISTORIC DISTRICT. Results of Archeological and Historical Research. U. S. Department of the Interior. December, 1978.

Fortuine, Robert. CHILLS AND FEVERS. University of Alaska Press, 1989.

Fraser, J. D. TWO YEARS IN ALASKA. Self-published, 1923.

French, M.D., L. H. NOME NUGGETS. Montross, Clarke & Emmons, 1901.

_____.SEWARD'S LAND OF GOLD. Montross, Clarke & Emmons, ND.

Friesen, Richard J. THE CHILKOOT PASS AND THE GREAT GOLD RUSH OF 1898. National Historic Parks and Sites Branch, Parks Canada, 1981.

Gard, Wayne. FRONTIER JUSTICE. University of Oklahoma Press, 1949.

Gilbert, Kenneth. ALASKAN POKER STORIES. Robert D. Seal, Seattle, 1958.

Goetzmann, William H. and Kay Sloan. LOOKING FAR NORTH, The Harriman Expedition to Alaska, 1899. Viking, New York, 1982.

Gruening, Ernest. AN ALASKAN READER. Meredith Press, New York, 1966.

Grinnell, Joseph. GOLD HUNTING IN ALASKA. David C. Cook Publishing Company, 1901.

Harris, A. C. ALASKA AND THE KLONDIKE GOLD FIELDS. Self-published, 1897.

Heiner, Virginia Doyle. ALASKA MINING HISTORY. State of Alaska, Division of Parks, Office of History and Archaeology, 1977.

Heller, Herbert L. SOURDOUGH SAGAS. World Publishing Company, 1967.

Helms, Andrea R. C. and Mary Childers Mangusso. "The Nome Gold Conspiracy," Pacific Northwest Quarterly, January, 1982.

Hinckley, Ted C. ALASKAN JOHN G. BRADY. Ohio State University Press, 1982.

Higginson, Ella. ALASKA, THE GREAT COUNTRY. Macmillan, 1923.

Hines, John Chesterfield "Jack." MINSTREL OF THE YUKON. Greenberg, New York, 1948.

Holeski, Carolyn Jean and Marlene Conger Holeski. IN SEARCH OF GOLD. Alaska Geographic Society, 1983.

Hunt, William R. DISTANT JUSTICE. University of Oklahoma Press, 1987.

_. GOLDEN PLACES, The History of Alaska-Yukon Mining. National Park Service, nd.

_. NORTH OF 53. Macmillan, 1974.

Hunter, Kathy. ALASKA NICKNAMES. Lazy Mountain Press, 1988.

IDITAROD GOLD RUSH TRAIL. Department of the Interior, ND.

"Index to the Early History of Alaska as Reported in the 1903-1907 Fairbanks Newspapers," Occasional Paper of the Elmer E. Rasmuson Library, UAF, 1980.

Janson, Lone E. THE COPPER SPIKE. Alaska Northwest Publishing, 1975.

Jenkins, Thomas. THE MAN OF ALASKA. Morehouse-Gorman, New York, 1943.

Johnston, Alva. THE LEGENDARY MIZNERS. Farrar, Straus and Young, 1953.

Jordan, Jed. FOOL'S GOLD. John Day Company, New York, 1960.

Jordan, Philip D. FRONTIER LAW AND ORDER. University of Nebraska Press, 1970.

Kelly, Emma L. "A Woman Pioneer in the Klondike and Alaska," Short Stories, December, 1912.

Kettell, Brian. GOLD. Ballinger Publishing Company, 1982.

Kirby, Edward M. THE RISE AND FALL OF THE SUNDANCE KID. Western Publications, 1983.

Kirchhoff, M J. HISTORIC MCCARTHY. Alaska Cedar Press, 1993.

Kitchener, L. D. FLAG OVER THE NORTH. Superior Publishing, 1954.

Kleinschmidt, Captain F. E. Kleinschmidt. "A Day of Blood," Pacific Monthly, June, 1910.

Klengenberg, Christian. KLENGENBERG OF THE ARCTIC. Edited by Tom MacInnes. Johnathan Cape, London, 1932.

Kosmos, George. ALASKA SOURDOUGH STORIES. Robert D. Seal, Seattle, 1956.

KOYUKUK. Alaska Geographic, 1983.

Kutz, Kenneth J. NOME GOLD. Gold Fever Publishing, 1991.

Kynell, K. S. A DIFFERENT FRONTIER. Northern Michigan University, 1991.

L'Ecuyer, Rosalie E. PROSPECTING AND MINING ACTIVITY IN THE RAMPART, MANLEY HOT SPRINGS AND FORT GIBBON MINING DISTRICTS OF ALASKA, 1894 TO THE PRESENT ERA. United States Department of the Interior, Bureau of Land Management, Alaska State Office, 1997.

Lenz, Mary and James H. Barker. BETHEL, THE FIRST 100 YEARS. City of Bethel, 1985.

Levi, Steven C. ALASCATTALO TALES, A TREASURY OF ALASKAN HUMOR. McFarland, 1993.

_____. COMMITTEE OF VIGILANCE, THE LAW AND ORDER COMMITTEE OF THE SAN FRANCISCO CHAMBER OF COMMERCE, McFarland, 1983.

LEWIS & DRYDEN'S MARINE HISTORY OF THE PACIFIC NORTHWEST. Superior Publishing, 1966.

Lokke, Carl L. KLONDIKE SAGA. Norwegian-American Historical Association, 1965.

Lomen, Carl J. FIFTY YEARS IN ALASKA. David McKay Company, 1954.

McAdam, Eban. FROM DUCK LAKE TO DAWSON CITY. Western Producer Prairie Books, 1977.

McCurdy, H. W. THE H. W. McCURDY MARINE HISTORY OF THE PACIFIC NORTHWEST. Superior Publishing, 1966.

McDonald, Donald. "I Remember Iditarod," Alaska Journal, September, 1969.

McDonald, Lucile. ALASKA STEAM. Alaska Northwest Publishing, 1984.

McElwaine, Eugene. THE TRUTH ABOUT ALASKA, THE LAND OF THE MIDNIGHT SUN. Self-published, 1901.

MacGowan, Michael. THE HARD ROAD TO THE KLONDIKE. Routledge and Kegan Paul, London, 1962.

MacInnes, Tom, editor. KLENGENBERG OF THE ARCTIC. Jonathan Cape, 1932.

McKay, Wallace Vincent. "The Saga of Belinda," Seattle Times, August 12, 1962.

McKeown, Martha Ferguson. THE TRAIL LED NORTH. Macmillan Company, 1948.

McKee, Lanier. THE LAND OF NOME. Grafton Press, New York, 1902.

McMichael, Alfred G. KLONDIKE LETTERS, The Correspondence of a Gold Seeker in 1898. Alaska Northwest Publishing Company, 1984.

Martin, Cy. GOLD RUSH NARROW GAUGE. Trans-Anglo Books, 1969.

——. WHISKEY AND WILD WOMEN. Hart Publishing, 1974.

Martinsen, Ella Lung. TRAIL TO NORTH STAR GOLD. Metropolitan Press, 1969.

Mathews, Richard. THE YUKON. Holt, Rinehart and Winston, 1968.

Minter, Roy. THE WHITE PASS, GATEWAY TO THE KLONDIKE. University of Alaska Press, 1987.

Moffit, Fred H. THE FAIRHAVEN GOLD PLACERS, SEWARD PENINSULA, ALASKA, USGS, Washington D. C. , 1905.

Moore, J. Bernard. SKAGWAY IN TIMES PRIMEVAL. Vantage, 1968.

Morgan, Murray. ONE MAN'S GOLD RUSH. University of Washington Press, 1967.

Murray, Keith A. REINDEER AND GOLD. Western Washington University, 1988.

Naske, Claus-M. and Ludwig J. Rowinski. FAIRBANKS, A PICTORIAL HISTORY. Donning Company, 1981.

_and Herman E. Slotnick. ALASKA, A HISTORY OF THE 49TH STATE. William B. Eerdmans Publishing, Grand Rapids, MI, 1979.

_. "The Red Lights of Fairbanks," Alaska Journal, Spring, 1984.

Nichols, Ph. D., Jeanette Paddock. ALASKA, A HISTORY OF ITS ADMINISTRATION , EXPLOITATION AND INDUSTRIAL DEVELOPMENT DURING THE FIRST HALF CENTURY UNDER THE RULE OF THE UNITED STATES. Arthur H. Clark Co., 1924.

NOME AND SEWARD PENINSULA, History, Description, Biographies and Stories. E. S. Harrison, Seattle, 1905.

O'Connor, Harvey. THE GUGGENHEIMS. Covici Friede, 1937.

O'Connor, Richard. HIGH JINKS ON THE KLONDIKE. Bobbs-Merrill, 1954.

Orth, Donald I. DICTIONARY OF ALASKA PLACE NAMES. United States Department of the Interior, 1967.

Ostrogorsky, Michael. "Women Were Everywhere," Columbia, Spring, 1994.

Phillips, James W. ALAKSA-YUKON PLACE NAMES. University of Washington, 1973.

Pitcher, James S. SOURDOUGH JIM PITCHER. Alaska Northwest Publishing Company, 1985.

Pointer, Larry. IN SEARCH OF BUTCH CASSIDY. University of Oklahoma Press, 1977.

PROCEEDINGS OF THE CONFERENCE ON ALASKA HISTORY. "Frontier Alaska." AMU Press, 1968.

Ravitz, Abe C. REX BEACH. Western Writers Series No. 113, Boise State University, 1994.

Ray, Dorothy Jean. "Sinrock Mary," Pacific Northwest Quarterly, July, 1984.

Reed, Irving McKenny. BOYHOOD IN THE NOME GOLD CAMP. University of Alaska, 1969.

_. "Frank Yasuda," Alaska Sportsman, June, 1963.

Remmington, C. H. ("Copper River Joe"). A GOLDEN CROSS (?) ON TRAILS FROM THE VALDEZ GLACIER. White-Thompson, Los Angeles, 1939.

Rickard, T. A. THROUGH THE YUKON AND ALASKA. Mining and Scientific Press, 1909.

Rickard, Mrs. Tex. EVERYTHING HAPPENED TO HIM. Rich & Cowan, 1937.

Ricks, Melvin B. ALASKA'S POSTMASTERS AND POST OFFICES. Tongass Publishing, 1965.

Robbins, Elizabeth. RAYMOND AND I. Macmillan, 1956.

Robertson, Frank C. and Beth Kay Harris. SOAPY SMITH, KING OF THE FRONTIER CON MEN. Hastings House, New York, 1962.

Samuels, Charles. THE MAGNIFICENT RUBE, THE LIFE AND GAUDY TIMES OF TEX RICKARD. McGraw-Hill, 1957.

Savage, A. H. DOGSLED APOSTLES. Sheed & Ward, New York. 1942.

Satterfield, Archie. CHILKOOT PASS. Alaska Northwest Publishing, 1973.

_____. KLONDIKE PARK. Fulcrum Publishing, Golden, Colorado, 1993.

Schrader, Frank C. and Alfred H. Brooks. CAPE NOME GOLD REGION, ALASKA. United States Government Printing Office, 1900.

Scott, Elva. HISTORIC EAGLE AND ITS PEOPLE. Eagle City, 1993.

Shiels, Archibald. SEWARD'S ICEBOX. Union Printing, 1933.

Shirley, Glen. WEST OF HELL'S FRINGE. University of Oklahoma Press, 1978.

Smith, Michael E. ALASKA'S ROADHOUSES. State of Alaska, Office of History and Archaeology, 1974.

Solka, Jr., Paul. ADVENTURES IN ALASKA JOURNALISM SINCE 1903. Commercial Printing, Fairbanks, 1980.

Solstice, Sarah. "A Woman in Alaska," <u>Alaska-Yukon Magazine</u>, March 1907.

Stacey, John F. TO ALASKA FOR GOLD. Ye Galleon Press, 1973.

Steffa, Don. "Tales of Noted Frontier Characters, III, 'Soapy Smith,' Bad Man and Bluffer," The Pacific Monthly, October, 1908.

Stefansson, Vilhjalmur. DISCOVERY. McGraw-Hill, 1964.

Stewart, Robert. SAM STEELE. Doubleday Canada, 1979.

Stone, David and Brenda. HARD ROCK GOLD. Juneau Centennial Committee, 1980.

Stuck, Hudson. ALASKAN MISSIONS OF THE EPISCOPAL CHURCH. Domestice and Foreign Missionary Society, 1920.

_. TEN THOUSAND MILES WITH A DOG SLED. Charles Scribner's Sons, 1914.

Sutherland, Dan. "Gold Rush Pioneer and Politician," <u>Alaska History</u>, Spring, 1995.

Tabbert, Russell. DICTIONARY OF ALASKAN ENGLISH. Denali Press, Juneau, Alaska, 1991.

Thomas, Jr., Lowell. THE TRAIL OF '98. Duell, Sloan and Pearce, New Yorik, 1962, Tornfelt, Evert E. and Michael Burwell. SHIPWRECKS OF THE ALASKAN SHELF AND SHORE. United States Department of the Interior, OCS Report MMS 92-0002.

Tower, Elizabeth A. BIG MIKE HENEY. Self-published, 1988.

_____. READING, RELIGION, REINDEER. Self-published, 1988.

Ulibarri, George. S. DOCUMENTING ALASKAN HISTORY. University of Alaska Press, 1982.

Walden, Arthur Treadwell. DOG-PUNCHER ON THE YUKON. Houghton Mifflin, 1931.

Wallace, John B. Four articles on his experiences in Nome which appeared in the *Alaska Sportsman* in August, October, November and December of 1939.

Washburn, Bradford. A TOURIST GUIDE TO MOUNT MCKINLEY. Alaska Northwest Publishing, 1971.

Webb, John Sidney. "The River Trip to the Klondike," *The Century Magazine*, March 1898.

Weimer, M. D. K. KLONDYKE. Self-published, 1903.

Wells, E. Hazard. MAGNIFICENCE AND MISERY. Doubleday, 1984.

Wendt, Ron. GOLD, GHOST TOWNS & GRIZZLIES. (self-published, 1994).

Wharton, David. THE ALASKA GOLD RUSH. Indiana University Press, 1972.

White, E. J. "Stroller." TALES OF A KLONDIKE NEWSMAN. Mitchell, 1969.

Whiting, M. D. F. B. GRIT, GRIEF, AND GOLD. Peacock Publishing, 1933.

Wickersham, James. OLD YUKON TALES – TRAILS – AND TRIALS, Washington Law Book, 1938.

Wiedemann, Thomas. CHEECHAKO INTO SOURDOUGH. Binford & Mort, 1942.

Willey, George Franklyn. "Lady Luck and the Cold Deck," *Alaska Sportsman*, October, 1954.

Wilson, William. "To Make A Stake," Alaska Journal, Winter, 1983.

Wilson, William H. "Alaska's Past; Alaska's Future," *Alaska Review,* Spring/Summer, 1970.

de Windt, F.R.G.S., Henry. THROUGH THE GOLD-FIELDS OF ALASKA TO BERING STRAITS. Chatto & Windus, London, 1899.

Woods, Henry F. GOD'S LOADED DICE. Caxton Publishers, 1948.

WOODSTOCK LETTERS, A HISTORICAL JOURNAL OF JESUIT MISSIONARY AND EDUCATIONAL ACTIVITIES. Academic Editions, 1987.

WORLD ALMANAC OF BOOKS AND FACTS, 1995.

Wyman, J. N. JOURNEY TO THE KOYUKUK. Pictorial Histories, 1988.

Young, S. Hall. ADVENTURES IN ALASKA. Fleming H. Revell, 1919.

YUKON RIVER IN ALASKA'S HISTORY. Papers Presented at the Annual Meeting of the Alaska Historical Society, October 7-9, 1993.

Primary Sources

Alaska Packers Association Records, microfiche, in the possession of the Z. J. Loussac Library.

Alaska Trial Courts Criminal Files, RG 21, National Archives – Alaska Region.

Alig, Joyce L. OLD GOLD RUSH TO ALASKA DIARIES OF 1898-1900. Messinger Press, Ohio, 2001.

Axe, B. E. Papers in the possession of the University of Washington.

Barrett, W. T., M. D. Papers in the possession of the Sisters of St. Ann Archives, Victoria, B. C.

Bufvers, John. Diary in the possession of the Z. J. Loussac Library, Anchorage, Alaska.

Burr, A. Regina. Diary in the possession of the Anchorage Museum of History and Art.

CAPTAIN J. D. WINCHESTER'S EXPERIENCE ON A VOYATE FROM LYNN, MASSACHUSETTS TO SAN FRANCISCO, CAL. AND TO THE ALASKAN GOLD FIELDS. Newcomb & Gauss Printers, 1900.

Cavanaugh, Albert B. Papers in the possession of the University of Washington.

Chilton, Robert S. Personal papers in the possession of Duke University.

Circle, Bylaws of the Miners of. Alaska State Library.

Circle, Commissioners Records. Alaska State Library.

Clum, John P. Papers in the possession of the University of Arizona.

Coghill, William A. "An Account of Some of the Alaskan Experience of W. A. Coghill as told to William Coghill Jr." in the possession of the University of Alaska, Fairbanks.

Collins, Henry A. Papers in the possession of the Huntington Library.

Cravez, Pam. SEIZING THE FRONTIER, ALASKA'S TERRITORIAL LAWYERS, 1984, unpublished in the possession of the Z. J. Loussac Library in Anchorage.

Crosby, Hartley. Collection of seven letters in the possession of the Alaska State Library.

Dawson Funeral Index in the possession of the Rasmuson Library, UAF.

DICTIONARY OF THE CHINOOK JARGON OR INDIAN TRADE LANGUAGE OF THE NORTH PACIFIC COAST. Victoria B. C., 1899, in the possession of the Anchorage Museum of History and Art.

Dey, Robert L. Diary in the possession of Dartmouth College.

Farnsworth, Robert J. Personal narrative in the possession of the Archives, University of Alaska, Fairbanks.

Glenn, Edwin F. Papers in the possession of the Archives, University of Alaska, Anchorage.

Goodwin, Freida. Oral history of her life in the possession of Richard Miller of Anchorage.

Governors' Papers of Alaska. The originals are in Washington D. C. at the National Archives but a microfilm copy of the documents are available at the National Archives – Alaska Region.

Hadley, Martha. THE ALASKAN DIARY OF AN ALASKAN PIONEER MISSIONARY. Self-published, 1969.

Harris, Richard T. Harris. Papers in the possession of the University of Alaska Anchorage.

Hartnett, Maurice. Diary of M.A. Hartnett on trip to Kotzebue Sound, Alaska, 1898, photocopy in the possession of the University of Washington.

Hartshorn, Florence. Papers in the possession of the University of Washington.

Herdman, James. MY FIRST STAMPEDE. Columbia Publishing Company, Long Beach, WA., nd. Hekrdle, Captain Kevin D. "Dangerous Passage: Gold Rush Shipwrecks of 1898,"

ALASKA HISTORICAL COMMISSION STUDIES IN HISTORY, No. 194, June, 1986. This monograph was found in the Z. J. Loussac Library in Anchorage Alaska.

Herning, Orville George. Diaries in the possession of the Anchorage Museum of History and Art.

Hubbard, II, Charles Goodyear. Papers in the possession of the University of Alaska, Anchorage.

Jacobs, Myna. Personal papers.

Jackson, Sheldon. Papers in the possession of the Sheldon Jackson Library, Sitka.

Jenks, Issac. Papers in the possession of the Huntington Library.

Johnson, Kirke E. Letters in the possession of the Oregon Historical Society.

Kappleman, Frank. Letter to his family in the possession of the Z. J. Loussac Library, Anchorage, Alaska.

Lillo, Waldemar Engvald. "The Alaska Gold Mining Company and the Cape Nome Conspiracy," Ph. D. Dissertation, University of North Dakota, 1935.

Mackey, Billy E. "Iditarod: Portrait of an Alaskan Gold Community," Ph. D. Dissertation, Northern Arizona University.

Martin, George D. "Reminiscence About a 250 Mile Trek in Alaska," in the possession of the Kansas State Historical Society.

Marx, Walter J. "History of Teller," ND in the possession of the Lois Morey Papers, University of Alaska, Anchorage.

Merritt, Fred T. Papers in the possession of the University of Washington.

Milroy Papers in the possession of the University of Washington.

Morey, Lois. Papers in the possession of the University of Alaska, Anchorage.

Nome Police Records, Alaska State Library.

Norby, "Yakima" Pete. Interview in the possession of the Yakima Valley Historical Society.

Norris, Frank. "Gawking at the Midnight Sun," Alaska Historical Commission Project No. 170, June, 1985.

Orth, Donald J. DICTIONARY OF ALASKA PLACE NAMES. USGS, Department of the Interior, Professional Paper 567, 1967.

Perkins, William T. Papers in the possession of the University of Washington.

Poppe Family Reminiscents. Document in the possession of the University of Alaska Anchorage Archives.

Pugh, Arthur. Diary in the possession of the State Historical Society of Wisconsin.

Ray, Captain P. H. "Relief of the Destitute in Gold Fields," 56thCongress, 1st Session, Senate Report No. 1023.

Record of Prisoners Received, U.S. Penitentiary, McNeil Island, RG 129, National Archives – Pacific Northwest Region.

Reick, Addie. Diary in the possession of the Western Historical Manuscript Collection, Columbia, Missouri.

Reid, Shad. Diary, copy in the possession of the Alaska State Library, Juneau.

Remich, J. E. DINGO, DUMPY NED AND MIKE KEENE. Self-published and undated, in the possession of the Z. J. Loussac Library in Anchorage, Alaska.

REPORT OF THE CRUISE OF THE U.S. REVENUE CUTTER **BEAR** AND THE OVERLAND EXPEDITION FOR THE RELIEF OF THE WHALERS IN THE ARCTIC OCEAN. United States Government Printing Office, 1899.

Robe, Cecil Francis. "The Penetration of an Alaskan Frontier, The Tanana Valley and Fairbanks," Ph. D. dissertation, Yale University, 1943.

Robertson, Frank C. and Beth Kay Harris. SOAPY SMITH, KING OF THE CON MEN. Hastings House, 1961.

Rock Island log book in the possession of the Huntington Museum.

Rodey, Bernard. "A random, unrevised account of a midwinter "Mush" or overland trip from Nome to Cordova, Valdez and Seward, Alaska with his philosophical, economic and political views regarding the great territory, and his journal of the trip, by B. S. Rodey, U.S. District Attorney at Nome" in Claus-M. Naske's A History of the Alaska Federal District Court System, 1884-1959, and the Creation of the State Supreme Court System prepared pursuant to RSA 410059 between the Alaska Court System and the Geophysical Institute, University of Alaska, Fairbanks, Alaska, in July of 1985 in the possession of the Law Library at the Alaska State Court in Anchorage.

St. Michael, Commissioner Records. Alaska State Archives.

Samms Diaries. Location of the original Quaker diaries is not known. Poor photocopies of these Quaker diaries were found in the archives at Whittier College in Southern California.

Shotwell, Margharete Ross. Personal Papers in the possession of the University of Washington.

Smith, Kathleen Loop. "A Pioneer Family in Alaska, Ellen Loop's Letters" unpublished collection in the possession of the University of Alaska, Anchorage.

Seitz, Dr. Louis Seitz. Letter in the possession of the Margaret I King Library, University of Kentucky.

Spencer, Arthur C., III. Papers in the possession of the University of Washington.

Sutherland, Dan. Papers in the possession of UAF.

Templeton, Archie. Papers in the possession of the University of Alaska Anchorage.

United States Government. Admiralty Register, United States District Court in the possession of the State of Alaska Archives, Juneau.

.....ANNUAL LIST OF MERCHANT VESSELS OF THE UNITED STATES.

.....Census of 1900 in the possession of the Z. J. Loussac Library.

.....Census of 1910 in the possession of the Z. J. Loussac Library.

.....Custom Service, original documentation from St. Michael, 1898-1905, in the possession of the Z. J. Loussac Library in Anchorage.

.....Dispatches of the U. S. Consuls in Dawson City in the possession of the National Archives – Alaska Region.

.....Index by District to U. S. Coast Guard Reports of Assistance, in the possession of the National Archives – Alaska Region.

.....Records of Alaska Customhouses in the possession of the National Archives – Alaska Region.

.....Records of the United States Department of the Interior in the possession of the National Archives – Alaska Region.

.....Records of Entries and Liquidations, Eagle, in the possession of the National Archives – Alaska Region.

.....Revenue Cutter Service, Alaska File, in the possession of the National Archives – Alaska Region.

..... REPORT UPON THE CUSTOMS DISTRICT, PUBLIC SERVICE, AND RESOURCES OF ALASKA TERRITORY BY

WILLIAM GOUVERNEUR MORRIS, 1879 in the possession of the Z. J. Loussac Library.

.....U. S. Coast Guard Casualty and Wreck Reports in the possession of the National Archives – Alaska Region.

Wade, George. Documents regarding his criminal record are in the possession of the United States Bureau of Prisons.

Watts, C. W. Papers in the possession of the Huntington Library.

Whyte, Bert. Papers in the possession of the University of Washington.

Wickersham, James. Papers in the possession of the University of Alaska, Fairbanks and the Huntington Library. Author's note: There is a free-floating collection of Wickersham letters and files on microfilm. The originals may be in Washington D. C.

Wonderlin, Fred N. Diary in the possession of the State Historical Society of Kansas.

Newspapers and Magazines

49th Star
Alaska Capital
(Juneau)
Alaska Citizen
(Fairbanks)
Alaska Daily Guide
Alaska Forum
Alaska History
Alaska Journal
Alaska Magazine
Alaska Prospector
Alaska Sportsman
Alaska Traveler's Guide
Alaska Truth
Alaska Weekly
Alaska-Yukon
Magazine
Alaskan World
(Fairbanks)
All Alaska Review
Bennett Sun
Bertillion Eye
Bijougram
Boston Alaskan
Chena Times
Chitina Leader
Cordova Daily Alaskan
Council City News
Daily Industrial

Worker
Daily Prospector
Bulletin
Diamond Drill
Dyea Press
Dyea Trail
Eagle City Tribune
Eskimo Bulletin
Fairbanks Daily New
Miner
Fairbanks Daily Times
Fairbanks Evening
Alaskan
Fairbanks Evening
News
Fairbanks Facts
Fairbanks Free Press
Fairbanks Gazette
Fairbanks Leaders
Fairbanks Weekly
News
Fort Wrangell News
Free Press
Hot Springs Echo
Hot Springs Post
Iditarod Nugget
Iditarod Pioneer
Innoko Miner
Interloper

Juneau Alaskan
Juneau Journal
Midnight Sun
Midnight Sun (Seattle)
Miner's Union
Bulletin
Musher
Nenana News
Nome Chronicle
Nome Gold Digger
Nome Industrial
Worker
Nome News
Nome Pioneer Press
Northern Light
(Fairbanks)
Northern Light
(Unalakleet)
Pathfinder
Pony Express (San
Francisco)
Rampart Miner
Riverside Daily
Enterprise (Riverside,
California)
Seattle Post-
Intelligencer
Seattle Times
Seward Daily Gateway

Sitka Cablegram
Skaguay Budget
Skagway News
Tanana Daily Star
Tanana Leader
Tanana Miner
Tanana Tribune
Tanana Valley Socialist
Teller News
Truth
Valdez Daily News
Valdez News
Vancouver Province
(British Columbia)
Yukon Press
Yukon Valley News

(ENDNOTES)

1.   Kepner-Crane, July 24, 1897.

2.   Cole, page 10.

3.   "Circle City Deserted," *Seattle Times,* October 18, 1897.

4.   "An Innocent Smuggler," *Seattle Times*, August 25, 1898.

5.   de Windt, pages 161-2.

6.   Dunham, page 840.

7.   This quote and the others in the section identified simply as "Darrell" came from Cash J. Darrell's "Eagle on the Yukon," *Alaska Life,* December, 1946. This author has no way of knowing if these quotes are accurate, apocryphal or generated under the guise of literary license.

8.   Darrell.

9.   Darrell.

10.   Darrell.

11.   Darrell.

12.   Scott, page 6.

13.   DeArmond, JUNEAU, page 33.

14.   "A Gold Find Near Sitka," *Seattle Times*, March 30, 1898; "Pande Basin, Alaska," *Seattle Times,* April 1, 1898.

15.   "News from Cape Yaktag," November 15, 1902, *Valdez News.*

16.   "Bristol Bay is a Big Fake," *Nome Chronicle*, September 10, 1900.

17.   "Iliamna Lake Find Created by Fake Prospector," *Alaska Daily Record,* September 8, 1909.

18. "Rich Strikes Reported North of Cook Inlet," *Seattle Times*, November 29, 1898.

19. "Gold from Cook Inlet," *Seattle Times*, October 12, 1897.

20. "Route to Copper River," *Seattle Times*, October 14, 1897.

21. "Gold in Sheets," *Seattle Times*, April 14, 1899.

22. "Treasure Trove in far Alaska," *Seattle Times*, April 4, 1899.

23. "Susitna Stampede," *Nome Pioneer Press*, December 28, 1907.

24. There is only one verse to this song and that verse can be found, among other sources, in Burl Ives' SONGBOOK.

25. Gould, page 22.

26. Cole, NOME, page 66.

27. Jordan, pages 71-2.

28. Carpenter, page 175.

29. Jordan, page 72.

30. Jordan, page 71.

31. Jordan, page 75.

32. "An Alaskan Character was "Billy the Horse," *Iditarod Pioneer*, April 29, 1916.

33. Jordan, page 75 and 170. The biography of Bishop Rowe indicates that Billy the Horse didn't know he was talking to the Bishop. Jordan's memoirs say he did.

34. "William M. Elliott Boosts the Nelchina," *Seward Daily Gateway*, October 20, 1913 and "An Alaskan Character was "Billy the Horse," *Iditarod Pioneer*, April 29, 1916.

35. Willey, George Franklyn, "Lady Luck and the Cold Deck," *Alaska Sportsman*, October, 1954. This may very well be of an incident that took place in Dawson.

36. "An Alaskan Character was "Billy the Horse," *Iditarod Pioneer*, April 29, 1916.

37. Gould, Hal, "Lazy John Was Proud of His," *Alaska Sportsman*, November 1938, page 22.

38. Hines, page 120.

39. Gould, Hal, "Lazy John Was Proud of His," *Alaska Sportsman*, November, 1938, page 9; "Blueberry Kid" Story, *All Alaska Weekly*, March 30, 1928.

40. Kosmos, pages 23-4.

41. Forselles, pages 77-81.

42. Cole, GHOSTS, pages 20 and 21; Fairbanks Civil File #2154, Box 33, NA-AR.

43. "Klondike Gambling King," *Seattle Post-Intelligencer,* September 20, 1898; "Alaska Man's Mind a Blank," *Cordova Daily Alaskan*, March 5, 1909.

44. Hines, page 120.

45. Hines, page 120.

46. Gould, page 22.

47. "Perforated his Pants," *Nome News,* April 17, 1901.

48. Forselles, page 39.

49. Young, ADVENTURES, pages 64-5.

50. "Billy Burns Described in Juneau Paper," (Fairbanks) *Alaska Citizen*, April 19, 1915.

51. Cole, GHOSTS, page 29.

52. Jarvis to Department of the Treasury, July 30, 1899, RCS, NA-AR.

53. Gould, page 22.

54. "The Better Way," *Tanana Leader,* August 18, 1910. The actual assault charge was "threatening to make a widow out of an old tillicum of his."

55. Fairbanks Criminal File #695, Box 31, NA-AR.

56. Dearmond, JUNEAU, page 146.

57. Juneau Criminal File #70, Box 3, NA-AR.

58. Gould, page 26.

59. "Commissioner's Court," *Tanana News*, September 6, 1913.

60. Jordan, pages 76-77.

61. Cole, BARNETTE, page 37.

62. Jordan, pages 78-81.

63. "'Megaphone Kid,'" *Northern Light,* September 29, 1906.

64. Hines, page 120.

65. Jordan, page 191.

66. Hines, page 120.

67. Clifford, page 46.

68. Jordan, page 72.

69. Anchorage Criminal File #91, Box 11,NA-AR.

70. Gould, page 26.

71. Cole, BARNETTE, page 117.

72. Gould, Hal, "Lazy John Was Proud of His," *Alaska Sportsman*, November 1938, page 9.

73. Jordan, page 75.

74. Sitka *Alaskan*, March 7, 1891.

75. Guiteau, Luther W., "Down the Klutina," *Alaska Sportsman*, December 1940, page 27.

76. Jordan, pages 74-5.

77. Hines, page 101.

78. Anchorage Criminal File #5091, Box 31, NA-AR.

79. Ketchikan Civil File #269, NA-AR.

80. Gould, page 26.

81. Carpenter, ALASKA, page 175.

82. *Hot Springs Echo*, August 22, 1911.

83. Shiels, page 152.

84. Clifford, page 46.

85. Carpenter, page 175.

86. Chase, POT, page 45.

87. Gould, Hal, "Lazy John Was Proud of His," *Alaska Sportsman*, November 1938, page 9.

88. He is mentioned in both Grinell and Hartnett.

89. "Hootch Albert Says J. Hayes Got His," *Tanana Tribune*, October 27, 1898.

90. "Foster is Pardoned," *Skagway Daily Alaskan*, December 10, 1899.

91. Hines, page 102.

92. Cole, GHOSTS, page 36.

93. "Death by Drowning," *Council City News*, July 19, 1902.

94. Hines, page 120.

95. Willey, George Franklyn, "Lady Luck and the Cold Deck," *Alaska Sportsman*, October 1954.

96. Gould, Hal, "Lazy John Was Proud of His," *Alaska Sportsman*, November, 1938, page 22.

97. Gould, Hal, "Lazy John Was Proud of His," *Alaska Sportsman,* November, 1938, page 9.
98. Gould, page 26.
99. *Tanana News,* July 19, 1913.
100. Cole, BARNETTE, page 60.
101. Hines, page 120.
102. Gould, Hal, "Lazy John Was Proud of His," *Alaska Sportsman,* November, 1938, page 9.
103. Gould, page 22.
104. Fairbanks Criminal File #453, Box 21, NA-AR.
105. United States vs. C. F. Cheek, C. M. Summers and Henry Shattuck, Juneau Criminal File #643.
106. "'Six Shooter Sam' Harris in New Role," *Alaska Daily Record,* September 7, 1909. Harris was said to be armed with a "gigantic 'smokestick,'" which this author interprets to mean that he had sported a large cigar.
107. "Cowardly Assault is Made on Jerry O'Neil," *Alaska Daily Record,* September 20, 1909.
108. United States vs. A. R. O'Brien, Juneau Criminal File #647, Box 21, RG 21, Alaska State Library. Of passing interest, Hopp was the editor of the *Fort Wrangel News* that covered the Bachelor's Club.
109. United States vs. L. S. Keller, Juneau Criminal File #649, Box 21, RG 21, Alaska State Library.
110. United States vs. Edward C. Russell, Juneau Criminal File #644B, Box 21, RG 21, Alaska State Library.
111. United States vs. W. C. Ullrich, Juneau Criminal File #645, Box 21, RG 21, Alaska State Library
112. United States vs. W. C. Ullrich, Juneau Criminal File #646, Alaska State Library
113. United States vs. A. R. O'Brien and C. M. Summers, Juneau Criminal File $641.
114. United States vs. C. F. Cheek, C. M. Summers and Henry Shattuck, Juneau Criminal File #643, Alaska State Library.
115. United States vs. A. R. O'Brien, Juneau Criminal File #647, Alaska State Library; United States vs. Charles A. Hopp, Juneau Criminal File

#648, Alaska State Library; "O'Brien Fine Will Amount to $230.00," *Alaska Daily Record*, October 28, 1909; "Ketchikan Jury is Out but Ten Minutes," *Alaska Daily Record*, October 25, 1909; "*Transcript* Forced to Suspend This Morning," *Alaska Daily Record* September 10, 1909;

116. Gould, page 22.
117. Gould, page 26.
118. Copper River Joe, pages 15-6.
119. "Bob Herrold Siwashed," *Yukon Valley News*, November 26, 1910. This article refers to the arrest of Herrold for selling liquor to Indians. Interestingly, the colloquial use of the term Hot Air Company in 1902 was for the company that delivered the mail – and do so very badly. In fact, in March of 1902 when the residents of St. Michael were "nearly wild for mail," a postal inspector had to snatch 1,000 pounds of mail and make sure it got delivered because the to Hot Air Company wasn't doing its contractor job.(Wilson, page 110.)
120. Gould, page 22.
121. Hines, page 102.
122. Forselles, page 38.
123. Hines, page 120.
124. Jordan, page 157.
125. Wharton, page 160.
126. Wickersham, YUKON, page 123.
127. Gould, page 22.
128. Gould, page 26.
129. *Hot Springs News*, May 23, 1908.
130. Hines, pages 119-120.
131. "Missouri Jack Married Now," *Fairbanks Daily News Miner*, April 19, 1909.
132. Shiels, page 152.
133. Carpenter, page 175.
134. Hines, page 102.
135. Seward Court Journal, July, 1915, page 11.
136. *Council City News*, November 24, 1906.
137. Windt, page 25.

138. Gould, page 26.
139. Gould, page 22.
140. Webb, *The Century Magazine,* page 681.
141. Webb, *The Century Magazine*, page 681.
142. Skagway Criminal File #191, Box 4, NA-AR.
143. Walden, page 47.
144. Hunt, JUSTICE, pages 226-227.
145. *Hot Springs Echo*, December 8, 1912,
146. Shiels, page 152.
147. Gould, page 22. There was also a Kangaroo O'Kelly from Cork who might have been the same man, (MacGowan, page 86-7.)
148. "'Rube' Pioneer," *Nome Pioneer Press*, October 29, 1907.
149. "Yukon River," page 167.
150. *Tanana Tribune*, October 20, 1912.
151. *Alaska Sportsman,* February, 1968, page 17.
152. Gould, Hal, "Lazy John was Proud of His," *Alaska Sportsman*, November, 1938, page 8.
153. Wendt, page 38.
154. Gould, Hal, "Lazy John Was Proud of His," *Alaska Sportsman,* November, 1908, page 8.
155. Gould, page 22.
156. Jordan, page 75.
157. Gould, page 22.
158. Jordan, page 78.
159. "Chena Notes," *Hot Springs Echo,* November 19, 1910.
160. Gould, Hal, "Lazy John Was Proud of His," *Alaska Sportsman*, November, 1938, page 22.
161. Cole, GHOSTS, page 29.
162. Carpenter, page 175.
163. Gould, page 22.
164. "Siberia Is Now Open," *Nome News,* March 24, 1900.
165. "Cleary Thief Is Arrested," *Fairbanks Times,* July 16, 1906.
166. United States Park Service brochure.
167. Yukon Valley News, November 26, 1910.

168. Juneau Criminal File #472, Box 13, NA-AR.
169. Gould, Hal, "Lazy John Was Proud of His," *Alaska Sportsman,* November, 1938, page 9.
170. Johnston, page 99.
171. Johnston, page 103.
172. Sullivan, pages 136-9.
173. Johnston, pages 100-101.
174. Hunt, page 198. Author's note: With gold at $18 an ounce and a drink at $.25, it would have taken a great many minute particles of gold to buy a shot of whiskey much less retire to the lap of luxury.
175. Clifford, page 46.
176. Cole, BARNETTE, pages 52 and 53.
177. Chase, POT, page 45.
178. Chase, POT, page 45.
179. Gould, page 22.
180. Fairbanks Criminal File #592, Box 26.
181. Fairbanks Criminal File #171, Box 1, NA-AR.
182. Gould, pages 22 and 26.
183. Hines, page 119.
184. Fairbanks Criminal File #453, Box 21, NA-AR.
185. Gould, page 22.
186. Jordan, page 42.
187. Jordan, page 75.
188. Jordan, page 71.
189. Jordan, pages 73-4.
190. Norby, page 4.
191. Fairbanks Criminal Case 306, December 28, 1908; NARA RG 21.
192. Jorday, page 74.
193. "'Happy Jack' is Again In Jail," *Fairbanks Evening News,* August 12, 1905.
194. Berton, pages 18-19.
195. Gould, page 26.
196. "Yukon River," page 166.
197. "Left Corpse in the Chapel: Went to the Potlatch," *Tanana Leader,* January 6, 1910.

198. Chase, POT, page 45 and Jordan, page 75.
199. Clark, CHOQUETTE, page 123.
200. Willey, George Franklyn, "Lady Luck and the Cold Deck," *Alaska Sportsman,* October, 1954.
201. Webb, The Century Magazine, page 681.
202. Hines, page 120.
203. Gould, page 26.
204. Hines, page 120.
205. Hines, page 120.
206. Forselles, pages 31-32.
207. Yukon River in Alaska's History, page 171.
208. Couch, Jim. "The Wizard of Eagle," *Alaska Sportsman,* February, 1957, pages 16-17, 33; "Dig Pioneer's Body from Cake of Ice," *Anchorage Weekly Times,* December 6, 1940.
209. Whiting, pages 79-81, Shiels, page 152, and Tower, HENEY, page 14.
210. Gould, Hal, "Lazy John Was Proud of His," *Alaska Sportsman,* November, 1938, page 22.
211. *Hot Spring Echo,* August 22, 1911.
212. Webb, *The Century Magazine,* page 681.
213. Gould, page 26.
214. Carpenter, pages 175-6.
215. Wendt, pages 58-9 and "From Ketchikan to Barrow," *Alaska Sportsman,* September, 1946, pages 22-3.
216. "'Scrap Iron Jake' Leaves City Jail," *Tanana Tribune,* March 24, 1909.
217. Sitka Criminal File #342, Box 7, NA-AR.
218. Park Service Brochure.
219. Hines, page 102.
220. Juneau Criminal File #333, Box 9.
221. Carpenter, page 175. There are also references to "Short and Dirty," possibly the same woman, in the Robert J. Farnsworth papers at the University of Alaska, Fairbanks Archives.
222. "Returns with his Captive," *Council City News,* November 8, 1902.
223. Jordan, pages 81-85,
224. Shiels, page 152.

225. Hines, page 102.

226. *Juneau City Mining Record,* April 28, 1892.

227. Clifford, page 46.

228. Gould, Hal, "Lazy John Was Proud of His," *Alaska Sportsman*, November, 1935, page 8.

229. Jordan, page 87.

230. Fairbanks Criminal File #384, Box 17, NA-AR.

231. *Hot Springs Echo,* March 18, 1909.

232. Carpenter, page 175.

233. Webb, *The Century Magazine,* page 681.

234. Gould, Hal, "Lazy John Was Proud of His," *Alaska Sportsman*, November, 1938, pages 9 and 22.

235. Gould, Hal, "Lazy John Was Proud of His," *Alaska Sportsman*, November, 1938, page 22.

236. Ketchikan Criminal File #363, Box 5, NA-AR.

237. Kirchhoff, pages 21-2.

238. Carpenter, page 175.

239. Jordan, pages 124-129.

240. Gould, page 22.

241. Gould, page 22.

242. "Found Dead in his Cabin," *Tanana Leader*, January 6, 1910.

243. Gould, page 22.

244. "Yukon River," page 166. The actual quote comes from Cash J. Darrell's article "Eagle on the Yukon," *Alaska Life*, December, 1946, but there is no way of knowing if the quote is accurate. The sentiment, however, probably was.

245. Gould, page 22.

246. Chase, POT, page 45.

247. Webb, *The Century Magazine*, page 681.

248. Gould, page 22.

249. Carpenter, page 175.

250. Gould, page 22.

251. L'Ecuyer, pps. 13-14.

252. Chase, POT, page 45.

253. *Council City News,* May 5, 1906.

254. "Robbery is Cleared," *Fairbanks Times,* July 28, 1906.

255. Ketchikan Criminal File #247, Box 1, NA-AR.

256. Hines, page 120.

257. Cole, GHOSTS, pages 36 and 37.

258. Gould, page 26.

259. Gould, Hal, "Lazy John Was Proud of His," *Alaska Sportsman,* November, 1938, page 22.

260. Gould, Hal, "Lazy John Was Proud of His," Alaska Sportsman, November, 1935, page 8.

261. Gould, page 22.

262. Gould, Hal, "Lazy John Was Proud of His," *Alaska Sportsman,* November, 1938, page 9.

263. Wharton ,page 173.

264. Cole, BARNETTE, pages 29-32. There are a few more details in Wickersham, YUKON, pages 142 through 143.

265. Gould, page 22.

266. Chase, POT, page 45.

267. Gould, page 26.

268. Chase, POT, page 45.

269. Gould, page 22.

270. Gould, page 22.

271. Juneau Criminal File #369, Box 3, NA-AR.

272. WHO'S WHO IN ALASKAN POLITICS, page 105; KLONDIKE NEWSMAN.

273. Davies, Fred C., "On the Valdez Trail," *Alaska Magazine,* June, 1965, page 22.

274. Cole, GHOSTS, page 19.

275. Nichols, page 293.

276. Gould, Hal, "Lazy John Was Proud of His," *Alaska Sportsman*, November, 1938, pages 8 and 9.

277. Forselles, page 38.

278. Hines, pages 100-111.

279. Austin, page 54.

280. Gould, page 26.
281. "Risked All For Nothing," *Nome Chronicle,* August 13, 1900.
282. "French Joe Bound Over," *Nome Chronicle,* August 15, 1900.
283. Chase, MOORE, pages 128-9.
284. "Frank Manley is Arrested and Released," *Fairbanks Daily Times,* October 25, 1908.
285. Coghill, page 11.
286. "Two Clearyites Have Dancing Booby Prize," *Fairbanks Daily Times,* December 27, 1908.
287. Barry, page 94.
288. Jenkins, pages 70 and 73.
289. Jenkins, pages 73 and 74.
290. Norby, pages 3 and 4.
291. Wickersham, YUKON, page 126. Wickersham pulled this from the Yukon Press, March 17, 1899.
292. Dietz, page 16.
293. Abercrombie, COMPILATIONS, pages 758-9.
294. Shiels, page 155.
295. "Educating the Eskimo," *Nome Pioneer Press,* March 14, 1908.
296. "Frozen but Will Recover," *Nome Pioneer Press,* January 21,1908.
297. Shiels, page 151.
298. Sitka Criminal File #369, Box 3; Seward Civil File in the Juneau Civil File boxes, File #580, Box 5, NA-AR.
299. "Hunters are Threatened," *Nome Pioneer Press,* February 18, 1908.
300. Andersen, page 123.
301. Andersen, page 170.
302. Dietz, pages 72-5.
303. Cole, GHOSTS, page 40.
304. "First Conviction for Gambling is Secured," *Fairbanks Daily Times,* November 21, 1908.
305. "Hot Springs News," Hot Springs Echo, November 19, 1910.
306. Hines, pages 109-111.
307. Carpenter, page 176.
308. "Stove Inventor Insane," *Alaska Citizen,* May 24, 1915.

309. Cole, GHOSTS, page 18.
310. Cole, GHOSTS, page 15.
311. Jordan, pages 164-5.
312. "Are Getting in Shape," *Nome Pioneer Press*, January 21, 1908; ALASKA ALMANAC.
313. All of the stories from the 1910 Census come from the ABSTRACT OF THE CENSUS for 1910 and can be found on pages 568-70.
314. Shiels, SEWARD'S, page 155.
315. "'7 Up' Changed to "Gates City," *Yukon Valley News*, August 31, 1904.
316. Wickersham, YUKON, pages 262-265.
317. "When and How to Outfit," *Skaguay News,* December 31, 1897.
318. "Local Doctor Under Arrest," *Fairbanks Times,* July 28, 1906.
319. "Still After the Doctor," *Fairbanks Times*, August 30, 1906. The author assumes that the trunk was empty. In fact, the news article actually said that when the trunk was opened it was found to contain "the doctor's principal stock in trade" rather than his surgical instruments.
320. "Still After Doctor," *Fairbanks Times,* August 30, 1906.
321. "Case goes to the Jury," *Fairbanks Evening News*, June 27, 1906.
322. "Dr. Joseph Weyerhorst Gone," *Fairbanks Daily Times*, August 29, 1906; "Still After Doctor," *Fairbanks Times*, August 30, 1906; Fairbanks Criminal Case #174.
323. "Got Benefit of the Limit," *Fairbanks Times*, July 29, 1906; "No Blame on Doctor," June 28, 1906, *Fairbanks Times;* "Inquest is Held," June 27, 1906, *Fairbanks Times.* Of note, two issues dicussed at the inquest were 1) the size of the incision to remove appendix and 2) whether the doctor and his wife had removed their rings before the operation. The name of the deceased was Fred G. Brose. Brose died at the Weyerhorst Sanitarium. An full page advertisement for the sanitarium can be found in the Fairbanks Times on June 5, 1905.
324. "Weyerhorsts in the Divorce Court," *Tanana Tribune,* May 30, 1908 and "Has New Troubles to Face," *Yukon World,* Dawson, January 18, 1908.
325. Juneau Criminal Files 771, 894, NA-AR.
326. "Dr. J. Weyerhorst Dies Tuesday A. M.," *Great Falls Tribune,* October 12, 1921.

Weyerhorst's death certificate does not give any leads to the historian. He was listed as "single," and "about 50." His father is listed as "—— Weyerhorst" with a birthplace as "Holland." His mother is listed as "unknown" and her nationality as "unknown." He had moved to Montana three years before his death.

327. Newland, page 2.
328. United States vs. J. G. Brady, Sitka Criminal File #182, Box 3, RG 21, NA-AR.
329. Milroy, page 7.
330. Dietz, page 172.
331. Charles Goodyear Hubbard to Bird, July 4, 1898, UAA Archives.
332. Jordan, pages 166-7.
333. "Strange Case of Hypnotism," *Nome Chronicle,* August 16, 1900.
334. "The Mystery of a Pair of Sox," *Alaska Forum,* September 9, 1905.
335. "At the Yukon Dog Yard," *Seattle Times,* November 9, 1897.
336. "Wounded the Horse Thief,*" Council City News,* August 2, 1902.
337. "Fate of Three Deserters," *Seattle Times,* September 14, 1897.
338. "Ferguson Writes He Is Out of Booze," *Tanana Tribune*, October 23, 1908.
339. *Worldwide,* 1904, page 207.
340. MANIILAQ, pages viii-ix.
341. "Out on a Bike," *Skagway Daily Alaskan,* December 14, 1899.
342. "Fire Insurance in Limited Amounts," *Skagway Daily Alaskan,* May 16, 1899.
343. McLean, page 54.
344. Wharton, page 236.
345. "Fear Pirates," *Seattle Times*, July 30, 1897.
346. "Disturbed Proceedings," *Juneau Daily Record,* September 20, 1909.
347. "The Famous Egg Man," Victoria B. C. *Daily Colonist,* March 20, 1898.
348. Hoggatt to Roosevelt, July 8, 1908, Governor's Papers.
349. "Tow and Sell Icebergs," *Seattle Times,* February 28, 1898.
350. "Dogs or Goats, Which?" *Seattle Times,* January 15, 1898.
351. Stuck, ALASKAN MISSIONS, pages 83-84.
352. *Chitina Leader,* December 10, 1910.

353. "A Fiery Corpse in a Coffin," *Seattle Times*, March 24, 1899.

354. "Should Act," *Interloper*, May 5, 1908.

355. "A Face in the Window," *Hot Springs Echo*, May 29, 1909.

356. "Discoverer of Nome in San Francisco Battle," *Daily Alaska Dispatch*, March 3, 1917.

357. Crad, pages 36-7.

358. FORT EGBERT AND THE EAGLE HISTORIC DISTRICT, page 73.

359. Woods, pages 251 to 253.

360. Cole, NOME, page 65.

361. McKeown, page 120-1.

362. Bockstoce, page 242.

363. Bockstoce, page 282.

364. Brown, pages 122 and 124.

365. L'Ecuyer, page 79.

366. L'Ecuyer, page 15.

367. Brown, page 117.

368. Brown, pages 116-7.

369. Kosmos, pages 27-8.

370. Gilbert, pages 19-20.

371. Gilbert, pages 27-29.

372. *Stikeen River Journal*, June 24, 1899.

373. Young, page 159.

374. Harris, page 218.

375. Harris, page 225.

376. Harris, page 227.

377. FACTS & DATES, 697.

378. WORLD ALMANAC.

379. Ravitz, page 7.

380. "Yukon River in Alaska's History, page 83.

381. Hartshorn, Dyea, page 3.

382. Moffit, page 47,50,61, and 18.

383. "Noah's Ark," Valdez News, July 12, 1902; August 10, 1902, *Nome Nugget;* May 9, 1906, *Dawson Daily News*. The article in the Dawson Daily News indicated that the structure could have been a Russian fort which

had floated away in high water. But how such a structure could have floated away and become beached "on a high hill" was not explained.

384. Cole, BARNETTE, pages 42-3.

385. "Broke Jail," June 14, 1902, *Valdez News;* "Koon Case," *Valdez News,* June 21, 1902.

386. "Horror of the Klondike," *New York Times,* June 20, 1899.

387. "Were Starving," August 31, 1901, *Valdez News.*

388. Farnsworth, page 24.

389. "Indian Eats his Family," *Nome News,* April 27. 1906.

390. "Skaguay Preacher Skips," June 24, 1899, *Stikeen River Journal.*

391. "Nearly Lynched," June 18, 1906, *Fairbanks Times.*

392. "Horses Eat Up the Street," June 2, 1905, *Fairbanks Times.*

393. "Picturesque Indian is Dead," *Seward Daily Gateway,* October 1, 1908.

394. "**SANTA CLARA** Arrives," *Seward Daily Gateway*, October 16, 1905.

395. "Dam Breaks at Valdez," Seward Daily Gateway, August 28, 1905.

396. "Outwitted the Thug," *Nome Chronicle,* December 1, 1900.

397. Barry, page 66.

398. "Saloon Men Are Notified," *Nome Daily News,* September 15, 1900.

399. Earp, page 160.

400. Pointer, page 219 and Kirby, page 111. Butch Cassidy, according to Pointer, lived into the 1930s in Spokane, Washington, under the alias of William T. Phillips. The Sundance Kid, according to Kirby, lived under the alias of Hiram Bebee and died in 1955 at the Utah State Prison in Salt Lake City. With regard to historical documentation regarding Cassidy in Alaska, this author could find none.

401. Jenkins, page 185.

402. Savage, page 81.

403. "Home for Indigent Dogs," *Nome Chronicle,* August 22, 1900.

404. "Suffering at Circle City," *Seattle Times,* April 27, 1899.

405. *Chitna Leader,* December 10, 1910.

406. "Stored His Ice," *Council City News,* May 24, 1902.

407. Goodwin interview.

408. Jordan, page 19.

409. Jenkins, page 186.

410. "From a Woman's Standpoint," *Skaguay News*, December 31, 1897. Anna Hall Strong was the wife of J. F. A. Strong, Governor of the Territory of Alaska form 1913 to 1918.

411. "Alaskans Are In Big Demand for Husbands," *Fairbanks Times*, July 19, 1906.

412. *Fort Wrangel News*, June 15, 1898.

413. "The Bachelor's Club," *Fort Wrangel News*, August 31, 1898.

414. "The Bachelor's Club," *Fort Wrangel News*, September 7, 1898.

415. "the Bachelor's Club," *Fort Wrangel News*, September 14, 1898.

416. "Left Banks to Pay the Bills," *Nome Chronicle*, November 17, 1900.

417. "Locks Up the Captain's Bride," *Nome Chronicle*, September 24, 1900.

418. Engstrom, page 46.

419. "Finlanders in Alaska," *Seattle Times*, February 1, 1898.

420. "Colonize Alaska," April 4, 1903, Valdez News. This was a reprint of a "dispatch" that had been published in the *Seattle Post Intelligencer.*

421. "Lapps to Colonize Alaska," July, 1897, *The Eskimo Bulletin.*

422. Dietz, pages 69-70.

423. "Indians Neglected," *Valdez News,* August 16, 1902.

424. "Many Died," November 16, 1901, *Valdez News.*

425. "Mumpy Stephen Drowned," *Seward Daily Gateway*, November 11, 1905.

426. Anderson, page 237.

427. Jordan, page 201.

428. "Stampeders Line Trail," *Fairbanks Weekly News*, August 9, 1905.

429. Wendt, page 21.

430. "Captain Barnette Buys Wonderland," *Fairbanks Daily News,* March 12, 1909.

431. Fortuine, page 222.

432. Robertson, page 51.

433. Berton, pages 122-123; Morgan, 161; "A Gun to Guard Gold," *Post-Intelligencer,* August 28, 1897; "In the Drydock with a Maxim Gun," *Post-Intelligencer,* September 3, 1897. The last article includes a freehand sketch of the gun and its mount.

434. Davis, SOURDOUGH, page 225.

435. "**MOONLIGHT** Goes Tonight," *Seattle Times,* August 24, 1897.
436. **ROCK ISLAND** log book, May, 30, 1898.
437. Fitz, page 46.
438. Conger, page 209.
439. "A New Dogsled," *Seattle Times,* September 17, 1897.
440. "Is a Locomotive a Klondike Possibility," *Seattle Times,* December 4, 1897.
441. "Whatcom Klondike Scheme," *Seattle Times,* November 27, 1897.
442. "A Yukon 'Go-Devil,'" *Seattle Times,* December 31, 1897.
443. Newland, page 1.
444. Morgan, pages 159 to 168. Purely by accident the author came across a microfilm of the scrapbook of Erastus Brainerd at the Rasmuson Archives at UAF. Alas, the microfilm was so poor that I could not make out any the articles. The original scrapbook is in the Library of Congress and appears to be a a collection of news articles and letters.
445. "City will Advertise," *Post-Intelligencer,* August 31, l897.
446. The special Klondike issue for l897 appeared on October 13, l897.
447. "All Questions Answered," *Post-Intelligencer,* March 27, l898.
448. Berton, pages 113-114.
449. Speidel, page 332.
450. "Convincing Evidence that Seattle has the Great Bulk of the Alaska Trade," *Post-Intelligence*r, October 20, l898.
451. "Yukon River in Alaska's History," page 83.
452. Governor John G. Brady to Secretary of the Interior, June 29, 1901, Revenue Custom Agent Files, NA-AR.
453. "Unfortunate Skaguay," *Seattle Times,* October 2, 1897.
454. Collier, pages 249-252.
455. Pillips, page 43.
456. Axe, February 3, 1898.
457. "Post Office Business," *Skaguay News,* February 18, 1898.
458. Watts, January 20, 1898.
459. Sullivan, page 107.
460. "When and How to Outfit," *Skagway News,* December 31, 1897.
461. Johnston, MIZNER, pages 86-7.

462. Morgan, pages 39-40.
463. "War Spreads to Alaska," *Nome Semi-Weekly News,* August 12, 1904.
464. Cole, BARNETTE, pages 47-8.
465. "McKinley Brouhaha Goes to Court," *Anchorage Daily News*, February 4, 1996.
466. Webb, *The Century Magazine,* March, 1898.
467. "Shanghaied on Nome Streets," *Nome Pioneer Press*, June 1, 1908.
468. "A Big Boom in Booze," *Council City News*, October 25, 1902.
469. "Two Men Meet Death – Are Eaten by Dogs," *Pioneer Press*, March 31, 1908.
470. Letter is in the Law and Order file of the Office of the Territories papers, National Archives – Washington D. C.
471. *Nome Daily News,* August 30, 1900.
472. Cravez, page 24.
473. Dey, page 14.
474. "Destination is Unknown," *Juneau Record Miner*, March 31, 1900.
475. Ravitz, page 7.
476. Herdman, page 15.
477. "A Man Fit to Become A Legend," *Anchorage Daily News*, April 17, 1995. There is a photograph of Max Gottschalk in Burnham's RIM OF MYSTERY facing page 48.
478. "Mystified by Sheep Drive," *Fairbanks News Miner,* May 26, 1909,
479. Bylaws of the Miners of Circle, Alaska State Library.
480. "The Alcoholic Thermometer," *Nome Chronicle,* August 11, 1900.
481. CORDOVA TO KENNECOTT, pages 9-13.
482. Dean, page 72.
483. "An Innocent Smuggler," *Seattle Times,* August 25, 1898.
484. "Sorcery is Practiced," *Skaguay News*, December 16, 1898.
485. United States vs. John Panter, Sitka Criminal file, Box 15, RG 21, NA-AR.
486. Skagway Criminal File #191, Box 4, NA-AR.
487. United States vs. Shorty Johnson and Mrs. Shorty Johnson, Sitka Criminal File #695, Box 22, RG 21, NA-AR.

488. Hines, pages 123-136. It is rumored but cannot be confirmed that Albert Fink was later the lawyer who defended Al Capone.
489. "Lawyers Fight in Court," *Council City News,* January 27, 1906.
490. Kitchener, pages 1-3.
491. Ravitz, page 10.
492. "Nearly Lynched," *Fairbanks Times,* June 18, 1906.
493. "Vigilantes to Assist Federal Officials," *Alaska Forum,* June 3, 1905.
494. McGinley vs. Cleary, *Alaska Reports,* Vol. 2, Third Division, Fairbanks, August 8, 1904.
495. Hatch to Collector of Customs, June 28, 1900, Customs.
496. "Death from Starvation," *Nome News,* March 10, 1900. Author's note: The length of time between the incident and the news story is probably due to the lack of ability of news to get to Nome during the winter.
497. Lenz, pages 22-3.
498. "News of the Northwest," *Valdez News,* November 16, 1901.
499. Donald H. Smith to United States Attorney General, January 28, 1899, Custom Service Records.
500. "'Good Injun Gone Muckey,'" *Council City News*, August 9, 1902.
501. The line came from "News of Whalers," published in the *Nome Nugget* on June 15, 1904. This author's source was the Revenue Cutter Service records, NA-AR.
502. Hamlet to Secretary of the Treasury, November 12, 1904, RCS.
503. Burnham, pages 68-9. There is a photograph of some of the bones and skulls at Kukulook opposite page 96.
504. Bockstoce, WHALES, pages 332-4.
505. ALASKA'S HISTORIC ROADHOUSES,page 20.
506. Campbell, CAPE NOME, page 5.
507. "Siberia is Open," Nome News, March 24, 1900 and "To Develop Siberia," *Teller News,* August 29, 1901.
508. "Next a Railroad," *Nome News,* December 23, 1899.
509. Jordan, pages 40-1.
510. Lomen, page 21.
511. Jordan, page 34.
512. Jordan, 36.

513. Clum, March 28 and 29.

514. Morgan, page 40.

515. Hines, page 5.

516. Brady to Secretary of the Interior, May 18, 1903, RCS, NA-AR.

517. McKeown, page 95.

518. Clum's notebook which has no page numbers.

519. Chase, SOURDOUGH, pages 173-174.

520. Fitz, page 67.

521. Nome Grand Jury to the United States District Court of the Second Division, in the papers of the Department of the Interior, April, 1905, National Archives.

522. "Natives Suffering," *Valdez News,* May 26, 1906.

523. "The Copper River Code," Victoria B. C., *Daily Colonist,* March 29, 1898.

524. "Gold Output of Alaska," December 22, 1906, *Fairbanks News.*

www.ingramcontent.com/pod-product-compliance
Lightning Source LLC
Chambersburg PA
CBHW060258100426
42742CB00011B/1800